Accessible Housing

Accessible Housing considers the role and significance of house builders in influencing the design and construction of accessible housing that can meet the needs of disabled people. Its primary focus is the speculative house building process, and the construction of private (for sale) dwellings. The book describes and evaluates the socio-institutional political, and technical relations that underpin the design and construction of housing. These, so it is argued, shape builders' reluctance to design and construct housing that is flexible to accommodate variations in bodily needs and performance.

A feature of the book is the exploration of disabled people's experiences of inaccessible dwelling spaces, and the role of law and regulation relating to the provision of accessible housing. Legal provisions and processes do little to influence builders to adopt design and construction practices that will provide usable or sustainable dwelling spaces. Rather, they encourage small-scale, incremental changes to the physical design of housing that are insufficient to provide a context for dignified living or lifestyles for disabled people.

While the book's primary focus is experiences in England and Wales, there is substantial discussion of legal and building practices in the USA in relation to the physical access needs of disabled people.

Rob Imrie is Professor of Geography at King's College, University of London. He is author of *Disability and the City*, co-author of *Inclusive Design*, and co-editor of *British Urban Policy* and *Urban Renaissance? New Labour, Community and Urban Policy*.

Accessible Housing

Quality, Disability and Design

Rob Imrie

Routledge
Taylor & Francis Group

LONDON AND NEW YORK

First published 2006
by Routledge
2 Park Square, Milton Park, Abingdon, Oxon OX14 4RN

Simultaneously published in the USA and Canada
by Routledge
270 Madison Ave, New York, NY 10016

Routledge is an imprint of the Taylor & Francis Group

© 2006 Rob Imrie

Typeset in Frutiger Light by Wearset Ltd, Boldon, Tyne and Wear
Printed and bound in Great Britain by Bell & Bain Ltd, Glasgow

Every effort has been made to ensure that the advice and information
in this book is true and accurate at the time of going to press.
However, neither the publisher nor the authors can accept any legal
responsibility or liability for any errors or omissions that may be made.
In the case of drug administration, any medical procedure or the use
of technical equipment mentioned within this book, you are strongly
advised to consult the manufacturer's guidelines

British Library Cataloguing in Publication Data
A catalogue record for this book is available from the British Library

Library of Congress Cataloging in Publication Data
A catalog record has been requested for this book

ISBN 0-415-31891-2 (hbk)
ISBN 0-415-31892-0 (pbk)

To my Mum and Dad

Contents

The author

Rob Imrie is Professor of Geography in the Department of Geography at King's College, University of London. His research interests include geographies of disability, the design of the built environment, and urban policy and politics. He is co-author (with Peter Hall) of *Inclusive Design: designing and developing accessible environments* (2001, Spon Press, London), author of *Disability and the City* (1996, Sage Publications, London, and St Martin's Press, New York), and co-editor (with Huw Thomas) of *British Urban Policy* (1999, Sage Publications, London) and (with Mike Raco) *Urban Renaissance? New Labour, Community and Urban Policy* (2003, Policy Press, Bristol).

Acknowledgements

In producing the book I am indebted to many people. I would like to thank the participants in the research for giving up their valuable time to share their experiences with me. In this respect, I would like to thank the members of the Carlisle Access Group, including Elaine Barnett, Margaret Easton, Peter Emmerson and Judith Holmshaw; 'Disability Bournemouth', including Becky Brookwell, Trish Pashley, Ann Simpson and Heather Trenchard; Bracknell Users Group, including Toni Barker, Carol Dann, Ann Groves and Sandra Marks; Wrexham Access Group, including John Carr, Harry Prankard and John ap Richards; and the members of the Elmbridge Access Group, including Hugh Ashton, Jenny Stone and Colin Wheatley. Other individuals who were supportive include: Edward Bannister, Andy Beyer, Kevin Blunden, Mike Donelly, Bill Malleris, Simon Moore, Ed Nolte, Steve Norwood, Kamla Pattni, Darrell Price, David Rogers, David Sharp, Mick Watts, Mark Webb and Peter Neumann, who organized an important study visit for me to Germany in November 2001.

The following house builders were interviewed as part of the research: Arncliffe Homes; Ben Bailey Homes Ltd; Barratts Developments plc; Bellway plc; Bennett plc; Bett Homes; The Berkeley Group plc; Bewley Homes plc; JS Bloor Ltd; Henry Boot Homes Ltd; John Coltman Homes; Chartdale Homes Ltd; Countryside Properties plc; Crest Nicholson plc; Croudace Ltd; William Davis Ltd; Fairclough Homes Ltd; Fairview New Homes plc; Gleeson Homes; Haslam Homes Ltd; Robert Hitchens Ltd; Hubert C Leach Ltd; Jelson Ltd; Jones Homes; Laing Homes Ltd; Linden plc; McCarthy & Stone (Developments) Ltd; Morris Homes Ltd; North Country Homes; Octagon Developments Ltd; Pasquinelli Homes; Persimmon plc; J.A. Pye (Oxford) Ltd; Redrow Group plc; Rialto Homes plc; Rydon Homes Ltd; Saxon Homes; Michael Shanly Homes; Shepherd Homes Ltd; Stamford Homes Ltd; Story Homes; Sunley Estates plc; Swan Hill Homes Ltd; Taylor Woodrow; Try Homes Ltd; Walton Homes; Ward Homes; Weaver Homes Ltd; Westbury plc; Wilson Connelly plc; David Wilson Homes Ltd; George Wimpey plc.

I am grateful to a number of individuals who supported the research by commenting on various drafts of questionnaires and advising on different stages of the research process. These include Neil Cooper, Trisha Gupta, Marian Kumar, Stewart McGough and the late Nancy Robertson. I am particularly grateful to Sarah Langton-Lockton, Chief Executive of the Centre for Accessible Environments, for supporting the research and providing access to a range of relevant resources. The structure of the project's research design was improved by the incorporation of the comments of anonymous referees of the original research application into a redesign of the research proposal. Likewise, an anonymous reader of a draft of the book helped me to overcome some (if not all) errors of style and argument in the text. A wonderful source of support and encouragement over the years has been Peter Cleland, and he has unfailingly provided me with constructive guidance and appropriate advice. He got the research 'kick started' by kindly arranging my first interview with a house builder, Newfield Jones Homes, based in Lytham St Anne's in Lancashire.

The Department of Geography at Royal Holloway, which I have since left, proved to be a supportive environment, and I am grateful to various colleagues there for their encouragement and support, particularly Mike Dolton and Wen-I-Lin. I am indebted to the ESRC and the Joseph Rowntree Foundation for providing the funds to do the research reported in the book. I am especially grateful to Sarah Fielder for providing pointed comments on different parts of the manuscript, and for supporting, more generally, the research that the book is based on. The same applies to Will Hawkesworth for his sharp wit and lucid observations (about the book and everything else!), and especially to Marian Hawkesworth who has been my main source of intellectual support over the years. She has unfailingly read and commented on manuscripts and papers, and listened, with patience, to my half-formed and often-rambling thoughts.

Finally, I owe a special thanks to my mother and father for their friendship and support over the years, and for providing me with the opportunities to pursue the things which matter most to me in life. I dedicate this book to them.

Illustration credits

I acknowledge the editors and publishers of journals for permission to use three of my previous publications for use as part-chapters within this book. Chapter 4 is substantially reproduced from an article in *Housing Studies* (2004, 19, 5). Parts of Chapter 5 were published in *Housing Studies* (2003, 18, 3), and parts of Chapter 6 were published in *Environment and Planning B* (2004, 31, 3).

Except where acknowledged, all illustrations in this book are the property of Rob Imrie. The author and the publisher would like to thank the following individuals and institutions for giving permission to reproduce illustrations:

Jonathan Hill for permission to reproduce Figure 1.6
Keith Lilley for permission to reproduce Figure 1.5
Will Hawkesworth for permission to reproduce Figures 5.5(a) and 5.6
Erick Mikiten for permission to reproduce Figure 2.3.

The authors and publisher are grateful to all who gave their permission for the use of copyright material. They apologize if they have inadvertently failed to acknowledge any copyright holder, and will be glad to correct any omissions that are drawn to their attention in future reprints or editions.

Introduction

Disabled people have the lowest incomes and worst housing circumstances of all social groups in society (OPCS, 2001). As Rowe (1990: 10) notes, 'the housing needs of disabled people are rarely considered within the general area of housing provision'. In 1971, the Office for Population Censuses and Surveys (OPCS, 1971) said that 800,000 people with physical impairments in the UK were living in unsatisfactory housing, a figure that was estimated to be over 1 million by 2001 (OPCS, 2001). Owner occupation is beyond the incomes of the majority of disabled people, while social housing is limited in quantity and location and is not always appropriate. Not surprisingly, most disabled people live with another family member, and in situations that do not always encourage or support independent living. In a context where government ministers in the UK are stressing the importance of developing an inclusive society, disabled people's inability to gain access to housing which meets their particular needs reinforces their partial citizenship.

This partiality is compounded by poor domestic design that inhibits disabled people's physical access to, and movement and mobility around, housing environments. For instance, the English House Condition Survey (ODPM, 2002) indicates that 95 per cent of dwellings in England were, in 2001, inaccessible to wheelchair users. Karn and Sheridan's (1994) study of design quality in a sample of new housing constructed in the UK in 1991/92 suggests that there is nothing new about this, in that only 4 per cent of housing association property and 2 per cent of private sector homes provided main entrance accessible thresholds to permit ease of wheelchair access.[1] Other studies concur in suggesting that, because of inappropriate design, disabled people are often dependent on others to get around their homes (Barnes, 1991). Thus, Oldman and Beresford's (2000: 439) research, of the housing experiences of disabled children, notes that children often feel stranded in one part of the home because of physical impediments and have to rely on an adult to move them around.

This book considers the processes that shape such experiences. It describes and discusses the underlying social relationships that influence the design of private (for sale) dwellings, and asks, how and why is domestic design inattentive to the needs of disabled people? Its primary focus is the role of the speculative house-building process, and the documentation of the attitudes, values and practices of house builders in relation to responding to the dwelling needs of disabled people. In particular, the book considers the role of regulation in relation to access, and documents how far housing quality can be attained for disabled people by recourse to legal regulation and rule. In this respect, much of the book is an evaluation of the role and relevance of Part M of the building regulations, introduced to England and Wales on 25 October 1999.[2] This regulation requires all new, privately constructed, dwellings to incorporate minimum standards of accessibility for disabled people. As Table I.1 and Figure I.1 illustrate, it is particularly aimed at providing ease of access through the principal entrance of a dwelling for wheelchair users, and, once inside, access to a downstairs WC.

Such (rule-based) design specifications reflect, I would argue, broader values based on the primacy of modernist values and practices. Since the late eighteenth century, the divine and transcendent, as a basis of knowledge and belief, have been rejected in favour of reason and natural science. In a world seemingly characterized by chaos and disorder, modernist values, by propagating a belief in 'linear progress, absolute truth, and rational planning', offered the possibilities of human control over the environment for the betterment of people (Harvey, 1989: 35). The order of the rule or regulation, linked to an understanding of society as interlocking parts or systems, became core to the rise of industrial systems and bureaucratic and technical organization. By the late nineteenth century, the rise of professional expertise and practice revolved around belief in the power of human calculability and purposive action as the basis of 'the good society'. The objective was the mastery of complexity, by seeking to reduce

Table I.1 The main features of Part M.

The main objective of Part M is to ensure that housing is 'visitable', or that the provision of particular design features will permit ease of entry of disabled people to a house so that they can visit friends or relatives. The objective is not to create livable spaces throughout the dwelling. The main design features include the following:

- A level or ramped approach to the house which is at least 900 mm wide
- An accessible threshold at the entrance to the house
- An entrance door which provides a minimum clear opening of 775 mm
- A toilet in the entrance storey which wheelchair users can access
- Corridors and hallways in the entrance storey sufficiently wide to allow circulation by a wheelchair user
- No changes of level on the entrance storey apart from on steeply sloping sites
- Switches and sockets sited between 450 mm and 1,200 mm from the floor
- The provision of lifts in flats is not a requirement
- Where a lift is provided in flats, a minimum lift capacity and dimensions will be recommended
- Where a lift is not provided, the common stair to be designed to suit the needs of ambulant disabled people.

NB: the provisions apply to flats as well as houses

Source: DETR, 1999a.

(a)

(b)

(c)

(d)

I.1 A montage of Part M design features. The montage features different aspects of design related to Part M. Photographs (a) and (b) show contrasting ramp features, and (c) and (d) show, respectively, the position of power points at 450 mm and the WC facility with the door opening out.

human and social systems to functions based on a singular set of rules and/or laws (see also Rowe, 1993).

The primacy of this modernist paradigm, in contemporary social and political practices, has shaped policy-makers' understanding of, and approaches to, the design of dwellings and the attainment of housing quality (Rowe, 1993; King, 1996). This understanding is one that conceives of 'housing as a system', or a place fit for the functions it has to perform (see Goodchild, 1997: 78). Thus, like all building regulations or standards, Part M is underpinned by a discourse of urban design that seeks to influence the form and content of the physical fabric of the dwelling to satisfy 'the convenience, safety and comfort of the occupants' (Goodchild, 1997: 78). This discourse takes the structure of the average dwelling as a given, and seeks to do no more than 'add on' design features in order to facilitate some flexibility of use. The basic layout and design of dwellings is not questioned by the regulation; the facilitation of access is purely a matter of small changes in design details. For Borsay (1986: 77), this is problematical because 'tinkering with the structure of ordinary housing does not spell access to suitable accommodation for many disabled people'.

This focus on technical standards is, as I shall argue, likely to fail to deliver the quality of housing that disabled people require because, in and of themselves, they do little to address an important determinant of deficient design – that is, the underlying values, attitudes and practices of builders, and those with responsibilities for the design and construction of dwellings. In particular, the social relations of speculative house building are underpinned by the rationality of real estate economics and its institutions that, in general terms, serve to encourage a one-dimensional conception of, and response to, housing quality. Such rationality, as chapters will discuss, underpins the production of a product (i.e. the dwelling) characterized by volume throughput and minimal variations in design from one dwelling to the next. This, for Turner (1976: 104), is a problematical aspect of the building industry because 'housing is unique by definition', and while it is simple to construct and assemble it has, as he suggests, 'an immensely complex and variable set of uses'.

Such complexity is, as the book suggests, rarely acknowledged or understood by builders, building control officers and others involved in the design and construction of housing. In relation to disabled people's housing needs, most builders do not regard these as a legitimate concern (for them), and rarely see disabled people as part of their target market. They are generally hostile to Part M because they see it as a cost and an irrelevance to the majority of their customer base. Building control officers regard the interpretation and implementation of Part M as relatively straightforward, although most see the regulation as 'half-hearted'. There are, however, no singular responses to Part M by builders or building control officers, but much variation based on a complexity of factors relating to the construction site, the attitudes of individual actors, the resources of builders, etc. The combination of such factors indicates, as I argue in the book, that the provision and regulation of access in dwellings, in any particular instance, has to be understood in relation to specific, contingent, often site-specific, social and institutional relations.

Alongside developing this (and related) arguments, I also want to suggest

that housing quality for disabled people will remain limited unless a fundamental issue is tackled: housing researchers' and practitioners' relative disinterest in issues about disability and dwelling. With some notable exceptions,
issues regarding disabled people and housing are conspicuous by their
absence from research council funding or the thematic priorities or agendas
of research councils. Likewise, disabled people and their needs rarely
feature in academic or policy debates about housing quality (although, for
exceptions, see Harrison and Davis, 2001; Heywood *et al.*, 2002; Imrie,
2003a; Dewsbury *et al.*, 2004; Heywood, 2004; Milner and Madigan,
2004). A perusal of research monographs and journals reveals little or
nothing written about disability and housing over the years. For instance,
the main outlet for scholars in housing research, the journal *Housing
Studies*, has, since its inception in 1983, published very few articles or features about the interrelationships between dwellings and disability.

While this neglect of disability and dwellings has been addressed, in
small part, by the publication of a special issue of *Housing Studies* on the
topic, the situation reflects a broader intellectual and/or academic disinterest and neglect in the subject matter of disability and impairment in society
(Imrie, 2004a). An example, amongst many others, is Burrows and Wilcox's
(2000) study of owner-occupiers with low incomes, which does not refer
to disabled people. Using data from the Survey of English Housing and the
English House Condition Survey (EHCS), the authors compare and contrast
low-income homeowners in terms of categories such as ethnicity, gender
and age. While the study is important, it is not clear why impairment, as a
category of potential significance in influencing people's dwelling choices
and experiences, is missing. It cannot be because there are no data, for
both surveys used by the authors ask questions of respondents about
impairment.

One of the reasons for the neglect of disability and impairment is that,
like most disciplines, housing studies conceives of disability as a minority
concern that is insignificant in an understanding of social patterns and
processes. Disability is not seen as constituted by, or constitutive of,
broader housing patterns and processes. For Allen (1999: 14), in a far-
reaching and important review of housing research and disability, the issue
is more profound in that, as he suggests, housing and comparative
community care research is 'substantively and epistemologically reductionist and, as a result, disablist'. Thus, Allen (1999: 15) notes that most
housing research on disability takes as given the status of the disabled
body as 'functionally incompetent, or a consequence of biological or bodily
malfunctions'. In concurring with Allen, the book, in part, seeks to take up
his challenge by (re)situating disability, as a theoretical referent, in the
broadcloth of social and environmental factors and processes.

This challenge ought not to be confined solely to the academe, because
the neglect of (and reductive frames of reference towards) disability and
housing is also reflected in policy and practice. For instance, in the USA a
range of reports on disabled people and housing have, time and again,
suggested that 'state and local officials do not give a high priority to the
housing needs of disabled people' (O'Hara and Miller, 1998: 3). Thus,
Stephen-Kaye (1997) notes that the National Organization on Disability's
(2002) Annual Report for 2002 did not mention the issue of housing.

Likewise, in the UK disabled people are characterized as 'vulnerable' persons by the EHCS, while Part M of the building regulations defines disability in terms of bodily deficit and deficiency. As the book will suggest, the former conception reinforces the erroneous yet widely held view that disabled people are dependent, even feeble, beings, while the latter, problematically, draws attention to bodily impairment as the causal (or determinant) feature of disabled people's lives.

The book is based primarily on information gathered for an Economic and Social Research Council (ESRC)-funded project entitled 'Responding to the housing needs of disabled people' (Grant number R000239210) that ran between July 2001 and June 2003 (Imrie, 2003b). The research was a joint collaboration with the Centre for Accessible Environments, and it involved the use of postal questionnaires sent to builders and building control officers in England and Wales, follow-up interviews, interviews with key actors, case studies of building projects, and focus groups and interviews with disabled people. Supplementary materials were gathered in study visits that were made to the USA, Germany and the Netherlands (for details of the research design and methods, see Appendix 1). The Joseph Rowntree Foundation also supported the research by providing a grant. This permitted an extension and development of aspects of the work for the ESRC, and the findings have since fed into the government's review of Part M (Imrie, 2003a; ODPM, 2004).

Collectively, the research projects explored the attitudes and practices of house builders and other building professionals in relation to responding to disabled people's physical access needs, and assessed the scope and relevance of building codes or regulations as one of the legal means for securing housing quality for disabled people. The results of the projects form the basis of the book, which will seek to develop and provide insights into three themes and/or debates about the interrelationships between housing quality, disability and design:

1 *Disability and domesticity.* In what ways are disabled people's lives affected by the nature of the design of domestic environments, and how far is domestic design and architecture implicated in inhibiting or facilitating the mobility and movement of disabled people? Are the design principles and practices of domestic architecture attentive to bodily impairment, or are disabled people excluded from the 'domestic ideal'? The book will provide analytical and empirical insights into how far conceptions of domesticity and design seek to incorporate, and respond to, the (bodily) needs of disabled people.

2 *House builders and disability.* To what extent are the building professions responsive to the dwelling needs of disabled people? There is limited knowledge about how designers and house builders are reacting and responding to government regulation, codes of practice, good practice guides, etc., in relation to accessible domestic design, or how the needs of disabled people are being incorporated, if at all, into the design of domestic environments. In seeking to redress this, the book will evaluate the attitudes, policies and practices of house builders and related property professionals in relation to the housing needs of disabled people.

3   *Regulation and the control of access.* What is the nature of government regulation and policy in relation to disability and the design of home environments? Increasingly, many countries are producing design guides, codes of practice and statutes to guide designers and builders towards the design of housing that meets some of the needs of disabled people (see, for example, Michailakis, 1997). The book documents the range of regulatory approaches to accessible design in housing, and seeks to assess how far policies and practices are adequate (or not) in creating accessible home environments for disabled people.

The research focuses primarily on the experiences of wheelchair users because the broad remit of Part M, particularly as builders and building control officers understand it, is to facilitate access to dwellings for people who use a wheelchair. This is not to deny the importance of the diverse nature of disability and impairment in society, nor of the heterogeneity of disabled people's interactions with domestic design. Rather, it was a conscious choice to limit the scope of the study within what might be regarded as a manageable and logical frame of reference. In addition, the book is not a design guide manual about best practice in relation to domestic design, nor does it seek to provide prescriptive advice and guidance about how best to achieve accessible dwelling spaces. There are such publications elsewhere, but none that have investigated the substance of builders' and building control officers' understanding of and responses to the dwelling needs of disabled people (see Steven Winter Associates, 1993, 1997).

The book is divided into three parts and eight chapters. Part I, Concepts and contexts, sets out broader debates in relation to the book's themes and, in particular, suggests that an understanding of disabled people's dwelling circumstances has to be situated in the context of the rationalities of real estate, and the reluctance of governments to legislate, in any effective way, against builders' design and construction practices. Chapter 1 describes disabled people's housing circumstances, and develops the argument that the dominant conceptions of housing quality, based on the attainment of physical and technical standards of construction, rarely refer to, or acknowledge, disabled people and their needs. Rather, principles and practices of housing design predominantly revolve around providing for non-impaired people in family units. This perpetuates, as material in the chapter suggests, the potential for undignified domestic lives for many disabled people, in which their independence of movement and mobility is limited or even denied to them.

In Chapter 2, I discuss the proposition that the disabling nature of domestic design is related to and conditioned by the social relations and structures of building provision, or the rationalities of real estate, that underpin the operations of the speculative house-building industry. Such structures operate around a profit/cost rationality that determines, in part, builders' approach to the design and construction of dwellings. This rationality, when wedded to most builders' partial understanding of disability and the domestic design needs of disabled people, tends to perpetuate a series of problematical and erroneous assumptions by builders about the impact of accessible design upon the costs and operations of the construction process. It is commonly assumed by builders that there is no effective demand for accessible housing, and that such provision will add significantly to development costs and reduce the design quality of dwellings. As I show in the chapter, such assumptions are flawed and have no real substance or credibility.

Chapter 3 suggests that the practices and outcomes of the speculative building industry are not wholly determinate but, rather, are conditioned by principles of law, legal regulation and practice, or broader social, political and regulatory contexts (Blomley, 1994; Imrie and Hall, 2001a). Referring to a range of countries, including the USA, the UK and Australia, the chapter explores the role and importance of access codes and regulations in seeking to ensure that house builders respond to the design needs of disabled people. The evidence shows that there is variable and uneven legal coverage of access issues within and between most countries, and governments are usually reluctant to legislate in relation to disabled people's access to dwellings. I develop the contention that the particular form of rules and regulations concerning disability and design standards, are, more often than not, part of the problem, not the solution, and are not likely, in their present form, to create usable domestic environments for disabled people.

Part II, Securing accessible homes, develops the broader concepts and ideas outlined in Part I by investigating, empirically, disabled people's feelings about domesticity and design, and documenting builders' and building control officers' attitudes and practices in relation to responding to the housing needs of disabled people. In Chapter 4, I develop the argument that while aspects of the home may provide for privacy, sanctuary, security and other aspects of 'ideal' domestic habitation, such provisions are always contingent, never secure, and likely to be challenged by, amongst other things, the onset and development of bodily impairment. However, explorations of the meaning of the home, and housing studies more generally, rarely consider the body and impairment and its interactions with domestic space. In this chapter I suggest that the quality of domestic life, and housing quality more generally, has to be understood, in part, with reference to the body and conceptions of corporeality – something which does not feature as part of the conceptual schema and practices of the building professions.

Chapter 5 explores house builders' attitudes about, and knowledge of, disability and disabled people. It is based on the observation that a key to an understanding of disabling domestic design is to explore the social relations of the design and construction process (see also Imrie and Hall, 2001b). The chapter considers the different ways in which builders are responding to the needs of disabled people through the context of Part M of the building regulations. As the material shows, builders have little or no knowledge about disabled people, and regard them as part of a minority group that is not relevant to their target markets. Most builders see Part M, as already intimated, as imposing additional cost burdens on the industry for the sake of what they regard to be a half-hearted and tokenistic regulation. However, despite builders' initial misgivings about Part M, few have had problems in interpreting the regulation – although, as the chapter shows, there are significant, sometimes problematical, variations in its implementation and/or the final design outcomes.

While the persistence of poor domestic design, in relation to disabled people's needs, can in part be explained by the attitudes and practices of builders, Chapter 6 suggests that the processes underpinning regulatory interpretation and implementation of the building regulations are not unimportant in influencing the content of domestic design. In developing this point, the chapter describes and evaluates the role and relevance of the building regulations in seeking to deliver design quality in dwellings, with reference to Part M. The research shows that officers regard Part M as one of the 'lesser' building regulations, time consuming and costly to regulate, and a burden on the building industry. The evidence also shows that officers' understanding of the requirements of Part M is variable, leading to inconsistencies in its application and outcomes. Such attitudes and practices, combined with the limited scope of the regulation, suggest that the regulation is unlikely significantly to raise housing quality (in relation to the needs of disabled people).

An important part of housing quality is user involvement in the design and construction process. This is the theme of Chapter 7, which considers the proposition that housing quality is likely to be limited for disabled people unless the form and content of their involvement with builders, and building professionals more generally, is significantly changed. Habraken (1972), Turner (1976) and others note that the provision of sustainable housing, or dwellings which are responsive to the corporeal, emotional and material needs of people, is beyond prescription by builders or regulators. However, as the chapter shows, there is no legal requirement for builders, or any other professional involved in house-building, to meet, consult or interact with disabled people about the design of dwellings. Not surprisingly, the evidence suggests that disabled people rarely meet builders or their representatives and that, conversely, builders have little knowledge or understanding of who disabled people are or what their design needs in dwellings might be.

In the final part of the book, Promoting accessible housing, I draw out the broader relevance of the research findings, and develop the argument that contemporary design and construction practices are problematical because they perpetuate forms of spatial injustice in which disabled people are, potentially, denied particular rights of habitation. In Chapter 8, I suggest that the development of housing quality, appropriate to the needs of disabled people, will require a transformation of the social and institutional relations and practices of the speculative house-building industry, and of the systems of regulatory control. One way to conceive of such changes is, as King (2003) suggests, by recourse to the adoption and development of vernacular housing strategies (see also Habraken, 1972; Turner, 1976). I discuss what vernacular housing strategies are, or ought to be, and suggest ways by which they could become part of viable housing futures for disabled people.

PART I
CONCEPTS AND CONTEXTS

1 Accessible housing, quality and design

1.1 Introduction

Disabled people's consumption of housing continues to be hindered by poor design that inhibits their access into, and ease of mobility around, dwellings. For instance, Mrs B., a client of the British charity Age Concern, recounted a familiar, everyday, tale: 'poorly designed housing doesn't merely limit my independence, it makes it impossible . . . I use a wheelchair all the time and cannot manage a step' (Age Concern, 1995: 1).[1] Rookard (1995: 1) recalled a similar situation with her father's difficulties in using a wheelchair: 'we are unable to visit my nephew and his wife in their new home due to the layout of their entrance area . . . Are disabled people supposed to sit in their own home all day?' Likewise, Edward Bannister (2003), a disability advocate who lives in Bolingbrook near Chicago, identified the limitations of design in relation to catering for his mobility impairment: 'me and my family were living in a town house, my bedroom was on the second floor and it got to the point where I couldn't get up and down to my bedroom'.[2]

Such sentiments are commonplace, and highlight the limitations of the design of domestic environments in relation to the needs of disabled people. Most dwellings are designed and constructed as 'types' that comprise standard fixtures and fittings that are not sensitive to variations in bodily form, capabilities and needs (Imrie and Hall, 2001b; Imrie, 2003c; Milner and Madigan, 2004). Builders, building professionals and others assume that (disabled) people will be able to adjust to the (pre-fixed) design of domestic space (see the discussion in Chapter 2). Such attitudes are endemic to the house-building industry in the UK, the USA and elsewhere, and are symptomatic of a disabling, and disablist, society that fails to recognize or understand that disabled people's abilities to adjust or adapt to design are likely to be conditioned by the nature of the design itself (and the underlying values and practices that shape it).

In developing such arguments, the next part of the chapter briefly outlines the broader patterns and process that characterize disabled people's housing circumstances. As the Introduction to the book intimates, disabled people have rarely had access to good-quality housing, or had the means to exercise meaningful choice in housing markets. More often than not, disabled people are confined to dwellings provided by a local authority or a social housing provider or, alternatively, reside in an institutional setting (Barnes, 1991; Ravatz, 1995). In particular, disabled people's pre-1948 experiences of domestic environments revolved primarily around either dependence on care in the family home, or the application of a mixture of punitive and charitable actions by a range of state and voluntary organizations. I suggest that these and related dwelling circumstances serve to potentially (re)produce undignified domestic circumstances for disabled people, and can be conceived of as perpetuating what Dikec (2001) refers to as spatial injustice.

I then turn to a discussion of the concept of housing quality and its relevance to the dwelling needs of disabled people. Housing quality is, as Lawrence (1995) suggests, a multifaceted and complex term that ought to encompass not only a consideration of the architectural and technical aspects of dwellings, but also the broader social and political contexts that shape their provision and availability. However, for Lawrence (1995) and others, policy-makers and built environment professionals more generally tend to emphasize the former at the expense of the latter, thus conceiving of the dwelling as a piece of hardware – that is, a physical or technical system operating more or less independently of socio-economic contexts or conditions (Goodchild and Furbey, 1986; Karn and Sheridan, 1994; Goodchild, 1997; Carmona, 2001; Franklin, 2001; Imrie, 2003a). Building codes and regulations relating to access reflect this concept of housing quality and, as I shall argue, this can potentially lead to a one-dimensional approach to and understanding of disabled people's dwelling needs.

This approach emphasizes that housing quality can be achieved first and foremost by recourse to the application of physical design or technical solutions, such as the standards relating to or derived from Part M (1999), life-time homes (LTH), smart homes and/or flexible or demountable fixtures and fittings. However, while the application of such standards is necessary in attaining particular aspects of housing quality (i.e. physical design standards), I will develop the argument, outlined by Franklin (2001: 83), that the 'mechanistic and deterministic formulations' underpinning them will fail, in and of themselves, to produce the quality of livable spaces responsive to the differentiated and complex needs of people (see also Turner, 1976). As Arias (1993: xvi) suggests, too many resources have been 'wasted on engineering and architectural solutions that do not answer the human concerns that turn houses into a home'.

In this respect, the penultimate part of the chapter will explore the possibilities of developing and applying a concept of housing quality that revolves around what Goodchild (1997) refers to as the house as a home or a place of personalization. For Goodchild (1997) and others, the quality of dwelling resides in its use, and this, for Arias (1993), is closely related to personal taste and human practice. As Arias (1993) suggests, housing quality, as a lived and tangible reality, must be related to and given content by the affective desires and emotions of dwellers. I relate such ideas to broader concerns, raised by Turner (1976), Habraken (1972) and others, that housing quality must involve a decentralization of control over the processes of planning, design and production of dwellings, part of what King (1996) refers to as a vernacular housing process (see also Rowe, 1993; Hill, 2003).

1.2 Indignity, disability and housing

For some commentators, disabled people's housing circumstances have rarely been dignified (Barnes, 1991; Harrison and Davis, 2001; Heywood *et al.*, 2002). Until the passing of the National Assistance Act (1948) in the UK, disabled people either lived with a family member or, if the family was unable to support them, in a private asylum or a workhouse (see Figure 1.1; Rostron, 1995). After 1948, while local authorities were empowered to provide specialist accommodation for disabled people, less than 50 per cent had done so by the 1980s.[3] Most provision, outside of the family setting, was by voluntary sector organizations, such as the Leonard Cheshire Homes and The Thistle Foundation. These were, and still are, regarded by many disabled people as perpetuating paternalistic and undig-nified forms of housing consumption (Hannaford, 1985; Morris, 1991). Hannaford (1985: 61) refers to such places as where disabled people were blamed for their circumstances: 'disability tends to be seen within social work analysis; it becomes a social problem'.

1.1 Institutional living.

Since the early 1950s, British local authorities have been encouraged to provide for disabled people's housing needs through a mixture of, primar-ily, non-statutory policy programmes (see Borsay, 1986). These have ranged from the adaptation of existing housing, such as the removal of front doorsteps and their replacement with ramped access and accessible thresholds, to the construction of homes designed to cater for wheelchair users and people with mobility or ambulant impairments. Until 1970, and the passing of the Chronically Sick and Disabled Persons Act (CSDP) (Department of Health, 1970), few purpose-built houses were constructed and most local authorities did little to respond to the housing needs of dis-abled people. Thereafter, the CSDP made it a statutory duty for local authorities to have regard 'to the special needs of chronically sick and dis-abled persons' when devising local housing policy (Department of Health, 1970: 3). In combination with related legislation, such as the 1974 Housing Act and the Local Government and Housing Act of 1989, the CSDP provided a framework for, potentially, changing the housing circum-stances of disabled people.[4]

However, assessments of the CSDP, and related legislation, note that the legal provisions were beset by problems of vagueness and ambiguity, and were rarely used to their full potential by local authorities (Armitage, 1983; Borsay, 1986).[5] For instance, Laune's (1990) review of housing and independent living for disabled people documents the decline in provision of wheelchair and mobility dwellings in the 1980s. In 1979, housing associations in England constructed 129 new wheelchair-standard proper-ties, in contrast with 571 constructed by local authorities (see Figure 1.2). By 1995 these figures had fallen, respectively, to 67 and 69 dwellings. Over the same period, the numbers of new mobility-standard properties declined from 2,136 (housing associations) and 5,950 (local authorities) to 102 and 469 respectively.[6] Such figures were at odds with the Conservat-ive government's statement in 1989 that 'it remains the government's

1.2 Completion of wheelchair dwellings in England by local authorities, 1970–96.
Source: Department of the Environment, 1974, 1991; ODPM, 2002.

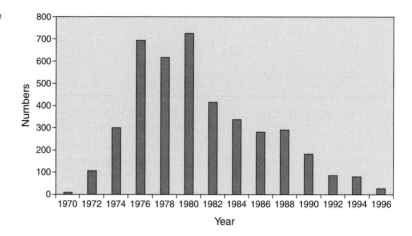

policy to provide the building of accessible housing and this is an area where housing associations and housing authorities have taken a lead' (Department of Health, 1989: 4).

In contrast, Laune (1990: 35) notes that, far from taking a lead, general needs housing associations rarely considered disabled people as potential tenants and, as he concluded, 'it is difficult to find examples of good practice with regard to housing provision for disabled people within general needs housing associations'. If anything, a combination of social and political changes since the late 1980s has exacerbated the difficulties for disabled people in gaining access to dwellings that cater for their needs. A reduction in local authority building programmes, coupled with 'Right to Buy' legislation, has reduced the quantity of properties in the sector that is most likely to provide for disabled people's needs.[7] This was the principal observation of the Ewing Inquiry (1994: 31) which, in investigating the housing circumstances of disabled people in Scotland, noted that 'disabled people have little choice in housing ... this situation is getting worse because of Right to Buy and because the needs of disabled people are insufficiently recognised'.[8]

The shortage of accessible dwellings was exacerbated by the practices of the private sector. The legislation tended to ignore the activities of private housing developers, and did little to regulate for access in new housing built for sale (see Chapters 3 and 5, and section 1.3). Morris (1990: 12) notes that, apart from the construction of a few private-sector sheltered housing schemes, there was 'no record of housing being built to wheelchair or mobility standards in the private sector'. This reflected a broader, long-term, pattern whereby standards relating to the quality of housing in the private sector were never subject to stringent levels of government regulation. Rather, governments assumed that house builders were best able to identify and respond to consumer preferences in relation to house design and quality issues without recourse to regulation. Regulation was seen, so builders and their representatives argued, as adding to costs and stifling design innovation and responsiveness to shifting patterns of demand (see, for example, House Builders Federation, 1995).

Consequently, self-regulation through voluntary codes of practice was paramount in relation to issues about housing quality, disability and access. For instance, in 1981 the National House Building Council (NHBC, 1981) issued an advisory note to builders asking them to make new dwellings more suitable for elderly and disabled occupants.[9] Likewise, in 1982 the House Builders Federation (HBF, 1982) published its 'Charter for the Disabled', which encouraged builders to respond to the design needs of disabled people. Such documents were little more than advice to builders 'on avoiding the worst' (Goodchild and Karn, 1997: 165), and were usually ignored because, as Borsay (1986) suggests, builders do not regard disabled people as a sufficiently large enough market to build speculatively for them. By the early 1990s it was clear that builders were failing to respond to advisory notes and other miscellaneous advice about disabled people's access to housing, and, as Barnes (1991: 158) observed, 'the stock of inaccessible housing continues to grow'.

For many disabled people, their functional capacities are potentially reduced by inaccessible dwellings. King's (1999) research of the housing circumstances of 478 wheelchair users in the UK shows that their dwellings did not fully meet their needs and that most said that they wanted to move.[10] Chamba et al.'s (1999) study also notes that in ethnic minority households with a mobility-impaired child, three out of five famil- ies stated that their home was unsuitable for their disabled child's needs. Only a quarter of the sample were able to afford to make adaptations to their home, and most of these were homeowners. Not surprisingly, the English House Condition Survey (EHCS) (ODPM, 2002) shows that only 7,000 dwellings in England have the design features that are seen by government as comprising the minimum requirements for wheelchair accessibility in dwellings (i.e. a level threshold, level access to the dwelling, a WC on the entrance storey, and 750 mm clear door openings), and that most of these are in the social rented sector (see Table 1.1, Appendix 2).[11]

The implication is that most of the dwelling stock in the UK, and else- where, is not designed to respond to the needs of people with different types of impairment (see also Karn and Sheridan, 1994). This is particularly so with regard to individuals with mobility impairments, and where the use of a wheelchair is required. For instance, Figure 1.3 (page 20) shows that 1 per cent of private flats and houses in England in 2001 had ramped access, and only 1 per cent of private houses had a WC converted for dis- abled people to use (ODPM, 2002).[12] Likewise, the Scottish House Con- dition Survey (Scottish Office, 1996) estimated that only 5,000 dwellings met wheelchair accessibility standards, with less than 40 per cent of these occupied by wheelchair users.[13] A similar survey, of housing and planning needs in Bournemouth in the UK, revealed that nearly two-thirds (62 per cent) of those relying on a wheelchair lived in homes not suited to wheel- chair use (Bournemouth Borough Council, 1998). Only a quarter (25 per cent) of wheelchair users lived in dwellings that had been adapted.[14]

Such disadvantage is portrayed by some researchers and government officials as the result of the debilitating effects of impairment, or the physiological deficit or medical problems that individual disabled people have. The prognosis is that disabled people ought to be subject to medical intervention, care and, ideally, cure and rehabilitation to ensure that they are able to fit into and interact with the prevalent patterns of domestic design. In this scenario, the problems relating to inaccessible dwellings are

Table 1.1 Dwellings (000s) having features or adaptations making them more suitable for use by people with disabilities, 2001.

		Flats			Houses		
		Private	Social	All flats	Private	Social	All houses
Level access							
Yes	num	1,027	1,156	2,183	10,974	1,748	12,722
	col %	49	62	55	74	75	74
No	num	1,077	694	1,772	3,885	579	4,464
	col %	51	38	45	26	25	26
Total	num	2,104	1,851	3,955	14,858	2,327	17,186
	col %	100	100	100	100	100	100
Flush threshold							
Yes	num	635	847	1,482	2,050	473	2,524
	col %	30	46	37	14	20	15
No	num	1,469	1,004	2,473	12,808	1,854	14,662
	col %	70	54	63	86	80	85
Total	num	2,104	1,851	3,955	14,858	2,327	17,186
	col %	100	100	100	100	100	100
Doorsets/circulation							
Yes	num	382	444	826	2,136	355	2,491
	col %	18	24	21	14	15	14
No	num	1,722	1,407	3,129	12,723	1,972	14,695
	col %	82	76	79	86	85	86
Total	num	2,104	1,851	3,955	14,858	2,327	17,186
	col %	100	100	100	100	100	100
Ramps							
Yes	num	25	83	108	117	109	225
	col %	1	4	3	1	5	1
No	num	2,079	1,768	3,847	14,742	2,218	16,960
	col %	99	96	97	99	95	99
Total	num	2,104	1,851	3,955	14,858	2,327	17,186
	col %	100	100	100	100	100	100
Grab rails							
Yes	num	102	284	385	468	268	735
	col %	5	15	10	3	12	4
No	num	2,003	1,567	3,570	14,391	2,059	16,450
	col %	95	85	90	97	88	96
Total	num	2,104	1,851	3,955	14,858	2,327	17,186
	col %	100	100	100	100	100	100
Bath/WC at entrance level							
Yes	num	1,314	1,237	2,551	5,195	812	6,007
	col %	62	67	64	35	35	35
No	num	791	613	1,404	9,664	1,515	11,178
	col %	38	33	36	65	65	65
Total	num	2,104	1,851	3,955	14,858	2,327	17,186
	col %	100	100	100	100	100	100

Table 1.1 continued.

		Flats			Houses		
		Private	Social	All flats	Private	Social	All houses
Bathroom adapted for disabled use							
Yes	**num**	76	275	350	304	222	527
	col %	4	15	9	2	10	3
No	**num**	2,028	1,576	3,605	14,554	2,105	16,659
	col %	96	85	91	98	90	97
Total	**num**	2,104	1,851	3,955	14,858	2,327	17,186
	col %	100	100	100	100	100	100
WC adapted for disabled use							
Yes	**num**	81	187	267	207	133	341
	col %	4	10	7	1	6	2
No	**num**	2,023	1,664	3,688	14,651	2,194	16,845
	col %	96	90	93	99	94	98
Total	**num**	2,104	1,851	3,955	14,858	2,327	17,186
	col %	100	100	100	100	100	100
Kitchen adapted for disabled persons' use							
Yes	**num**	29	62	91	77	33	110
	col %	1	3	2	1	1	1
No	**num**	2,075	1,789	3,864	14,781	2,294	17,075
	col %	99	97	98	99	99	99
Total	**num**	2,104	1,851	3,955	14,858	2,327	17,186
	col %	100	100	100	100	100	100
Electrical modifications							
Yes	**num**	52	174	226	100	107	207
	col %	2	9	6	1	5	1
No	**num**	2,053	1,677	3,729	14,759	2,220	16,979
	col %	98	91	94	99	95	99
Total	**num**	2,104	1,851	3,955	14,858	2,327	17,186
	col %	100	100	100	100	100	100
Lift present							
Yes	**num**	231	484	717	na	na	na
	col %	11	26	18	na	na	na
No	**num**	1,873	1,367	3,238	na	na	na
	col %	89	74	82	na	na	na
Total	**num**	2,104	1,851	3,955	na	na	na
	col %	100	100	100	na	na	na

Source: English House Condition Survey, ODPM (2001).

less to do with the broader processes shaping the nature of domestic design, and more the outcome of individual bodily deficits or deficiencies. Impairment, and the individuals it resides within, is the causal mechanism, or the matter that determines disabled people's experiences of domesticity and habitation. In turn, impairment is often understood as illness and a health issue, rather than a social construction or part of physiology that, in interaction with pejorative societal attitudes and processes, renders the body disabled.

While rejecting the dominant, medical conceptions of disability, I do not

1.3 Dwellings having features or adaptations making them more suitable for use by disabled people, 2001.
(a) Dwellings in England with ramped access.
(b) Dwellings in England with a WC adapted for use by disabled people
Source: ODPM, 2002.

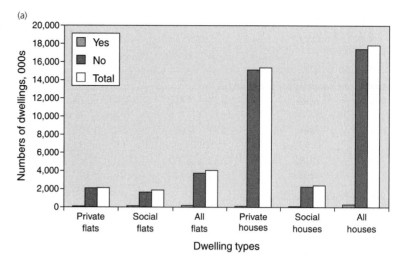

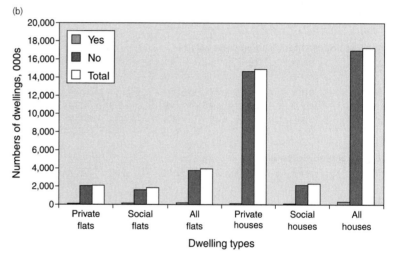

discount the significance of impairment in influencing aspects of the lives of disabled people (see also Imrie, 2004b; C. Thomas, 2004). However, I suggest, in different parts of the book, that the focus of attention, in terms of understanding the nature of disablement in relation to housing, ought to be shifted to the study of broader social, political and institutional relations and processes (see Allen, 2000). This directs attention to questions such as, what are the social, political and institutional processes and practices that shape domestic design, and how are they implicated in inhibiting or facilitating the mobility and movement of disabled people? Likewise, how far has domestic architecture, through the ages, been (in)attentive to bodily impairment, and to what extent have disabled people been excluded from the 'domestic ideal'? What do patterns of inclusion/exclusion in domestic environments reveal about attitudes and values in relation to disability and impairment in society?

In this respect, one way of thinking about disabled people's circumstances is that they represent, in part, a state of homelessness, not necessarily in the sense of an absence of access to a physical shelter, but more in the sense of what Edgar *et al.* (2002: 3) refer to as 'a denial of . . .

access to somewhere for basic human functioning'. Such functioning, for Waldron (1993) and King (1996), relates to basic or necessary forms of bodily reproduction, such as urinating and sleeping, which, if not undertaken, do not permit people, as King (1996: 55) suggests, 'to live at all'. While King's point is, perhaps, overstated, it helps to draw attention to the potential interactions between impairment and design in circumscribing, or making difficult, the exercise of basic (bodily) functions. For instance, Sharma (2002: 17) suggests that 'living in unsuitable accommodation causes major problems for families'. In one family, she notes that 'the father has to carry his 18-year-old daughter to and from the school bus because the entrance to the house is not big enough for the wheelchair' (Sharma, 2002: 18).

The denial of a person's capability to act is core to Nussbaum's (1999: 41) argument that there is a series of universal rights that relate to 'central human functional capabilities' or, as she implies, those functions that seem central in defining the very presence of a human life (see also Chapter 4; Young, 1990; Morris, 1991; King, 1996, 2003; Reinders, 2000; Somerville and Chan, 2001).[15] The exercise of these capabilities is, as Nussbaum (1999: 41) notes, core to being truly human, and one of these, amongst others, is bodily health and integrity which can be facilitated in part by 'being able to have adequate shelter'. While Nussbaum does not really define what 'adequate' shelter is, she suggests that it is not sufficient for human beings to be provided solely with the means of survival; life is, or ought to be, the pursuit of human dignity in which people are not subject to hunger or fear or lack of social or other opportunities.

However, disabled people lack support for, or opportunities to facilitate, some central human functions, such as 'being able to have adequate shelter'. This is because the denial of support or opportunity is, in Nussbaum's (1999: 54) terms, 'frequently caused' by their being disabled in social contexts that do not value or recognize the worth of individuals with impairment. For instance, the design of most dwellings is derived from a conception of the occupier or user that rarely identifies them with impairment. The consequence is, as Figure 1.4 shows, disabling design, in which the invisibility of disabled people to those that design and construct dwellings has the potential to lead to marked differences between disabled and non-disabled people in exercising bodily autonomy, or using the dwelling in ways that they might want to. Nussbaum (1999: 54) refers to such inequities as 'an unequal failure in capability', which is, as she says, a 'problem of justice'.

This problem can be understood, in part, as the perpetuation of patterns of spatial injustice, or what Dikec (2001) refers to as the systematic exclusion, oppression and domination of particular people and/or groups in relation to different parts of the built environment (see also Lefebvre, 1991, 1996). For some, steps into dwellings do not prevent ease of access, whereas for others (as Figure 1.4 indicates) steps are insurmountable barriers. Likewise, the division of dwellings into functionally separate spaces (i.e. the upstairs bathroom, the downstairs living room) has the potential, as Chapter 4 shows, to restrict ease of entry and/or use of dwelling spaces by some disabled people. The patterning of spatialized exclusion that sometimes results is reflective of the social production of space that

1.4 Photograph (a) depicts a new development that retains steps to the entrances of the two houses in the foreground, so rendering them inaccessible to wheelchair users. Photograph (b) shows a common problem, in which entry to the dwelling may have ramped and/or level access, but it lacks the same facility for access to the garden. This limits the usability of the house. Photograph (c) shows the back entrance to Anne's house, constructed in such a way that she is unable to use this route.

(a)

(b)

(c)

revolves around what Young (1990: 38) refers to as 'oppressive social relations' – that is, 'systematic institutional processes that prevent some people from developing and exercising their capacities and expressing their experiences'.

These processes are evident in many aspects of disabled people's interactions with dwellings, including the effects of legal rules and regulations governing the consumption of rented accommodation. The marginal labour market status of disabled people means that they tend to live in private or social rented dwellings, where barriers to entry, in financial terms, are usually less prohibitive than for owner occupation.[16] However, the rules of conduct, including those relating to the physical adaptation of dwellings, do not require private landlords in the UK to make their dwellings accessible, and tenants can only do so with the permission of the owner and at their own expense.[17] In one survey of housing need, of 293 disabled people in the privately rented sector, none was living in an adapted dwelling (Bournemouth Borough Council, 1998). In contrast, a much higher proportion of disabled people in owner-occupied (64 per cent) and socially rented (30 per cent) dwellings were living in adapted accommodation (see Table 1.2).

Such data are revealing of relations of domination, or what Young (1990: 38) defines as the institutional conditions that inhibit people from participating in determining their actions or the conditions of their actions. As she notes, people live within such structures of domination 'if other persons or groups can determine without reciprocation the conditions of their action' (Young, 1990: 38). The design and building process provide examples of this in which, as Chapters 4 and 7 reveal, disabled people's experiences of dwellings are not usually incorporated into clients' briefs, while architects and other building professionals rarely consult with disabled people about the design of residential developments. Rather, disabled people's needs are either ignored or (re)classified by professionals into problematical categories, such as 'special needs', which more often than not serve as a justification for confining disabled people to ghettoized environments (Morris, 1991; Imrie, 1996; Gleeson, 1998).

The potential effect is one whereby disabled people may not be able, with any ease, to determine their housing circumstances, due to what Somerville and Chan (2001) refer to as 'indignification' – that is, a general societal disrespect for particular groups and/or individuals in society (see also Maslow, 1970; Harrison, 2004; Heywood, 2004). As Somerville and Chan (2001: 2) suggest, human dignity is a sense of self and societal

Table 1.2 Properties adapted for wheelchair use, by tenure group.

	Owner occupier numbers (%)	Social renters numbers (%)	Private renters numbers (%)
Yes – purpose-built	41 (4)	166 (40)	0 (0)
Yes – adapted	293 (31)	124	0 (0)
No	606 (65)	124	293 (100)
Total	940 (100)	414 (100)	293 (100)

Source: Bournemouth Borough Council, 1998.

respect, the former understood in part as autonomy or the capacity for free will, insight and choice; the latter as acceptance and caring, or the valuation of an individual 'as an indispensable element of society' (Somerville and Chan, 2001: 3). For Somerville and Chan (2001), the objective of social policy, including housing policy, ought to be the attainment of human dignity, or what they refer to as 'that which is produced by a combination of care of the self with being cared about by others'.

However, the attitudes and practices of housing providers, including house builders, are far from dignified. For instance, the 1991 EHCS, like its 2001 counterpart, deemed a dwelling to be accessible 'if it had no more than two steps to the floor which provided kitchen, WC and bathroom facilities and at least two other rooms' (Department of the Environment, 1991: 44).[18] Using this definition, the data show that just over 25 per cent of the housing stock was accessible, and was primarily bungalows and flats with lifts. Local authorities and housing associations provided the most accessible dwellings. The EHCS definition of what constitutes an accessible dwelling is unsatisfactory. It is difficult to imagine how a dwelling with steps can facilitate the movement and mobility of disabled people, particularly those who are dependent on a wheelchair. In addition, the definition does not provide or specify the dimensions or measures of key rooms, such as the WC, that ought to be attained in achieving 'accessibility' in dwellings.

The result is the construction of dwellings that are not necessarily sensitized to disabled people and their needs, based on technical standards which, once absorbed into the practices of builders and building control departments, perpetuate patterns and processes characterized by what Somerville and Chan (2001) term 'institutional disrespect'. Such disrespect is not usually open or obvious, but is manifest through the subtle, everyday or taken-for-granted categories and related practices that define the operations of institutions (Oliver, 1990; Morris, 1991; Reinders, 2000). For instance, since 1993 general needs housing associations, as a condition of funding from government, have been required to construct dwellings to minimum levels of accessibility by implementing the Scheme Development Standards.[19] Likewise, as discussed in the Introduction to the book, private builders have been required, since October 1999, to construct all new dwellings to similar standards, through the context of Part M of the building regulations (see Table I.1).

While such standards are helping to increase the numbers of dwellings deemed to be 'accessible', they do so, I suggest, in ways that serve to reproduce indignities relating to disability. Both standards revolve around the use of design criteria that do not fit in with most people's idea of what they expect from a dwelling; that is, to be able to live in it and use it (without necessarily being dependent on others). Part M, as outlined in the Introduction to the book, only requires a dwelling to be 'visitable' – that is, to permit a person, specifically a wheelchair user, to gain access through the principal entrance to facilitate visits to friends and relatives. It does not require that they be given access to all parts of the dwelling, or that it should be usable (except in a rudimentary sense) (see also the arguments in Chapter 3). In this respect, dwellings constructed to (at the time of writing) current standards cannot optimize disabled people's autonomy, or provide the basis, easily, for self-determination – which, in Downie and Telfer's (1969) terms, means the destruction of personhood.[20]

1.3 Housing quality, standards and the reductive nature of design

The previous section demonstrates that most disabled people do not have access to good-quality dwellings in the UK. Rather, disabled people's housing circumstances, however one may wish to measure them, are characterized by an absence of quality, in the sense that they do little to facilitate ease of mobility, movement and use. The reference to quality is important, because government and academic debates about the nature of dwellings in society tend to revolve around a particular understanding of what housing quality is or ought to be (see the debates in Goodchild, 1997; Carmona, 2001). It is generally understood to refer to the development and application of technical standards that relate to the physical design of dwellings, in which the objective is to achieve 'habitability', or the development of environments to support and facilitate human life and health (Goodchild, 1997). This directs policy-makers' attention, as Goodchild (1997) suggests, to attaining minimum space standards and standards of physical amenity in dwellings.

Such standards have been set primarily through the context of town planning legislation and building regulation, although little has been done to regulate the amenity standards of dwellings or the functional performance-based aspects of habitation, particularly in private dwellings (although see the arguments in section 1.5). Indeed, most government directives and standards relating to the quality of dwellings apply to social or public, not private, construction, based on the *laissez-faire* understanding that private developers ought to be given the scope and freedom to determine the quality of housing design in relation to the expression of market or consumer preferences. Nonetheless, private builders have broadly (if not fully) followed guidance set by influential government reports on housing standards, such as Parker Morris (MHLG, 1961), yet, as Goodchild and Furbey (1986: 81–83) note, they have been reluctant to support standards relating to the overall size of the dwelling (i.e. the 'footprint') or to household activities.

While this potentially limits builders' definitions of what is or should be housing quality, this is arguably less important than the understanding, by builders, government officials and others, that housing quality can be attained by setting and seeking to attain physical design standards based on objective criteria or technical measures that relate to 'the good dwelling'. Since the Public Health Acts of 1874 and 1875, design criteria in relation to dwellings in England have propagated a physical design determinism in which physical layout and the provision of fixtures and fittings, such as lighting and drainage, are benchmarks of quality. However, as Harrison (2004) and others suggest, while physical fixtures and layout are a necessary part of the quality of habitation, they are insufficient and, in and of themselves, treat a dwelling as an abstraction from the home, or a place of meaningful social and cultural interaction that at root defines, for most people, what quality of habitation is (see also the arguments in section 1.5 and Chapter 4).

1.5 Le Corbusier's modular man is inscribed onto a Habitation de Grand Hateur (high-rise building) in the town of Firminy in France. It is part of a Unité d'habitation complex designed by Le Corbusier. The modular man reflects Le Corbusier's (1925: 83) understanding 'that man is a geometrical animal', or that the proportions of architecture can be derived from the (standard) measures of the (uniform) human body. Such measures are derived from a conception of the body as 'non-impaired', in which it is assumed that body parts are functioning according to medical definitions of the normal biological body. The outcome is generic design solutions in which flexibility of use, based on human physiological difference and diversity, are absorbed into and understood in terms of fixed and universal standards of function or performance.

In this respect, some observers note that the rationale for minimum standards of physical amenity, as the measure and mark of housing quality, is more 'with economic, technological, and political priorities in mind, whereas the lifestyle, domestic economy, health and well being of local populations have been largely undervalued' (Lawrence, 2002: 401). This chimes, in part, with the dominant conception of the dwelling in the early twentieth century as a technical system, or machine for living in, orientated towards efficient living spaces that will, as Le Corbusier stated, 'by order bring about freedom'. Rowe (1993), for instance, notes that scientific rationalism and management, and the application of Taylorist principles to the home, were deployed to deliver mass housing by using the technical standard to specify the rational disposition of physical layout and function in dwellings.[21] This revolved around a series of ergonomic or body-centred exercises that sought to promote efficient and productive living by designing spaces to eliminate wasteful movement and unnecessary expenditure of human effort (see Figure 1.5).

The application of scientific management to the home was particularly evident in the pages of *Ladies Home Journal* in the early part of the twentieth century, and given full justification in the influential publication *The New Housekeeping*, authored by Christine Frederick (1913) (see also Beecher and Beecher, 1869). As Frederick (1913: 13) suggested, 'there is an older saying that a woman's work is never done. If the principles of effi-

ciency can be specifically carried out in every kind of shop, factory and business, why couldn't they be carried out equally well at home?'. Such sentiments were translated into the standardization of many aspects of domestic design, in which the dwelling was arranged to what Llewellyn (2004: 48) refers to as principles of 'architectural efficiency rather than the needs of everyday life'. One example, depicted in Figure 1.6, was the Frankfurt kitchen designed in 1927 by the Austrian architect Grete Schulte-Lihotzky, which sought to facilitate efficient living in small spaces by deploying precise design standards or measures to ensure maximum productivity.

The design of the Frankfurt kitchen reflected the development and use of design standards that, in Rowe's (1993) terms, addressed issues of acceptable values. By this, Rowe (1993: 312) notes that housing quality standards comprise minimum physical dimensions and performance criteria that are supposed to 'hold for a majority of relevant cases' or even, as Callado (1995: 1666) suggests, 'to encompass the expectations of every-

(a)   (b)

1.6 The Frankfurt kitchen and the galley kitchen: Schulte-Lihotzky's design for the Frankfurt kitchen (a) is based on the gallery kitchen (b), which is an enclosed workspace that was designed to ease the perceived burden of (women's) domestic duties. Hill (2003) suggests that the design of the kitchen is problematical because it excludes, or seeks to suppress, an important dimension of housing quality; that is, user creativity and autonomy. For Hill (2003: 17), the Frankfurt kitchen is symptomatic of a one-dimensional approach to design quality that conceives of 'the user as passive and having constant and universal needs . . . the passive user learns to operate a space the way the technician learns to operate a machine – the correct way'. Likewise, Llewellyn (2004: 48), in commenting on the adoption of the galley kitchen concept by designers in the 1930s, notes that those who used them 'were often unhappy with the small size of the kitchens they came to inhabit' (see also Denby, 1934). Such design clearly lacks sensitivity to the bodily needs of people with mobility impairments, particularly those who are dependent on the use of a wheelchair (which could not easily operate in the minimal spaces of the galley kitchen).

one'. Such standards have been influenced by the idea of normalcy, which, as Canguilhem (1991: 109) comments, is the 'perfect ideological and technical solution to the paradox of the individual . . . of how it is possible to be an individual equal to other individuals' (see also Foucault, 1977; Hill, 2003). This became, and remains, the dominant value-orientation to the design of dwellings with influential architects, such as Walter Gropius (quoted in Conrad, 1964: 95), reaffirming the necessity of the norm or standard because 'on the whole, the necessities of life are the same for the majority of the population'.

The social values and technological norms that underpinned the setting of minimum design standards, of the types evident in the Frankfurt kitchen, have contributed to the indignification of disabled people because, as Canguilhem (1991: 247) suggests, they reflect 'an idea of society and its hierarchy of values' that consigns impairment to the margins of consciousness and societal consideration (see also Oliver, 1990; Reinders, 2000). This idea (of society) is one whereby the standards revolve around a conception of corporeality as a 'given' physiology (i.e. a medical fact) based on scientifically established criteria of bodily performance. That is, the standard of building design and performance as the embodiment of able-bodiness or bodies without impairment. The implementation of such standards is, so Canguilhem (1991: 247) notes, to 'impose a requirement on an existence', or 'a given whose variety, disparity, with regard to the requirement, present themselves as hostile'.

In this sense, the emergence of minimum standards of physical amenity and habitation reflected what the Congres Internationaux d'Architecture Moderne (CIAM) in 1929 referred to as the problem of the 'minimum house'; that is, 'the resolution of broad biological and psychological needs within the static system of the house itself' (Rowe, 1993: 57). The implication is the potential de-corporealization of the dwelling, transformed out of recognition or, as Vidler (1999: 64) suggests, 'not now of a particular individual for a once inhabited dwelling but of a collective population for a never experienced space'. For Vidler (1999), the standardized dwelling was no longer part of a place of habitation but had become an instrument – what Bachelard (1948: 6) referred to as the 'geometric cube' and the 'cement cell'. Others concurred with Adorno's (1974: 38) suggestion that 'dwelling, in the proper sense, is now impossible', referring to modern dwellings as 'living cases manufactured by experts for philistines . . . devoid of all relation to the occupant'.

The estrangement of being from dwelling, implied by Adorno's (1974) observation, is indicative of the reduction of housing quality to the attainment of normative standards for living (based on measures of central tendency). This was the basis of formative design standards in the UK, including the Tudor Walters report of 1918 that was significant in its recommendation of minimum space standards in public dwellings and its provision of guidance on amenities such as heating and lighting (Tudor Walters Committee, 1918). It also recommended that dwellings be adaptable to changing needs, and facilitate privacy for household members such as elderly people and children. Later reports, published by the Dudley Committee (Ministry of Health, 1944) and by Parker Morris (Ministry of Health and Local Government, 1961), continued in this vein in recommending modest improvements in space standards and the internal layout of rooms. The Parker Morris report observed that dwellings 'have steep stairs and mean halls and landings', and suggested that spaces ought to be adaptable to cater for changes in patterns of household use (MHLG, 1961: 3).

While these observations were in some respects ahead of their time, the dimensions of rooms recommended by Parker Morris did not provide much scope for changes in living patterns, or for flexibility in coping with changes in preferences or needs of households. Rather, the standards of dwelling design recommended by Parker Morris, Tudor Walters and a host of other publications paid little more than lip service to individual needs or lifestyles that did not conform to the nuclear family.[22] The Dudley Report, in recommending a minimum of three bedrooms, an upstairs bathroom and WC, was seeking to respond to the perceived needs of the family for individual privacy, but in doing so was implicated in the production of what Lefebvre (1991: 384) refers to as 'boxes for living in, of identical plans piled on top of another'.[23] The resultant spaces were, in Lefebvre's (1991: 384) terms, functional and hierarchical, controlling and managing activity with 'the emphasis being on private life, on the genital order of the family'.

Such order is, so some argue, reflective of the ideological and socially constructed nature of design and domestic space, in which modern domestic architecture is characterized by social and cultural norms that revolve primarily around family life, sex roles and particular patterns of social interaction (Wright, 1980, 1981; Ravatz, 1995; MacPherson, 1997; Chapman and Hockey, 1999; Hockey, 1999; Madigan and Munro, 1999). In this respect, housing quality, or people's experiences of domestic life and living, cannot be understood in isolation from the moral encoding or order of domestic design in which, as Lerup (1987: 16) suggests, 'the single family house is a disciplinary mechanism – morality manifest in form'. For Wright (1981: xv), this morality (of the modern dwelling) is closely associated with values propagating the capacity of the physical design to 'reinforce certain character traits . . . and assure a good society', to leave, as Gavin (1850: 23) comments, an 'impress' on the life of the people' (see also Evans, 1978).

For Lawrence (1987), the moral 'impress' of the modern dwelling has problematical, material and practical implications for the quality of habitation, a point which is core to MacPherson's (1997) study of governments' responses to the housing needs of migrant Samoan people in New Zealand in the 1960s and 1970s. During this period, successive governments in New Zealand provided subsidies to house builders to encourage them to construct affordable dwellings for sale to middle- and low-income groups. As a condition of the receipt of subsidies, builders were required to construct dwellings to government housing advisers' prescribed design briefs that, as MacPherson (1997: 152) suggests, 'made assumptions about the lifestyle and requirements of the typical family which required builders to design dwellings around the lifestyles of the European nuclear family' (see also Wright, 1980, 1981; Madigan and Munro, 1999).

The dwellings that were built were no more than three or four bedrooms in size. This was according to the directives of the Housing

Corporation, who suggested that dwellings be constructed around a maximum occupancy of two adults and two children, so responding to the needs of the dominant ethnic group and failing to acknowledge or provide for the needs of the largest group of potential homeowners, Samoan migrants. The objective of government was to provide basic housing, and little thought was put into the provision of additional or appropriate facilities in response to the needs of different types of consumers (MacPherson, 1997). This was problematical in relation to Samoan migrants because of their large family sizes, and, as MacPherson (1997) notes, problems with the design soon became apparent, including overcrowding and overworked cooling, heating and hot-water systems. In some instances, Samoan migrant families were forced to convert garages into additional living accommodation to try and meet their household needs.

This course of action was a predictable outcome of government advisers and ministers in New Zealand propagating a series of physical design standards that were not sensitized to social and cultural variations relating to the use of dwellings, nor to the bodily or corporeal needs of those that did not conform to a cultural stereotype (see Bloomer and Moore, 1977; Imrie, 2003c). As Chow (2002) suggests, the design of dwellings (in such instances) is often underpinned by a 'formulaic approach' that seeks to define new households and their lifestyles in general terms, and then supply a dwelling that is, as far as is practicable, a match. This 'predict and provide' mentality is enshrined in both housing policy and builders' practices, and it conceives of dwellings, as Chow (2002: 82) suggests, as 'static rather than temporal, limiting everyday and longer term choices'. This is particularly so for disabled people, who, as already intimated, have rarely featured as part of the 'formulaic approach' of housing quality standards.

The substance of the Tudor Walters (Tudor Walters Committee, 1918) report, for instance, barely recognized household structure outside of the family norm, or that specific members of a household, such as a disabled person, might require design standards that differed from those that were recommended. Its only concession was to provide some guidance about flexibility in the use of dwellings, suggesting that a ground-floor room 'could be used as a bedroom to suit an elderly or disabled person'. Likewise, the Parker Morris standards distinguished between 'family' and 'other' types of accommodation and, as Milner and Madigan (2004: 731) note, 'disabled people were considered to deviate from normative assumptions of the average family to such an extent that they were not even included under the category of "other" accommodation in the report', and consequentially they were rendered invisible.

Such indignities are also evident in the technical and other standards set by private builders through the auspices of the NHBC. It first established dwelling standards in 1967 to head off criticisms from government and others that the standards of design in private dwellings had fallen behind those in the public sector. The NHBC's response has been to adopt physical standards similar to those for public or social dwellings, particularly in reaffirming the dwelling as the domain of the familial 'normal body' (e.g. its reference to family rooms). Thus the NHBC website (www.nhbc.co.uk) states that its standards deal with each part of the building process, from foundations all the way through to painting and decorating. They include detailed guidance and sketches showing key parts of the construction. However, as King (1996: 23) suggests, dwellings tend to be understood as 'equipment that provides shelter', in which their objective is to solve technical and management problems rather than respond to specific human needs.

In this sense, the development of housing quality, by recourse to universal, minimum standards of physical fitness and function, is problematical for reducing human variation and needs to singular design types or solutions; that is, the propagation of design criteria that are insensitive to cross-cultural variations, or the differences in dwelling needs between, for example, men and women, disabled people, different ethnic groups and people of different ages. This orientation remains at the heart of contemporary building regulation and control, and it is limited because, as King (1996: 23) notes, it treats dwellings as 'material aggregations' – that is, as things or objects rather than as manifestations constituted by and constitutive of social and political processes (see also Lawrence, 2002). One way in which this issue has been addressed is in relation to the concept of flexibility, a theme I now turn to.

1.4 The relevance of flexibility?

The needs of disabled people, in relation to the design of dwellings, are often discussed by highlighting how impairment acts as a limitation on the use of domestic spaces (DETR, 1999b). The solution is, as intimated in section 1.2, either to rehabilitate and cure the medical problem or alternatively to provide special accommodation or physical adaptations to ensure that the design facilitates, as far as is practicable, the movement and mobility of the person. While Part M goes some way to facilitating such mobility and movement, it is limited because it prescribes standardized design features that fall far short of providing a usable domestic environment (see Chapters 3 and 6). Recognition of this has led some commentators to call for a greater range of standards, such as those for LTH (Lifetime Home Standards), to be incorporated into the construction of dwellings, with others suggesting that principles that promote flexible architecture, such as demountable walls and the use of assistive technologies, be part of a broader approach in facilitating adaptable domestic design (Dewsbury et al., 2004).

Such views chime, in part, with those of Lawrence (1987) and others who note that the idea of inherent and potential adaptability ought to be core to design thinking and practice in relation to the development of quality in dwellings (see also Collins, 1965; Rapoport, 1977; Pikusa, 1983; Forty, 2000; Hill, 2003). As Lawrence (1987: 23) suggests, inherent adaptability is the design attributes built into the initial design that 'make a wide range of interpretations possible' and comprise a 'minimum of design features that would not inhibit particular choices of us'. Potential adaptability relates to the design of construction techniques that make possible multiple uses of dwellings. Such ideas are not dissimilar to those of flexibility, a term which, as Hamdi (1990) notes, is a recognition of and response to rapid changes in family size and composition, and changing expectations of what ought to comprise minimum standards of comfort in the home (see also Forty, 2000; Hill, 2003).

The term 'flexibility' has its origins in debates about architectural process in the 1950s, and it was, at that time, a reaction against the deterministic excesses of functionalism, or the view that asserts that space (form) determines function or the use of the built environment. The debates about flexibility expressed some dissatisfaction with the modernist paradigm, particularly the conception of the architect as expert and purveyor of architectural quality through the context of design (see also Chapter 7; Bloomer and Moore, 1977; Bentley, 1999). Thus Walter Gropius (1954: 178) observed that 'the architect should conceive buildings not as monuments, but as receptacles for the flow of life which they have to serve'. In this respect, conceptions and practices of flexibility suggested that architectural quality ought to be developed, in part, in relation to use and the potential of buildings 'to absorb, or adapt to reflect, changes in use' (Forty, 2000: 31).

Such observations were not new, and reflected disquiet amongst many regarding the standardization of design and the reduction of much of the complexity of urban living to minimum standards (Habraken, 1972; Turner, 1976). Alvar Aalto (1940) echoed a general dissatisfaction with the idea of architecture as a utilitarian application. Rather, for Aalto (1940: 14) the purpose of architecture was 'to bring the material world into harmony with human life'. Likewise, Le Corbusier's (1923: 24) pronouncement on the design of dwellings was typical: 'God forbid that there should be any question in the architect's mind of mass produced housing . . . the home is the product of the spirit' (see also Figure 1.7). Others concurred with Habraken (1972: 13), for instance, suggesting that mass-produced dwellings were anathema to good human living: 'there is therefore nothing worse than to have to live among what is indifferent to our actions'.

The prognosis for proponents of modernist design and process was to generate flexibility in the design process. Hill (2003: 32) suggests that flexibility has many shades of meaning, but that at root it refers to the 'accom-

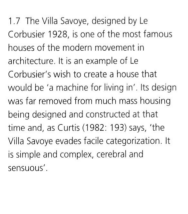

1.7 The Villa Savoye, designed by Le Corbusier 1928, is one of the most famous houses of the modern movement in architecture. It is an example of Le Corbusier's wish to create a house that would be 'a machine for living in'. Its design was far removed from much mass housing being designed and constructed at that time and, as Curtis (1982: 193) says, 'the Villa Savoye evades facile categorization. It is simple and complex, cerebral and sensuous'.

modation of changing relationships between events, context, and the use of space'. The most common meaning of flexibility is flexibility by technical means, which, as Forty (2000) notes, can be understood in relation to two types. The first is flexibility by movement or the reconfiguration of intricate elements in the dwelling (see also Collins, 1965; Bentley, 1999; Forty, 2000). Hill (2003: 32) describes Pierre Choreau's Maison de Verre, located in Paris, as an example of this type of technical flexibility, in which, as he notes, 'when open, the pivoting storage unit in the main bathroom screens the bather, while sliding screens on the ground floor, one glass, the others perforated metal, can be moved separately to create gradations of aural and visual privacy' (Figure 1.8).

1.8 Maison de Verre, Paris.

The second type of technical flexibility refers to the use of lightweight demountable fixtures and fittings, and moveable floors, walls and ceiling panels, including open-plan design (see Gann, 1992; Gann et al., 1999; Kendall and Teicher, 2000). Flexibility by use of moveable parts and/or open plan is, for Hill (2003), a description of use as much as form, and it is characterized by a loose fit between space and use. The flexibility of the space depends in part on the user, or, as Hill (2003: 38) suggests, change of use may well be 'less dependent on a physical transformation of the space than a change in the perception of the user'. An example of this is the Villa Madama, located in Rome, which, as Evans (1997: 64) notes, is characterized by 'no qualitative distinction between the way through the house and the inhabited spaces within it ... the villa was, in terms of occupation, an open plan permeable to the numerous members of the household'.

The principles of technical flexibility are core to a new orthodoxy in debates about disability and design. This suggests that the development and use of appropriate design standards (such as LTH) and design hardware, ranging from assistive technologies (such as bath seats, automated windows and tap controls) to demountable walls and ceilings, can be a panacea to poorly designed domestic environments. LTH, for instance, have their origins in debates about 'flexibility in use', and are related to design criteria first outlined by the Helen Hamlyn Trust (1989), later developed by the Joseph Rowntree Foundation.[24] The standards are, as Figure 1.9 indicates, committed to inclusive design in which the dwelling is adapted (or adaptable) to be responsive to the changing needs of people throughout their lifetime. As Milner and Madigan (2004) suggest, LTH are the new benchmarks of housing design quality in social housing in the UK, and are set to be incorporated into a revised version of Part M of the building regulations (ODPM, 2004).

Likewise, the application of open building principles and assistive technologies has the potential to enhance the quality of habitation for disabled people (Gann, 1992; Gann et al., 1999; Barlow and Venables, 2004; Dewsbury et al., 2004). For Gann (1992), open building aims to improve the range, flexibility and choice of dwelling types available to customers by the use of industrialized component parts. As Gann (1992) suggests, few builders have a customer focus and do any more than produce standardized house types, sometimes differentiated by minimal differences in design detail (see Chapter 2). For Gann (1992) and others, changes in the social and technical relations of the building process, including the

1.9 Lifetime Home Standards.

Access

1. Where car parking is adjacent to the home, it should be capable of enlargement to attain 3.3 metres width.

2. The distance from the car-parking space to the home should be kept to a minimum and should be level or gently sloping.

3. The approach to all entrances should be level or gently sloping (gradients for paths should be the same as for public buildings in the Building Regulations).

4. All entrances should be illuminated and have level access over the threshold, and the main entrance should be covered.

5. Where homes are reached by a lift, it should be wheelchair accessible.

Inside the home

6. The width of the doorways and hallways should accord with the Access Committee for England's standards.

7. There should be space for the turning of wheelchairs in kitchens, dining areas and sitting rooms and adequate circulation space for wheelchair users elsewhere.

8. The sitting room (or family room) should be at entrance level.

9. In houses of two or more storeys, there should be space on the ground floor that could be used as a convenient bed space.

10. There should be a downstairs toilet which should be wheelchair accessible, with drainage and service provision enabling a shower to be fitted at any time.

11. Walls in bathrooms and toilets should be capable of taking adaptations such as handrails.

12. The design should incorporate provision for a future stair lift and a suitably identified space for potential installation of a house lift (through-the-floor lift) from the ground to the first floor, for example to a bedroom next to the bathroom.

13. The bath/bedroom ceiling should be strong enough, or capable of being made strong enough, to support a hoist at a later date. Within the bath/bedroom wall provision should be made for a future floor-to-ceiling door, to connect the two rooms by a hoist.

14. The bathroom layout should be designed to incorporate ease of access, probably from a side approach, to the bath and WC. The wash basins should also be accessible.

Fixtures and fittings

15. Living-room window glazing should begin at 800 mm or lower, and windows should be easy to open/operate.

16. Switches, sockets and service controls should be at a height usable by all (i.e. between 600 mm and 1,200 mm from the floor).

Source: Joseph Rowntree Foundation, 2003.

integration of design, cost and production control, and the functional integration of different parts of building activity, are likely to deliver more flexible, customized design suited to individual needs than conventional approaches to construction (see Figure 1.10).

However, Barlow and Venables (2004) suggest that the application of LTH and open building principles will have limited value because they only apply to new construction. They comment that electronically enhanced assistive technologies, in conjunction with physical adaptation to the house, are likely to be of more widespread benefit because they can be fitted into established dwellings and reach a greater number of individuals (see also Dewsbury et al., 2004). They also note that while assistive technologies are critical tools in facilitating the use of dwellings, and are therefore part of housing quality, their significance should not be overestimated. Dewsbury et al. (2004) concur by suggesting that the extent to which assistive technologies will enhance usability of dwellings, hence raising the quality of habitation, depends in part on designers being sensitive to user needs or, as Sterling (2002: 255) observes, 'a home exists in order to shelter people, not to boss them around with algorithms'.

For Forty (2000: 142), technical flexibility, such as that proffered by LTH, open building or assistive technologies, is no more than the redemption of 'functionalism from determinist excess', because it does not challenge the underlying structures, values or operations of the architectural and construction professions. In other words, he is sceptical about how far the application of flexibility will transcend the dominant role of architects, or the continuation of functionalist applications of design (see also Hill, 2003). As Forty (2000: 2) suggests, architects are attracted to the incorporation of flexibility into design because it provides 'the illusion of projecting their control over the building into the future, beyond the period of their actual responsibility for it'. Others, like DeGory (1998), note that developers are attracted to flexibility in design because it provides (market) potential for increasing the exchange value of buildings through adaptation and re-use.

Discourses of technical flexibility, in relation to responding to disabled people's dwelling needs, reinforce the problematical view that flexibility is the characteristic of the building and/or the physical design. For instance, LTH are functional design solutions that impose prescriptive functions, or

---

- Different levels of building activity are made functionally and physically independent
- Occupier choice is maximized by re-engineering the building, its dependencies and lead times
- Production methods and locations are optimized to deliver occupier choice at controlled levels of quality
- Systems are developed that integrate design, cost and production control
- An effective system for delivering and installing occupiers' desired fit-outs on site is provided
- Sustainability, in the context of a flexible, adaptable product, is maximized
- The recycling of parts.

Source: Gann, 1992.

1.10 A comparison of open building principles and conventional approaches to construction.

forms of use of dwellings, that, as Milner and Madigan (2004) suggest, do not relate or respond to different types of users. Rather, as they suggest, LTH are far from inclusive in that they promote design that primarily caters for the needs of people with mobility impairments to the exclusion of others, such as children and vision-impaired people (see Allen *et al.*, 2002; Milner and Madigan, 2004). Likewise, Holland and Pearce (2002: 242) note that LTH are not that flexible and do not incorporate 'wider design related sensory features, such as temperature and draft control, sound insulation, lighting levels . . .'

It is difficult to see how far transformations in disabled people's lives can occur without the development of social or political programmes for change, and in this respect technical forms of flexibility and their design solutions are not helpful. Such solutions are presented as neutral and apolitical in that they barely recognize the interrelationships between the social, technical, political and economic processes underpinning building and design. Instead, technical strategies of flexible design proceed on the understanding that environmental change is a matter of developing and implementing a technical or design solution. In this respect, the provision of appropriate dwelling design for disabled people is a matter of physical adaptation from one type of design to another, reconfiguring the fixtures and features of a building and developing new procedural mechanisms for deploying resources and their management.

A technical and procedural response is, however, partial because it leaves intact the social and attitudinal relations which influence the form and content of design. These attitudes are broadly discriminatory, and there is no reason to suppose that technical adaptations, in and of themselves, will significantly change the lives of disabled people. Assistive technologies are corrective of, and compensatory mechanisms for, the loss of bodily functions, and are derived from a value system that seeks to change disabled people into 'normal' human beings. The objective is, as proponents of universal design suggest, 'to integrate people with disabilities into the mainstream' (Center for Universal Design, 2000: 1). Impairment, as far as technical flexibility is concerned, is regarded as something to be overcome or to be eradicated, rather than to be accepted as an intrinsic feature or part of a person and their identity. In this sense, technical flexibility, as a potential basis for the development and propagation of housing quality, is likely to be limited.

1.5 Seeking to enhance housing quality

In seeking to move beyond static and reductionist conceptions of housing quality, a range of writers, such as Habraken (1972) and Turner (1976), note that the quality of dwellings is related to much more than physical or technical design criteria. Likewise, commentators such as Harrison (2004) and Rowe (1993) express some caution, and doubt, about the relevance of an understanding of housing quality in terms of the dwelling as a physical product. For Rowe (1993: 287), housing quality is 'a process not simply a thing' (see also Habraken, 1972). Harrison (2004) amplifies in noting that the application of physical and/or technical standards to dwellings implies that positive outcomes are expected in relation to space standards, insulation, access, etc. However, he suggests that it is difficult conclusively to demonstrate benefits from physical dwelling changes because the range of 'confounding variables is wide' (Harrison, 2004: 698).

This echoes others who, like Rapoport (1982), suggest that the complexity of factors influencing housing quality ought to be defined and understood first and foremost in relation to how far the dwelling and environment supports and/or facilitates particular lifestyles, values and human emotions (Turner, 1976; Bloomer and Moore, 1977). In this respect, Goodchild (1997) argues that one way of thinking about housing quality is to differentiate between the house as a building, artefact or object, and the house as a home (see Chapter 4). Whereas the former refers to the dwelling as a system of physical and technical components, usually shaped by prescriptive quality standards (see section 1.2), the latter is more concerned with the socio-cultural aspects of the 'relationships between the environment and the users way of life, social structures and daily routines' (Goodchild, 1997; see also Lawrence, 1987, 1995).

This observation is important because it suggests that housing quality, in a physical sense, is only one part of the basic needs of people (irrespective of whether or not they have a bodily impairment). As Harrison (2004: 701) notes, other quality considerations in relation to dwellings include the meanings and expectations vested by individuals in their homes and neighbourhoods, including social interactions with neighbours and 'opportunities to "self manage" the residence experience'. For instance, Allen et al.'s (2002) research, of vision-impaired children living in a poor neighbourhood, showed that the quality of habitation was diminished by the children's confidence being undermined 'by their poor living environment (including anti-social behaviour and bullying)'. For Allen et al. (2002), children's quality of habitation was more likely to be influenced by broader environmental problems 'than any issues relating to poor urban design'.

Such experiences of dwelling are variable across time and space, and are likely to lead to diverse interpretations of what housing quality is or ought to be. For Lawrence (1995), housing quality is a compound concept in which quality of habitation is the intersection of the availability, affordability and physical condition and functioning of dwellings, as determined by a range of contextually specific and contingent socio-economic, institutional and political relationships. As such, an understanding of housing quality requires the integration of diverse subject matter, including studies of the supply of dwellings, the material characteristics of housing, and the characteristics and value systems of different types of residents. As Lawrence (1995: 1656) notes, little has been done (or achieved) by academics and policy-makers to 'address or define a broad integrated definition of housing quality', a process not helped by the marginalization of the subject in 'mainstream debate and decision making on housing policy'.

However, there is some evidence that debate about housing quality, beyond discourses of technical flexibility, has featured in government pronouncements in the UK. For instance, the Parker Morris (MHLG, 1961) report anticipated themes that government has only recently returned to in relation to housing quality, including the performance of the dwelling in relation to user requirements, and the importance of the dwelling's setting as part of the quality of habitation. As the Parker Morris report said:

'housing standards should be couched in terms which concentrate on the activities that the occupiers will want to pursue', while observing that 'in the past the setting of the home has too often been neglected' (MHLG, 1961: 5). Such exhortations have, however, usually fallen on deaf ears because successive governments in the UK have been preoccupied with a 'predict and provide' approach to housing policy – that is, with estimating changes in household formation and predicting, then seeking to supply for, the demand for new dwellings.

Since 1997 a change in emphasis has occurred, at least at the level of political and policy rhetoric. In a drive to improve the quality of dwellings, the ODPM (2000a: 1) has observed that 'little is done to measure the quality of the provision and determine whether the housing is likely to meet the current and future needs of occupiers'. Rather, in relation to social housing the government has noted that cost cutting has led to a 'bed spaces per pound' approach, 'with inadequate room sizes and poor estates facilities' (ODPM, 2000a: 1). In seeking to rectify this, the ODPM (2000b: 1) has sought to develop new yardsticks and measures of housing quality for social housing that *in the longer term should also be usable for all forms of private housing* (emphasis added). The result is the Housing Quality Indicator (HQI) system, which is a measurement and assessment tool that, as Figure 1.11 shows, comprises ten main indicators of the quality of a dwelling.

The objective of the HQI system is, so the ODPM (2000b) claims, to evaluate dwellings on the basis of quality rather than simply of cost, by assessing the quality of a dwelling's location, design and performance.[25] One of the quality criteria is accessibility, and, as the ODPM (2000b: 2) states in referring to statutory mechanisms of control, 'within dwellings, much more attention is paid to access to rooms rather than their usability'. The HQI system aims to rectify this by focusing on usability and performance.

1.11 Housing Quality Indicators.

The HQI allows an assessment of quality of key features of a housing project in three main categories:

1. Location
2. Design
3. Performance.

These three categories produce the ten quality indicators that make up the housing quality indicator system:

1. Location
2. Site – visual impact, layout and landscaping
3. Site – open space
4. Site – routes and movement
5. Unit – size
6. Unit – layout
7. Unit – noise, light and services
8. Unit – accessibility
9. Unit – energy, green and sustainability issues
10. Performance in use.

Source: ODPM, 2000b.

While a welcome change in focus, the HQI system is limited in scope because it does not need to be adopted by private builders. Moreover, the quality criteria are still wedded to directives and benchmarks developed and delivered by experts and professionals, and contain little by way of experiential input or viewpoint. The criteria (or benchmarks) are broadly physical in nature, and do not depart in any significant sense from the discourse of technical flexibility or the reliance on prescriptive standard setting as a tool or approach to housing quality.

What, then, should the components of housing quality be? Foremost, Lawrence (1995) notes that prescriptive principles of housing quality are problematical because they restrict or condition what ought to be achieved, and in doing so provide limited scope for innovation in design or departure from a regulatory process which is centrally controlled and directed. Others concur with Rowe (1993), suggesting that they offer no guidance to building activities well above the standards. However, most observers agree that prescriptive standards, in and of themselves, are not a bad thing, and do identity what is not acceptable. Commentators such as Prak and Priemus (1995) and Lawrence (1995) argue that the prescriptive approach to housing quality ought to be complemented by other approaches. For instance, Lawrence (1995: 1662) advocates proscriptive principles which, as he says, 'imply that what is not forbidden is permitted. They do not hinder a wide range of solutions to housing requirements.'

Likewise, Rowe (1993: 318) suggests that design ought not to be prefixed or based on what he calls 'superimposed categories and stereotypical views', but rather be sensitized to 'a status actually aspired to by the group'. This, for Rowe (1993: 318), will facilitate an important part of housing quality, that is, the celebration of 'redeeming and worthwhile aspects of the life and circumstances of the group concerned'. King (1996) also notes that policy-makers' primary concern for material standards and values potentially inhibits residents' control of their dwelling circumstances. For King, part of housing quality ought to be based on a vernacular housing process, or that which is self-made in distinction to being dictated from elsewhere. Thus, echoing the arguments of Illich (1992), King (1996: 167) argues that a dwelling is beyond the prescriptions of professionals: 'it can only be made by those experiencing and making it as an habitual and self made process' (see also Chapter 8).

A difficulty is how to translate such sentiments into practical action and change, especially in relation to dwellings provided by private-sector house builders. For some, the best route is a reliance on market mechanisms, in which builders are free from government regulation (HBF, 1995; King, 1996, 2003). Seeking to secure housing quality through market mechanisms may, however, lead to less than required by certain groups who, like some disabled people, are at the margins of the labour market and have limited capacity to exercise a market choice (in relation to their consumption of dwellings). Goodchild and Karn (1997) also note that, left to the market, the focus tends to be one of quality of construction rather than the quality of design, in which the non-tangible elements of habitation, or those aspects of the dwelling that relate to non-physical and technical criteria, are neglected or ignored.

The current dwelling standards of the NHBC, for instance, make few references to the overall size of dwellings, and little is said about the performance or adaptability of dwellings in relation to household activities. Housing quality, where it is mentioned, revolves primarily around discourses of technical flexibility. For instance, as Figure 1.12 shows, the NHBC has a quality checklist which instructs prospective customers what to look out for when buying a new house. It directs customers, when viewing property, to pose pertinent (perhaps naïve or self-evident) questions such as, 'is the brickwork clean and free from major chips...', 'do the downpipes and guttering appear secure?', and 'do garage doors open and shut properly?' There is, however, some vague recognition that the form of dwellings ought to fit the changing needs of the household, with the checklist inviting prospective customers to consider how far the size of the dwelling meets their needs 'in the present and in the future'.

The discourse of technical flexibility, evident in most NHBC publications, runs parallel to builders' focus, encouraged by government, on issues relating to managerial and systems efficiency. This is apparent in the UK

1.12 NHBC – a quality checklist.

What to look for:

- Check whether the homes are being built by an NHBC-registered builder. If so, your new home will have the benefit of NHBC's 10-year Buildmark warranty and insurance cover.
- Look out for PIJ flags and site boards – this means the new homes have been built by a 'Pride in the Job' award-winning site manager and indicates that the builder has been recognized for its exceptional standards.
- Once you have found a home you like, check out local amenities – find out where the nearest shops, schools and petrol stations are.

On site:

- Remember each construction site is unique, with hazards and exposures changing daily. Always wear strong, sturdy footwear and any protective equipment provided, e.g. hard hat.
- When crossing the site, use only man-made roads and tracts. Watch out for moving vehicles.

The new home:

Outside:

- Is the brickwork clean and free from major chips, and is the pointing neat and evenly finished?
- Do the downpipes and guttering appear secure?
- Do garage doors open and shut properly?
- Has debris from building work been removed from front and back gardens?

Inside:

- Take a tape measure to check your furniture will fit into your new home. It is also a good idea to see what storage space is available.
- Is there enough room for your needs in the present and in the future?
- Finally, try to imagine the house in good weather and bad, and in each season. It will help you imagine whether you will be happy there all year round.

Source: NHBC, 2003

government's approach to improving house-building, which is encouraging builders, amongst other things, to bring in 'board level expertise from manufacturing industry in order to implement new supply chain management techniques' and 'to develop better component systems to speed up construction' (DTI, 2000). Likewise, in the USA the National Housing Quality Award scheme defines quality achievement in relation to how well builders measure up to eight criteria, including leadership, customer satisfaction, human resources and business results (NAHB Research Center, 2003). Of 100 marks allocated across the quality achievement criteria, 30 are available in relation to 'business results', or what the NAHB (2003: 3) defines as the measurement of 'high performance business practices'.

Such schemes are bereft of measures of quality that relate to the performance of dwellings in relation to users' interaction with design, nor do they rate or quantify the provision of affordable or appropriate dwellings in relation to the specific needs of different types of potential consumers. One possible way of rectifying this is to respond to and develop the suggestion by Goodchild and Karn (1997: 174) that 'to improve quality of design in the private sector . . . the best mechanism is to strengthen consumer pressure'. However, this is likely to be a problematical route because, to be effective, consumer pressure will need (a) to be able to challenge the oligopolistic producer networks that dominate the design and construction of dwellings, characterized by, as Hooper (1999) suggests, low levels of responsiveness by builders to consumer demands; and (b) to overcome the unequal capacities and capabilities of different types of consumers to influence the attitudes and actions of builders.

One should not underestimate the complexity of the social-institutional, economic and cultural shifts required to broaden conceptions of, and practices related to, housing quality. In particular, given the context-dependent nature and rootedness of housing quality in specific socio-economic, political and cultural relationships, it may well be that it is neither possible nor desirable to specify its particular elements. However, broader principles, already alluded to, can provide some guidance about what housing quality ought to be, particularly in relation to the needs of those with mobility impairment and/or who are dependent on a wheelchair to facilitate all or part of their mobility:

- The objective of housing quality should be to facilitate processes that ensure that an individual's habitation is dignified. Following Somerville and Chan (2001), an important part of dignity is autonomy or the capacity for self-determination. However, for disabled people, like others, self-determination is constrained by a combination of circumstances, including their lack of income and employment opportunities, and the poor quality of physical accessibility of the housing stock (amongst other things). The attainment of housing quality requires, therefore, not only the rectification of the physical dimensions and performance of dwellings, but also the provision of the means for disabled people to be able to consume them.
- Housing quality is not solely about the production of physical spaces relating to the functioning of the dwelling. As Chow (2002: 82) suggests, the 'task of dwelling design is not to prescribe a fit between a

lifestyle's activities and a house's form'. While the attainment of physical criteria (or standards) is a necessary part of the qualitative experiences of habitation, it is not sufficient. In addition, a 'dwelling', in Habraken's (1972) terms, is a 'building', or something that facilitates what King (1996: 178) refers to as 'other intrinsic valuable relationships'. The dwelling is a conduit for personal meaning, privacy and a place that, as Norberg-Schulz (1985) suggests, opens up pathways into the world.

- In this respect, a dwelling is much more than a physical structure; it also provides a context for social interaction, familial engagement and the reproduction of bodily and cognitive functions (King, 1996; Somerville and Chan, 2001). Quality of habitation ought to be related to corporeal or bodily experiences of the environment, and the understanding that physical and mental bodily matter should not be reduced to a 'type' that revolves around a medicalized norm. While dwellings ought to be responsive to the universal needs of the human body (for warmth, water, defecation, etc.), how such needs are met will be dependent on the particular individuals.

- However, the mentalities of building standards are premised on the reduction of social complexity to type, and the facilitation of living for a standardized consumer that, more often than not, revolves around the family unit. The (officially) recommended numbers of rooms, including their prescribed dimensions, locations and functions, betrays ignorance of the dynamics of social relationships and the complexities of use to which dwelling space is subject. Conceptions of housing quality ought to transcend the focus of prescribed standards on familial (or other) norms, and instead seek to respond to the multiplicity of human interactions that revolve around the intersections between ethnicity, sexuality, gender, disability and other (meaningful) categories of social identity and process.

- The economics of speculative house building are not predisposed towards vernacular, or local, processes in which customized or individual dwelling design is paramount. If one accepts that housing quality is maximized by responding to individual needs, then the social and economic relations of the building industry need to be modified. For Chow (2002: 82), this means that the architect and builder needs 'to design for choices rather than to make prototypes to choose from'. Housing quality is the reverse of the 'type' or the prefabricated or the preset design that seeks to anticipate the interactions between bodies, human values and design. Housing quality, then, requires a fundamental restructuring of housing provision and the underlying values that shape it.

- Issues of governance are integral to housing quality and, following King (1996), the absence of housing quality is related in part to the mentalities of policy professionals, builders, developers, architects, etc., who tend to see housing as a 'thing' – that is, as an object rather than a 'process'. Modernist values and practices that have shaped housing provision and consumption define housing as a commodity that can be prescribed, developed and delivered by hierarchical systems of production, planning and control (King, 1996). Such systems of governance provide limited scope for individual intervention or determination of outcomes, and ought to be changed to reflect what Illich (1992) refers to as vernacular or self-made or taught forms of social interaction.

- The social relations of house building are, as Chapter 2 shows, top down, and rarely provide user input into the design and construction process. The use of consumer surveys and feedback by builders is a poor substitute for drawing on first-hand, experiential knowledge of habitation. Following Lefebvre (1991), it seems appropriate to reframe disabled people's right to good-quality housing in ways that expand on what democratic involvement and deliberation is (or ought to be). For Lefebvre, democratic deliberation ought not to be limited just to the formal institutions (and processes) of government, but also be applied to all decisions that contribute to social process and outcome. This means that the right to the city would, as Purcell (2002: 102) says, 'give urban inhabitants a literal seat at the corporate table'.

1.6 Conclusions

There has rarely been any substantial debate amongst academics or policy-makers and practitioners about the interrelationships between disability and housing quality, other than to discuss and develop a range of technical standards or measures that are designed to respond primarily to the access needs of wheelchair users. This is unsatisfactory because it reduces disability to a 'type' or a caricature of who a disabled person is, and assumes that the quality of domestic habitation can be facilitated by recourse to the implementation of a one-dimensional conception of housing quality. In contrast, the arguments in this chapter suggest that housing quality, as a multidimensional phenomenon, ought to relate design criteria to the complex, contingent and embodied processes that comprise disabled people's experiences of domestic design, and the built environment more generally (Imrie, 1996; Imrie and Hall, 2001b).

This will require significant changes in thinking about what disability is and, in particular, a rejection of categories that reduce disabled people to the (ontological) status of dependent, deviant and 'not normal' spheres of existence and being. Such characterizations and related categories remain powerful and centre stage, and they reaffirm rather than challenge builders' and building professionals' pejorative conceptions of what disability is, and how the housing needs of disabled people should be met. As later chapters will show, actors in the building industry tend to regard disabled people as a minority group who do not constitute a sufficient market demand and, consequentially, are not an attractive or legitimate target. This suggests that the attitudes and practices of speculative house builders and related agents are part of an enframing context which conditions, in part, the quality of habitation experienced by disabled people. I turn to this theme in the next chapter.

Further reading

For general overviews of the key debates about and insights into housing quality, readers should consult the excellent writings by Carmona (2001),

Franklin (2001) and Goodchild (1997). In relation to debates on disability and housing quality standards, readers should refer to the articles by Malcolm Harrison (2004) and Jo Milner and Ruth Madigan (2004). On broader debates about modernity and the rights to habitation (and the city), readers should look at Lefebvre (1991, 1996) and Dikec (2001). The interrelationships between modernity and the design of dwellings are very well covered in Peter Rowe's (1993) superb book, so too in the texts by Wright (1980, 1981). Jonathan Hill's (2003) book, 'Actions of Architecture', is excellent in dealing with themes about flexibility and the design process.

2 Disability, design and the speculative house-building industry

2.1 Introduction

All the houses they saw had a common quality for which she could find no word, but for which the proper word is 'incivility'. 'They build these 'ouses', she said, 'as though girls wasn't 'uman beings.'

(H. G. Wells, 1993, chapter 1, sections 2–3).

One of the important elements in understanding the interrelationships between housing quality and disability relates to the processes of production and provision of dwellings. Such processes are characterized by a complexity of social, technical and legal relationships that collectively condition the attitudes and actions of builders and other professionals in relation to the design and construction of dwellings. Competitive strategies of house builders revolve around the purchase of land, and the attempt to realize profit through land and house price inflation. Because of the high costs involved in the process, builders are reluctant to change tried and tested design, or to increase costs by recourse to customized production. Rather, the production of dwellings is driven by risk-averse least-cost strategies that reflect, in part, the tight profit margins of the house-building industry. This usually results in the perpetuation of standardized design packages or, as Carmona (2001: 125) aptly observes, 'the unique market circumstances in which house building occurs will continue to ensure the widely accepted (even amongst many house builders) devaluing of design . . .'.

The purpose of this chapter is to explore the persistent lack of accessible design in dwellings in the broader context of the rationale and operations of the speculative house-building industry. In doing so, I develop two interrelated observations. First, while most builders and building professionals hold pejorative views about disabled people and their design requirements, these in and of themselves do not explain the absence of accessible design in dwellings. Rather, its absence has to be related in large part to the broader social relations of housing production, or what I term the rationalities of real estate (see also Ball, 1983, 1996; Barlow, 1999; Nicol and Hooper, 1999). Second, building professionals tend to regard accessible design as compromising aspects of the building process by, for example, adding to their development costs and reducing design quality. However, I want to suggest that aspects of accessible design, far from detracting from developers' profits, can be combined with the building process to produce satisfactory outcomes for all parties.

I divide the chapter into three. First, I note that contemporary debates about the poor quality of dwellings produced by speculative builders are not new, but have their roots in the building booms of the nineteenth century (see Burdett, 1883; Dyos, 1961, 1968; Jackson, 1981; Burnett, 1986). Historically, the speculative builder has tended to be characterized as a purveyor of poor quality and the chief culprit in the production of a bland urban environment. Typical of this was the comment by Benjamin Disraeli (1847: 12) in relation to the impact of builders' practices on the design of new neighbourhoods in the mid-nineteenth century: 'it is impossible to conceive of anything more tame, more insipid, more uniform. Pancras is like Marylebone, Marylebone is like Paddington; all the streets resemble each other'. Such characterizations have entered into popular consciousness but, as I shall argue, they are unhelpful because they ignore, or deflect attention from, the broader social and political contexts and underlying processes that shape the attitudes and actions of builders and related professionals.

In this respect, I develop the contention that the speculative building industry is unlikely to be attentive to disabled people because of its adherence to the rationality of real estate economics. This rationality revolves around what Guy (1998: 207) describes as builders extracting 'as much surplus exchange value as possible from building construction with little regard to the eventual use value of the building'. It is characterized by, amongst other factors, the prioritization of economic objectives, the drive towards design reductionism and the standardization of the product, and a conception of the customer or home purchaser in general or abstract, non-specific terms (see Ball, 1983; Barlow, 1999; Hooper, 1999). This combination is, as I shall argue, problematical not only for disabled people but also for consumers more generally, who time and again suggest that dwellings are neither spacious or flexible enough to accommodate diverse and changing forms of habitation (Hooper, 1999; Carmona, 2001).

In the second part, I describe and evaluate the building industry's orientation towards disabled people, and in particular explore what I regard as the fallacies and falsehoods held by many builders in relation to responding to the domestic design needs of disabled people (see also Imrie and Hall, 2001a; Truesdale and Steinfeld, 2002; Burns, 2004; P. Thomas, 2004). One of these is builders' reproduction of the problematical or reductive understanding of disabled people that sees disability as an abnormal medical condition that requires special provision or treatment separate from the mainstream. In the context of housing, this means that builders propagate the erroneous view that they ought not to be required to provide for those that are deemed, by the building industry, to constitute a minority (for example, see the HBF, 1995). In addition, builders (and their pressure groups) tend to deploy data and argument that, as I shall argue, exaggerate the operational, and other, cost impacts of providing accessible design for disabled people.

I conclude by suggesting that while the rationalities of real estate are unlikely to be displaced, they can be modified by appropriate regulation by government and by the use of financial and other incentives to encourage builders to respond to the variegated, yet often unarticulated, needs of disabled people in the domestic environment.

2.2 Housing quality and the speculative house-building process

The speculative house-building industry attracts negative and often hostile comments in relation to the quality of dwellings constructed by its members. More than any other industry, house building is perceived by the general public as a process that seeks to minimize expenditure on design innovation and quality in order to maximize profits. For instance, Rogers' (1994) survey of consumers' views of speculative dwellings in the UK found that 90 per cent of respondents felt that builders were not providing enough choice in design. In addition, 60 per cent felt that what was on offer was not value for money, leading Rogers (1994: 8) to conclude that consumers are provided with 'little or no leverage over the content of domestic design'.[1] Likewise, in 2001 the Minister for Planning, Lord Falconer (2001: 2), in commenting on speculative new-build dwellings, noted that 'too many of these housing estates are designed for nowhere but found everywhere . . . they end up being soulless and dispiriting'.

Such sentiments are deeply rooted in the psyche of British culture, and have historical precedents. Jackson (1981: 2), in writing about nineteenth-century speculative building in London, notes that 'the speculative house remained an object of consternation and satirical derision'. Letters to *The Builder* magazine in the mid-nineteenth century frequently drew attention to the inadequacies of speculative housing. As one observer suggested: 'the practices adopted by builders in the erection of houses for their own private speculation are so radically unworkmanlike and dishonest' (Anon., *The Builder*, 1844: 473).[2] Others put it more strongly, with a feature in *Building News* suggesting that speculative builders' 'houses were ugly and vulgar . . . he always built on one pattern; it saved time, trouble and expense; and he never found that tenants cared for anything but cheapness' (Anon., *Building News*, 1873: 242).[3] Likewise, Burdett's (1883: 238) observations of jerry building in a poorer middle-class area of London, noted:

Here is a house, empty, which was completed and occupied two years ago . . . Now look at the floors. Not one of these is level; they are at all sorts of angles, owing to the sinking of the walls. You have to walk up and down hill, as it were, to cross each room in the house.

These observations about urban form were commonplace throughout the nineteenth century in which one commentary suggested that the effects of the speculative building process was to produce places that 'were not so much towns as . . . the barracks of an industry' (Hammond and Hammond, 1917: 39–40; Figure 2.1).[4] The speculative builder was reviled or, as a letter to *The Builder* (Anon, 1885: 896) said: 'he found a solitude and left

2.1 Images of the speculative dwelling.

a slum'. Others were scathing about builders' imposition of house-types on neighbourhoods, creating feelings of what one commentator described as the 'solemn monotony that reigns over the purely residential district' (*Our Rambler in Belgravia*, 1869: 89). A comment in *Punch* (1846: 178) magazine suggested that the street scene in London was affecting local residents: 'dull uniformity sends him into a fit of melancholy for a whole morning's walk'.

Later accounts and observations of the speculative builder were much more circumspect (Dyos, 1961, 1968; Jackson, 1981; Burnett, 1985). Jackson (1981: 6) refers to a feature in the *Building News* in 1908 in which it is suggested that 'it may well be doubted whether all bad building is speculative, or whether . . . all speculative building is bad'. Dyos (1961, 1968) also notes that pejorative comments about the building trade, while reflecting some builders' practices, were often exaggerated and failed to recognize that many speculative builders produced reasonable quality dwellings. Where poor quality of design and construction was evident it was not always the fault of the builder and, as Dyos (1961) argues, a significant determinant of building practices was the reluctance of governments to develop building codes which meant that builders could operate more or less to whatever standards they pleased.

Dyos's comments are helpful because they suggest that speculative house builders, and their products, were not all of a 'type', and that their actions were conditioned largely by social, economic and political circumstances often beyond their control. For instance, Dyos (1961) notes that government taxation on building materials in the 1870s and 1880s, a period of significant demand for new dwellings, did not encourage builders to purchase expensive or high-quality materials. This period was also characterized by the availability of cheap and plentiful credit which, aligned with the high demand for housing, encouraged many people to take up building as a trade, often without the know-how, skills or commitment required in the production of quality dwellings (Dyos, 1961). Not surprisingly, in places like Camberwell, South London, there was a surfeit of builders, with Dyos (1961) reporting that 416 were operating there between 1878 and 1880.

Burnett (1986: 260) develops a similar analysis to that of Dyos of the speculative house builder, in which he suggests that social comment and criticism was, often unfairly, directed at speculative builders in the interwar period because 'intense price competition . . . had forced down the quality of work and materials and obliged builders to concentrate on external appearance and gimmicks which would sell the product'.[5] Likewise, Richards (1973: 86) notes that rivalry among builders to produce cheap dwellings had led them to use 'cheap materials and mean dimensions and to rely on insufficiently skilled labour'. Comments in the *Illustrated Builder and Carpenter* (1935) reinforced this view by suggesting that the problems of poorly designed housing were due to 'the so called estate developers employing labourers who are carrying out the work of tradesmen without serving any form of apprenticeship'.

These observations suggest that competitive pressure, rather than wilful, pathological, actions, primarily influence builders' attitudes and practices towards the quality of their product. Such actions can be understood as being driven by the rationalities of real estate, or the nature of the specific products and markets that characterize house building. The speculative house-building process, in seeking to achieve scale economies and product throughput, post-1945, reflects the modernist paradigm and its legitimating of what Lefaivre and Tzoni (1983: 5) refer to as 'the norm of efficiency as the highest in all facets of human life'. This norm can be defined in relation to builders' prioritization of a range of building features not necessarily sensitized to user needs, including the minimization of the footprint of dwellings, the maximization of plot densities, the standardization of layout, the use of a range of limited house-types, and the encouragement of generic usages of space.

Such features are produced by a process which, as Carmona (2001: 111) suggests, is characterized by minimal time to develop and deliver good design; no detailed site analysis or visits; little quality control in relation to the design process; rarely any designer involvement in the construction phases of a project; and the attainment of cost targets above all else. In particular, dwellings have a high capital value 'with large amounts of developers' capital tied up in purchase of land and materials' (Carmona, 2001: 108). Such capital cannot be realized as profit until dwellings have been constructed, a process which is characterized by lengthy time scales. The imperative on builders is to speed up the design and construction of dwellings to permit rapid turnover, a process that is sometimes unhinged by factors beyond builders' control, such as volatility in demand and delays in obtaining appropriate planning and building control consents. Uncertainty, combined with low profit margins in the industry, pushes builders towards what Carmona (2001: 111) refers to as 'least costly solutions'.[6]

The rationale is, primarily, for builders to profit by, as Barlow (1999: 25) suggests, 'timing the sale of dwellings to benefit from house price inflation'. The industry's short-term horizons and prioritization of seeking to realize short-term profits militate against investment in product or process innovation in relation to aspects of housing design. As a consequence, builders are not likely to focus on innovation in design or layout as a source of profits because, as a range of commentators note, builders' primary source of profit is the land on which the dwelling is constructed rather than the dwelling itself (Ball, 1983; Bramley et al., 1995; Barlow, 1999; Hooper, 1999; Carmona, 2001). This emphasis has led to economists frequently referring to house building as 'the backwards industry' in which, as Barlow (1999: 32) suggests, 'houses are often completed to suit the requirements of the financial period rather than customers' needs' (see also Landis, 1983).

The underlying dynamics or rationalities of real estate manifest themselves in different ways, but, as Ball (1983: 141) recounts, one outcome is that private builders' behaviour in the post-Parker Morris period led to construction standards well below the recommended minimum, or a 'minimum for the then typical standard of living for the working class' (see also Goodchild and Furbey, 1986; Goodchild, 1997). Likewise, Leopold and Bishop (1983: 71), in comparing space standards and design quality in public and private dwellings, noted that the former far exceeded the latter. As they suggested, in relation to private new-build dwellings: 'in many cases rooms simply cannot accommodate the basic furniture necessary for its stated function ... rooms that cannot meet the basic requirements obviously offer no flexibility for sensible alternative arrangements' (Leopold and Bishop, 1983: 71; see also Ball, 1983; Hooper and Nicol, 1999).

The diminution in space standards in private dwellings was exacerbated by market and regulatory conditions and, due to recession in housing and property markets in the late 1980s and early 1990s, the additional fixtures and fittings and enhanced space standards recommended by Parker Morris were particularly unattractive to builders. Likewise, space standards were subject to more or less continual government deregulation post-1980, and this encouraged builders to reduce the square footage of housing, especially at the bottom end of one- and two-bedroom houses. For example, internal corridor widths and floor to ceiling heights were often reduced by builders, the latter as a consequence of the abolition of minimum standards in 1993. In effect, the reverse of what was had been encouraged by Parker Morris and related standards (i.e. enhanced space standards) was evident in much new-build housing by the end of the last millennium.

It was also suggested that the design limitations were such that not even adaptations would be able to create flexibility of use in the dwellings (Carmona, 2001). In part this is a reflection of the emergence of the house-type, in which builders construct a limited range of dwellings characterized by standardized design features and fixtures and fittings. As Hooper (1999: 12) notes, the use of a portfolio of standard design features enables builders to 'estimate accurately production costs and construction times under conditions of uncertainty'. This produces, at best, incremental behaviour, in which most builders are reluctant to change elements of the standard design package – or, as a builder that was interviewed by me said: 'At the end of the day it's all about money and making profit, and the more you over-subscribe, the less that profit will be, and regrettably, in this commercial world you've got to ignore the potential for overstepping the mark'. The implication of this, as Hooper (1999) observes, is one whereby potential customers have limited choice in relation to the design of new dwellings.

This is because speculative builders tend to perceive consumers as conservative in taste, and likely to react against dramatic shifts in style or design. Most house builders claim that they design and construct dwellings according to what consumers want and, as Alwyn Lloyd (1936: 122) suggests, 'the attitude of the builder to the planning and design of the dwellings he erects, naturally, to a large extent reflects the mentality of those who purchase them'. However, evidence from a range of research suggests that Lloyd's observation may be inaccurate in that, as intimated earlier in this part of the chapter, there seems to be much customer dissatisfaction with speculative housing, and little attention paid by builders to particular design features that customers say that they want. For instance, research seems to suggest that consumers are dissatisfied with aspects of new dwellings and want more choice in relation to their homes' interiors, including additional storage space and energy-saving features (Welsh, 1994; Barlow and Ozaki, 2003).

While Hooper (1999) and others note that a 'new perspective is emerging' whereby builders are increasingly sensitive to customer needs, Hooper

(1999: 15) adds caution by suggesting that it is 'unlikely that the UK house building industry will be able to adapt its increasingly standardised products to a rapidly changing demographic structure and the associated changes in lifestyle' (see also Barlow and Ozaki, 2003). Barlow (1999: 39) also notes that builders have 'a better awareness of articulated customer' and, given that disabled people are (according to builders) rarely seen or heard by them, the fear is that disabled people's demands will remain unarticulated and not likely to influence the design of new house-types. The problem, I would argue, is less to do with the relative absence of consumer pressure by disabled people (which, after all, can be ignored by builders) and more with the attitudes and values of building and construction professionals, as conditioned by the broader rationalities of real estates. This is a theme that I now turn to.

2.3 Deconstructing the values of the speculative building industry

The rationalities of real estate, underpinned by the broader structures of building provision, predispose builders to particular courses of action in relation to the design and construction of dwellings. As the previous section intimated, builders, while retaining some autonomy in influencing the scope and specificities of the design and building process, tend to operate within a narrow range of house-types that, in Chow's (2002: 87) terms, capitalize 'on the ability of people to adapt' (see also Ball, 1998; Barlow, 1999). This formulaic approach to the design of dwellings is endemic in the UK, the USA and elsewhere, and its cost-cutting/profit maximizing rationale underpins, in part, builders' antagonistic attitudes towards regulation or rules. This is particularly evident in relation to accessible design and disability, and, whenever and wherever governments have raised the issue, it has led to predictable comments and reactions by house builders.

For instance, the HBF (1995: 2) in the UK has characterized Part M of the building regulations as 'a wholly disproportionate response to a very limited problem' (see also Beazer Homes, 1995). They suggested that its introduction was likely to cause rain penetration through front doors due to the accessible thresholds, to increase building costs due to the use of additional materials, and to lead to the loss of one- and two-bed starter homes, too small to accommodate the increase in space standards.[7] In addition, the HBF (1995: 1) said that 'there is no evidence of particular difficulty in gaining access to new homes on a scale that justifies taking special measures to amend all new homes'. Instead, as they stated, 'if a disabled person visits a home owner, it is to be expected that they can be assisted over the threshold' (HBF, 1995: 2). They also objected to Part M on aesthetic grounds in noting that 'the provision of ramped access will in itself be ugly, increasing the amount of concrete or tarmac in front of houses' (HBF, 1995: 3).

The attitudes of the HBF, and house builders more generally, tend to be rooted in a medical conception of disability that blames victims for their plight. For instance, a report by the Volume House Builders Study Group (1995: 1) in the UK notes that:

unfortunately the situation of many disabled people (particularly the elderly) does prevent their normal participation in activities available to the majority . . . The remedy is to assume that visiting disabled people will be assisted from the point of entry to the dwelling. Where they are visiting an able bodied occupant then that person will be available to provide necessary assistance over the threshold, into a WC, etc.

Likewise, the Vice President of the House Builders Association of Illinois in the USA, Mark Harrison (cited at www.raggedgemagazine.com, 6 February 2002) has argued that the problem for builders is having to respond to the minority of the population (with abnormal bodily conditions): 'at what point do we stop taking away rights of healthy people in writing a standard for the handicapped?'

Disabled people, according to this opinion, are non-persons, or those who ought to be treated differently because of their impairments and unhealthy bodies. There is, however, nothing extraordinary in this view, because those builders who voice it are doing no more than replicating and reflecting broader societal conceptions of disability that suggest that disabled people are second-class citizens who, through bad luck, individual error or misfortune, are impaired (see Oliver, 1990; Imrie, 1996; Imrie and Hall, 2001b). The prognosis is 'self help', in which the onus is on the individual (i.e. the disabled person) to overcome social and environmental barriers. While this line of thinking is, as Chapter 1 suggested, detrimental to responding to the needs of disabled people, and implicated in their indignification, it becomes more so when aligned with what I regard as three problematical assumptions propagated by builders about the interrelationships between disability and the design and building process. These are that:

1 The provision of accessible dwellings will add significantly to development costs
2 Regulation relating to access is disproportionate as there is little demand for accessible dwellings
3 The implementation of accessible design will lead to a reduction in housing quality.

I discuss and evaluate each proposition in turn.

The provision of accessible dwellings will add significantly to development costs

The response of builders to legal regulation relating to access reflects the economic rationale of real estate that defines the value of a building primarily in terms of its monetary, financial or market valuation. For builders, the value of a dwelling is also related to the costs associated with its design, construction, marketing and sale – or, as a builder said to me in interview: 'regulations relating to access are costing us more and place an additional burden on the building industry'. Others concurred; as another builder in interview commented: 'take away all these regulations, and we would save thousands of pounds on each dwelling we construct' (see also the testimonials in Chapter 5). These views are part of a broader tradition within the building trade of characterizing any regulation as imposing a cost on construction activity, although, as Landis (1983) notes, there is disagreement about the precise effects of building codes or regulations on the cost of dwellings.

For instance, in describing the impact of the use of building codes in California, Maisel (1953: 249) suggests that 50 per cent of builders had their construction costs raised by less than 1 per cent for the typical home due to compliance with the uniform codes. Even in places where greater code restrictions were in place, a situation affecting 20 per cent of builders in the state, 'the increased costs did not run to more than 3 per cent above the uniform code areas' (Maisel, 1953: 249). In contrast, Burns and Mittelbach's (1968) analysis of the 1968 House and Home Survey in the USA indicated that up to 7 per cent of the cost of constructing a single family home could be saved by eliminating what they referred to as the most wasteful building codes. Others note that the strict enforcement of building regulations or codes is one of the causes of city centre decline in the USA, because, as Burby et al. (2000: 21) comment, 'it adds to the costs of development in unnecessary ways' (see also Culwell and Kau, 1982).[8]

This was the general view of builders towards the Department of the Environment's (DoE) announcement, in 1995, that Part M of the building regulations was likely to be extended to cover newly constructed dwellings in England and Wales. In written representations to the DOE, builders and/or their representatives and assorted lobby groups made it clear that they opposed Part M, primarily because of its cost implications. Their general comments about the cost implications of Part M had a familiar and repetitive refrain: 'it will have a massive cost effect on our industry as a whole, affecting every new dwelling built' (Goodman, 1995: 1); 'the additional costs are intolerable' (Wimpey Homes, 1995: 1); 'the cost implications of Part M will have serious consequences for all house builders...' (Finn, 1995: 2); and 'the extension would have compliance cost implications . . . as it would profoundly change the layout of many new dwellings' (Bright, 1995: 1).[9]

Some builders went to great lengths to prove the point by itemizing what they thought the cost implications of Part M were likely to be. For instance, a representative from Beazer Homes argued that if the regulation had been applied across all of their 5,350 housing completions for 1993–94, it would have cost the company an additional £5.35 million (Davis, 1995: 1). Others concurred, and the Senior Design and Planning Executive of Midland and General Homes estimated, as evident in Table 2.1, that the additional cost per plot of implementing Part M would be, for his company, £2,845 – with the consequence that, as he said, 'the marketability of our product will be decreased rather than enhanced by these new provisions' (Smith, 1995: 1). Likewise, the Managing Director of Wimpey Homes (1995: 1) suggested that 'our three bedroom house will have to be increased in size . . . with an associated cost of between £450 and £671 per house'.[10]

Builders also objected to Part M on the grounds that its implementation was likely to reduce the numbers of dwelling units achievable per acre, with a consequential reduction of profit. A representative for Beazer

Table 2.1 Estimate of the additional costs of Part M: Midland & General Homes.

Design features required to meet Part M	Costs of provision per dwelling (£)
Ramped entrance	140
Increases in door widths and internal modifications	80
Upsizing of site storm drainage	20
Additional site excavation and grading	75
Additional surfacing wall/drainage	655
Loss of 2 dwellings in every 50	1,875
Total additional cost	2,845

Source: Smith, 1995.

Homes said that, on an average mixed development of 12,000 square feet (of building) per acre, meeting 'the requirements of Part M was likely to increase footage by 250 to 300 square feet per acre or the equivalent of one unit per acre' (Davis, 1995: 1). In their representations to the DOE, Beazer Homes calculated that on a site with 75 plots there would be a loss of value of £400 per plot. This, so Beazer Homes claimed, would have translated into a non-recoverable loss of plot value of £2.14 million if the regulation had been applied to its total build of 5,350 units in 1993–94. Likewise, Barratts Development plc said that adapting one of its house types, The Palmerston, to meet Part M would require them to add 69 square feet per dwelling, resulting in the loss of 'one plot every 11 houses' and, consequentially, a major loss in profits (Finn, 1995).

However, some of the companies were less sure about the impact of certain aspects of the regulation, with the Planning Manager at Beazer Homes noting that 'it has to be said that across the 13 operating companies, no clear pattern emerges. In some areas it is more expensive to make small units comply than large units, and in other cases the exact opposite applies' (Davis, 1995: 1). For Davis, 'it is difficult to calculate an average cost per unit', suggesting that the bigger issue was redesign costs which 'will work out at £50 per unit'. Some builders, as Chapter 5 illustrates, admitted that their costing estimates submitted to the DoE had been crude – a point borne out by studies that have suggested that the cost impact of accessibility legislation was never likely to be as high as builders initially claimed (Schroeder and Steinfeld, 1979; Department of Housing and Urban Development, 1990; Steven Winter Associates, 1993; BCIS, 2003).[11] Thus, a report by BCIS (2003), on behalf of the ODPM, indicates that the estimated additional costs per house, as Table 2.2 shows, ought to be no more than between £935 and £1,495.

These views are confirmed further by studies that question, and even refute, builders' allegations that the adoption of accessible design is prohibitively expensive (Dunn, 1988; Truesdale and Steinfeld, 2002). For instance, Dunn (1988), referring to dwellings in the USA, suggests that the additional costs of constructing accessible dwellings ranges between 0.25 per cent and 4.2 per cent depending on the numbers and types of dwellings being constructed. As he notes, the additional increase would be less than 1 per cent if at least 10 per cent of all new dwellings in a development were constructed to accessibility standards. Likewise, Steven

Proposed measures	Estimated additional costs per dwelling (£)
Level or ramped access to dwelling	Nominal except on steep slopes
Level entry threshold	100–175
775 mm entrance door	Nominal
Entrance-level WC (where not provided)	835–1,320
Wider internal doors and circulation	Nominal
Accessible switches and sockets	Nominal
Flats: ambulant stairways	140 per flight
Total	935–1,495

Table 2.2 Estimated additional costs per dwelling for proposed Part M measures, private dwellings.

Source: Adapted from BCIS, 2003.

Winter Associates (1993) compared the costs of construction of non-accessible family dwellings on eight sites in the USA, and the comparative costs if constructed to the accessibility standards contained in the Fair Housing Accessibility Guidelines (see Chapter 3). The study showed that the cost differences between the two were insignificant, with a less than 1 per cent increase in costs to incorporate accessible design features.

In a similar exercise, Truesdale and Steinfeld (2002) hired building contractors to estimate the costs of visitable dwellings built in Buffalo and Rochester in New York State, and compared them against the cost of previous, non-visitable designs that the contractors were using. As Table 2.3 indicates, the costs of the visitability features are modest and, as Truesdale and Steinfeld (2002: 19) suggest, they are 'clearly affordable within the scope of home building projects' and furthermore 'would not be noticeable in the monthly mortgage repayment' (see also Carroll et al., 1999). For Truesdale and Steinfeld (2002: 19), what is important to emphasize, but rarely mentioned by the building trade, is that 'the redesign improved general livability considerably ... the cost difference resulted in increased value; the result was an improved home design, and the new owners are quite satisfied' (see also Sangster, 1997).

This has been the consistent message of those who, in the UK, have argued that Part M is modest and that, as a minimum, LTH standards ought to be adopted (Cobbold, 1997; Carroll et al., 1999). While LTH standards do not greatly exceed Part M, they seek to encourage livable environments that people can use and that are not prohibitively expensive for builders to design and construct (see Table 2.4). Sangster (1997) estimates that the cost of a LTH would be no more than an additional £295 per three-bedroom (private) dwelling, while O'Brien et al. (2002: 33) note that to incorporate all of the standards 'would cost a minimum of £165 and a maximum of £545', and would reduce related costs, such as those associated with reduced accidents in the home. Likewise, for the Access Committee for England (1995: 10): 'the average cost of between £180 and £400 ... is a small price to pay for such large long-term benefits, but it is also insignificant compared to other factors affecting house prices, such as geographical location, land price and interest rates'.

In this respect, builders' observations about the costs of regulation in relation to accessible design in dwellings are one-sided because they do not account for savings to governments' health care and welfare spending

Table 2.3 An estimation of the costs of visitability in new dwellings.

Main visitability criteria	Design changes	Itemized cost	Comments
1. No step entry	Grade site to provide driveway slope of 5 per cent and elevation change of 12 inches	No cost	This is the preferred option according to the contractor that was consulted. The fill from the basement excavation could be used to grade the site. The cost of the grading would be offset by eliminating the need to remove the excavated soil from the site
	Eliminate wood stairway and handrails at rear deck	$300–$500	
	Provide 6-foot long wooden ramp, with two handrails to the rear deck with railings on both sides, supported by the deck at the top end and a concrete pad at the bottom end.	Less than $500	
	Concrete front terrace level with interior floor with a slight pitch for drainage.	No difference in cost	
2. Accessible doors	Widen 5 hinged doors to 32 inches clear minimum	$25	Exterior doors are usually already wide enough
	Increase width of bedroom hallway from 36 inches to 42 inches	No cost – same wall length and total area	Width of hallway would be sufficient at 36 inches if doors were all on sides of hallway
	Cut 3 inches off the width of all bedrooms and add 6 inches to hallway width	No cost	

Table 2.3 continued.

Main visitability criteria	Design changes	Itemized cost	Comments
3. Access to one bathroom	Add approximately 10 square feet in one bathroom to allow door to close when wheelchair is in the room	No cost; compensated by slightly reduced area elsewhere	Many bathroom designs will not need additional space, just the reorganization of the fixtures
	Reduce living room, dining area by 10 square feet	No cost	Most houses will have enough space to accomplish this trade-off without any impact on livability

Source: Truesdale and Steinfeld (2002: 18).

Table 2.4 The minimum and maximum comparative costs for each of the life-time homes criteria across housing sectors.

Life-time homes design features	Social housing 2 bedroom or 3 person		Private housing 3 bedroom or 5 person	
	Cost		Cost	
	Minimum	Maximum	Minimum	Maximum
Extended parking	Nil	Nil	Nil	Nil
Level approach from parking	Nil	Nil	Nil	Nil
General levels gently sloping	Nil	Nil	Nil	Nil
Covered, illuminated entrance	Nil	250	41	255
Lift provided for wheelchair	Nil	Nil	Nil	Nil
Door and hallway width	Nil	Nil	Nil	21
Turning circles to ground-floor rooms	Nil	Nil	Nil	Nil
Living room at ground-floor level	Nil	Nil	Nil	Nil
Ground-floor bedspace	Nil	Nil	Nil	Nil
Ground-floor adaptions	115	115	98	98
Reinforce toilet walls	Nil	130	Nil	112
Future stair lift	50	50	43	43
Bathroom ceiling/wall adaption	Nil	Nil	Nil	Nil
Bathroom design	Nil	Nil	Nil	Nil
Glazing height	Nil	Nil	Nil	Nil
Switches and sockets	Nil	Nil	Nil	Nil
Automatic heating systems and controls	Nil	Nil	Nil	Nil
Total	165	545	182	529

Source: O'Brien et al. (2002: 33).

in relation to maintaining independent lives for disabled people; nor do they acknowledge the potential benefits of increased convenience, accessibility and sociability resulting from the implementation of Part M. However, research by BCIS (2003), on behalf of the ODPM, anticipates that the implementation of Part M will lead to savings in residential care costs due to elderly people being able to stay longer in their own homes. As BCIS (2003: 3) note, the unit cost for residential care in staffed homes in 1994–95 was £268 per person per week. Dwellings constructed to Part M standards offer 'a potential saving of £14,000 per year for every elderly person who is able to live in their own home for longer', comparing 'favourably with the average additional £238 to £381 that it will cost to build each new house' (BCIS, 2003: 3).[12]

Regulation relating to access is disproportionate as there is little demand for accessible dwellings

A common observation by builders and building control officers, about responding to the dwelling needs of disabled people, is that there is little or no need to do so in that disabled people are a minority and do not constitute an effective market demand (see also Chapters 5 and 6). This was one of the observations by the HBF (1995) in commenting on the draft proposals for Part M. As the HBF (1995: 1) said: 'it is highly improbable that most purchasers of new homes will ever be visited by anyone in a wheelchair'. Others in the building professions have voiced similar sentiments, with the Managing Director of the Redrow Group, Chris Lewis (1995: 1), suggesting that 'to impose draconian measures on all new home buyers for the possible benefit of such a small minority is, though well meaning, misguided and misplaced'. Likewise, a spokesperson from another building company noted that the government's plans to insist on the construction of accessible dwellings was impractical and 'unjustified when considered against very limited usage' (Blair, 1995: 1).

   Such views seem credible and unproblematic to most builders because, as they suggest, disabled people rarely purchase dwellings from them. For instance, a representative from the biggest volume house builder in the UK, Barratts Developments plc, noted that

> during the last nine years Barratts have offered to adapt any standard house type to mobility access standards, free of charge, provided the purchaser makes the request at an early stage of construction . . . in those nine years, 37 purchasers out of almost 100,000 have accepted this offer – just 0.037%. Why should such a minority set the standard trend for regulating?
>
> (Finn, 1995: 3)

Likewise, a representative of a major building company that I interviewed said that 'in my ten years working on site for this organization, only once has a wheelchair user come by and asked for a house, and that's it, so why should we have to provide something for which there's not much demand?' (see also Chapter 5; Imrie, 2003a).

   These views are, however, problematical in a number of ways (see also

Chapters 5 and 6; Imrie and Hall, 2001a).[13] Foremost, the discussion in Chapter 1 of this book suggested that the demand for accessible dwellings in the UK and elsewhere, while often unarticulated by disabled people, is significant. For instance, Thamesdown Borough Council (1994) estimated that in 1991 there were 2.4 million people in England and Wales in need of accessible housing. Likewise, PIEDA plc (1996: 1), commenting on the UK's housing stock, note that '1 in 4 households contain at least one person with some form of disability . . . the need for accessible housing is therefore substantial . . . the majority of the nation's existing housing is ill suited to the needs of disabled people, or of anyone whose mobility is impaired'. This is particularly the case given that, in a national UK survey of housing, only 29 per cent of disabled people living in private households thought they had all the necessary adaptations (see Barnes *et al.*, 1999: 120).

There is, then, no shortage of potential demand for accessible dwellings – an observation that is reinforced by the understanding that disabled people are not necessarily a minority, in that impairment is neither special nor specific to any particular individual or group (Zola, 1989; Bickenbach *et al.*, 1999; Imrie, 2004b). Rather, impairment is intrinsic to the human condition in that all human beings are likely, at some stage in their lives, to experience bodily or physiological changes that, will potentially affect the functioning of their bodies (see Salmen and Ostroff, 1997; Shantakumar, 1994). This fact of physiology is likely to become more important given the emergence of a population structure skewed towards older age groups, or those most likely to acquire impairment. As Figure 2.2 shows, it is estimated that by 2030 the proportion of the UK's population aged 65 years and over will have increased from 20 per cent to 30 per cent (Imrie and Hall, 2001a; OPCS, 2002).

The 'minority' label attached to disabled people is also based on the false premise, held by builders and others, that disability is equivalent to wheelchair use and/or forms of mobility or ambulant impairment (see also Chapter 5). For most builders, the (fallacious) logic is that if they don't see a wheelchair user on site, then they haven't encountered disability or a

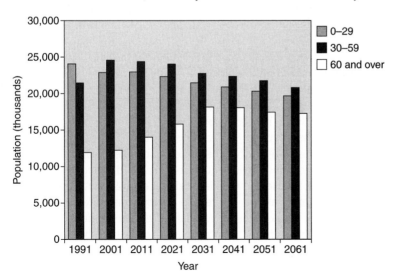

2.2 Projected population by age, 1991–2061, UK.

disabled person. However, as evidence shows, less than 4 per cent of (registered) disabled people in the UK use a wheelchair, and for the majority of these people the wheelchair is used only in certain circumstances (OPCS, 1987, 2002; Imrie and Hall, 2001a). In this respect, while builders are right to characterize wheelchair users as a 'minority', they are wrong to do this for disabled people as a whole. Such assumptions fail to acknowledge the differentiated nature of impairment in society, and are likely to lead to underestimations (by builders and others) of the demand by disabled people for private (for sale) dwellings.

Because builders tend to reduce disability to wheelchair users or users of specialized equipment, disabled people are seen as different from other customers, and more demanding in that they require (so builders perceive) customized and hence costly design (see also Barlow and Ozaki, 2001; Imrie, 2003a). However, research tends to emphasize that there is a much closer correspondence between disabled people's views of what constitutes good design quality in dwellings, and those of consumers more generally. As Chapter 1 indicated, most disabled people, especially wheelchair users and people with vision impairments, are critical of the lack of space in dwellings and suggest that what they need, above all else, is additional space to facilitate ease of access, mobility and storage of specialized equipment (like wheelchairs). Such views correspond with general consumer surveys of attitudes to housing, with Hedges and Clemens' (1994) research of a cross-section of consumers, indicating that there is felt to be a lack of space in dwellings.

Likewise, Haddon's (1998: 4) survey of visitors to the INTEGER Project in the UK, a demonstration project of an intelligent and environmentally sensitive dwelling, notes that, 'in all its guises space in homes remains so important ... if such homes fall below space expectations, perhaps because of a trade off with intelligent and green features, we might anticipate that the overall response to such homes might well be negative'. Bishop and Davidson's (1989: 42) research also suggests that flexibility in layout and spaciousness are important to purchasers, regardless of their bodily state or condition. A more recent survey of 1,000 owner occupiers, carried out by the Housing Forum (2000) in the UK, reconfirmed such views in that 83 per cent of the respondents wanted more flexibility in the design of dwellings, and more choice regarding the initial design. It appears, then, that people, regardless of whether they are disabled or not, have similar or shared feelings for what constitutes 'a good house'.

Builders' attitudes towards disabled people as potential customers are revealing about the paucity of customer focus or development within the speculative building industry more generally, and constitute, I would argue, a significant barrier to disabled people gaining access to decent dwellings. In this respect, while the barriers to disabled people constituting an effective demand for private (owner-occupied) dwellings include individual or personal factors, broader social and external factors, such as builders' ignorance of and indifference towards disability and domestic design, warrant some attention. Whereas builders and other building professionals tend to highlight the potency of the former – that is, individual deficiency, pathology and impairment as the source of the problem – I want to argue that social, structural and attitudinal relations and processes are potentially much more far reaching in influencing how far disabled people are able to gain access to accessible housing constructed by speculative builders.

One of the significant barriers to disabled people's access to private (owner-occupied) dwellings that limits their ability to exercise choice in housing markets relates to the ways in which information about dwellings is collated, organized and made available.[14] Information about private (for sale) dwellings is usually available from estate agents (or realtors), although private sales (through websites and other outlets) are increasing in volume. Typically, the information about dwellings for sale revolves around what the real estate industry regards as the main selling features of a dwelling. This includes the overall size of the dwelling, the numbers of rooms and their respective dimensions, but very rarely anything about accessible design features – a matter that is vital to disabled people in enabling them to evaluate the merits of a dwelling. Some estate agents belong to schemes to promote accessible dwellings and/or highlight accessible features in dwellings that they market, although they are few and far between (see Chapter 8 for a discussion of these schemes).

For many disabled people, just getting to the sales office and/or to view a dwelling can be an insurmountable barrier that can, potentially, prevent a purchase. For instance, Burns' (2004) research shows that a common problem is that disabled people, particularly wheelchair users, cannot easily access sales offices (see also Chapter 7; Imrie, 2004a; P. Thomas, 2004). As one of her respondents said: 'because it was a wee portacabin it was mostly my wife that was going in to ask the details because you can't get into them' (Burns, 2004: 765). Thomas's (2004) investigation of wheelchair users highlights similar experiences. For one of her respondents: 'I visited five city centre loft development sales offices . . . four of them were physically inaccessible, the fifth had a locked glass door . . . the member of staff had a look of surprise when she saw me . . . as if she wondered what a wheelchair user would possibly be doing at the sales office' (P. Thomas, 2004: 785).

These comments suggest that disabled people's encounters with sales staff and other professionals such as builders do not always encourage them to pursue a purchase or to persist with the search for a dwelling. For instance, Thomas (2004) notes that builders' indifference to disabled people is a factor in discouraging a house purchase (see also Burns, 2002). One of her respondents, Graham, recalled a typical experience: 'most of the developers in the area were not interested in helping me find a suitable property. It was a case of take it or leave it' (P. Thomas, 2004: 788). Another of Thomas' respondents, Gill, was put off by the poor behaviour of sales staff, who treated her as though she was invisible. As she said, the sales staff 'insisted on replying to my dad and asking him questions even though I had explained I was buying a place for myself . . . the estate agent said she was telling my dad because "you'll have problems finding it" ' (cited in P. Thomas, 2004: 786).

Disabled people are also discouraged from pursuing the search process because of previously poor and problematical experiences in which what they went to view was usually inappropriate or rarely incorporated the relevant design features to meet their needs (Burns, 2004). P. Thomas

(2004) provides a rich series of testimonies from disabled people, frustrated with the difficulties in finding suitable property. As one of Thomas' (2004: 789) respondents, Liz, said: 'we excluded most properties immediately, because it was obvious that they were not accessible . . . we did try to visit some properties but were not able to find any that were even suitable for adaptation. After so many disappointments we started to feel quite desperate.' Liz's partner, Steve, added that 'none of the large developers were building bungalows, nor were they interested in altering their plans to build anything accessible. So our preferred option of buying a new property was quickly discounted' (cited in P. Thomas, 2004: 787).

Steve's account highlights the problems with a system that is reactive rather than proactive in relation to consumer demands, and which is usually reluctant to depart from the pre-set designs of its house-types. One builder, interviewed by me, summed up the situation:

> We will accommodate it as much as we possibly can, but it's left to the individual to come on and say 'Well, I have a particular problem, can you do something for me?' And we'll say 'Yes, certainly.' You know, 'Give us enough notice and we will do it for you.' That's not a problem. But we don't, we don't make a concerted effort to go out and hit it as a market share and say 'Oh, come on, disabled people, we are building on this basis for you.'
>
> (Imrie, 2003a; see also Chapter 5)

Here the onus is on individual consumers to try and persuade builders to customize design, but, as P. Thomas (2004) suggests, this is not easy. Eve, one of Thomas' (2004: 788) respondents, recalls a typical situation: 'one major developer was completely unhelpful when the sales assistant said the specifications could not be changed at all'.

The implementation of accessible design will lead to a reduction in housing quality

While the rationalities of real estate orientate the building industry towards the standardization of the design and construction of the dwelling, this is not to say that design does not matter. Rather, far from the popular wisdom espoused about the building industry, a main impetus for builders is selling the product. This means that they can ill afford to ignore the importance of design in seeking to differentiate the dwelling from competitors'. As Leopold and Bishop (1983: 128) note, 'builders seek to achieve a balance by using a wide range of finishing materials in combination with minor distinctions in layout and landscape to confer individuality on a house which, in all other respects, may replicate its neighbour exactly' (see also Hooper, 1999; Carmona, 2001). Carmona (2001) refers to this as a process of 'facadism', in which builders seek to attract consumers by differentiating the external features of dwellings (the so-called 'kerb appeal') without altering (standardized) internal arrangements and layouts.

One of the HBF's (1995) main objections regarding Part M was its likelihood of reducing the quality of housing and leading to the development of design styles unacceptable to consumers. As the HBF (1995: 2) said, the regulation was likely to create an 'institutional feel' to domestic environ-ments by virtue of its requirement for the incorporation of ramps and other accessible design features. One builder argued that the overall quality of dwellings would be reduced, resulting 'in lost internal space, increased external envelope . . . and a front elevation with such a large front entrance protrusion that it kills the design' (Finn, 1995: 3). Likewise, Fraser (1995: 1), an employee of Westbury Homes, suggested that 'large scale ramping, ugly handrails, and significant areas of hard landscaping are completely at odds with the concept of good design', a point also made by Barratts Developments plc: 'ramped approaches will also provide more hard surfacing, at the loss of soft landscaping, which will no doubt prove detrimental to the attractive streetscapes we are attempting to achieve' (Finn, 1995: 3).

It was also suggested that safety in homes would be reduced or, as a representative from the NHBC noted, 'ramps and stepped ramps are viewed as a potential safety hazard' (Mills, 1995: 1). Others claimed that a reduction in the size of living space in dwellings, such as sitting rooms and bedrooms, was likely to occur in order to accommodate Part M speci-fications. Thus, the Chief Executive of Beazer Homes suggested that 'the need for increased circulation space within dwellings will inevitably result in the substitution of circulation space for living space, which is unpopular with purchasers' (Webb, 1995: 1). Likewise, Shepard Homes (1995: 1) noted that the regulation 'would lead to the loss of the understairs cup-board and reduction in the size of the lounge . . . the adaptations will have a negative effect upon the marketability of the house-type...'. For Barratts Developments plc, the implication of Part M for their popular three-bedroom detached unit, the Cleveland, was such that the internal layout was likely to lose 'ten foot from the living space' (Finn, 1995: 5).

Truesdale and Steinfeld (2002) suggest that builders' comments are not without some substance. They argue that builders' observations, about the 'institutional feel' created by accessible design features, is based on the understanding that the concept of accessible housing design often ignores aesthetic considerations in favour of the specification of functional design and equipment. Thus, the design guidelines in Part M's approved docu-ment (AD) provide purely functional advice. They offer no guidance to architects or builders about aesthetic form or principle, with the potential consequence that replication of the contents of the AD, from one housing development to another, is likely, so Truesdale and Steinfeld (2002) argue, to reproduce an 'institutional feel'. Truesdale and Steinfeld (2002) also note that the dominance of physical and technical standards in enframing builders' approaches to accessibility is likely to encourage the building industry to comply with official guidelines and advice rather than to pursue creative alternatives.

Such observations, however, seem to be overstated in that the experi-ences of builders on site indicate, as Chapters 5 and 6 show, that the fears of the HBF and builders more generally have not really materialized. This is not surprising because, as a builder who was interviewed by me sug-gested: 'the representations by builders to the government in 1995 reflected genuine fears but they were over the top and not based on sound reasoning'. Others concurred, and as another builder said:

I think if you want to instil a difference of appearance within the development, there's a greater need now to think harder about the surfacing materials, how they relate to the access for people of any situation, and landscaping. I think there's a greater need for a more developed architectural landscaping between all these areas of level access. Just to lift it slightly, otherwise it can look a bit mundane and barren running back in. But that's not a contentious issue. Like everything else, it can be absorbed within the design, it's never a problem.

(See Chapter 5 for further testimonials)

There are many examples of well-designed dwellings that are constructed to be fully accessible to, and usable by, wheelchair users. Figure 2.3 shows the Caldera Place Apartments, designed by Erick Mikiten and constructed in Concord, California, and winner of a prestigious award in 2002 for housing accessibility.[15] As Mikiten (2004: 4) said, 'my goal was to create exceptional access seamlessly integrated with great design', a view echoed by expert opinion voiced by representatives of the American Institute of Architects. In particular, they draw attention to the dwelling's

2.3 Caldera Place Apartments, California. Inspired both by his own need for wheelchair access and the dearth of independent-living apartments for the 14,500 low-income disabled people in Alameda County, California, the architect of Caldera Place Apartments, Erick Mikiten, set out to create a dwelling of accommodation and affordability. Following the federal government's 811 program guidelines on affordable housing for disabled people, Erick Mikiten has designed 12 apartments of artistic form and unique function. Thoughtful touches abound, from adjustable height counters and rollout shelving in the kitchens, and wheelchair-accommodating shower stalls in the bathrooms to height-adjusted electrical outlets that are easily reached from a wheelchair. Ramps cleverly serve the dual purpose of providing accessibility around the complex and denoting the boundaries of the residential courtyard. Consideration of historical neighbourhood design can be seen in the complex's front rock wall, which serves both as a visual anchor with the neighbourhood and as height-appropriate extra table or seating space for wheelchair users. The design of Caldera Place shows that, with forethought and understanding, wheelchair-accessible housing can be aesthetic as well as functional.

In developing the design for Caldera Place, Mikiten (2004) said: 'I varied the height of the front wall to provide a variety of heights for people to use. Some people might not be able to crouch down much, or have trouble getting up from a low seat, so portions higher than a normal seat are provided. These also work well for people in wheelchairs to roll up next to and use as a desk-height place to put something they may be doing. The lower sections are low enough to be easy to transfer onto for someone in a wheelchair. The seats are provided as an encouragement to friendly gathering by the residents as well as being a covered place to wait for someone to pick them up by car from the adjacent parking lot.'

composite lumber-surfaced ramp that connects the ground and first floors, and the varying height of bench walls that provide a diversity of seating. Likewise, Figure 2.4 illustrates a dwelling designed and constructed by the UK house builder, Octagon. It is an excellent design outcome, in which the builder has combined steps with level and/or ramped approaches in ways that complement, rather than detract from, the classical effect of the principal entrance.

The reactions of builders to the perceived diminution of quality of dwellings due to Part M is couched within the mentalities of physical design, in which quality is understood, as outlined in Chapter 1, to refer to the dwelling as a piece of hardware – that is, a physical or technical system. This, though, as already discussed, is a limited and limiting way of conceiving of housing quality, and an alternative way of evaluating the impact of accessibility codes or regulations on the quality of dwellings is to broaden the definition and understanding of what housing quality is or ought to be. In this respect, Chapter 1 suggested that housing quality, as a composite concept, refers to disabled people attaining a dignified state or status in relation to their consumption of dwellings. Thus it might be more appropriate for builders and others, in judging changes in housing quality, to evaluate how far accessible design features interact with impairment to secure dignified living environs and circumstances.

In this respect, some research suggests that accessible design, far from detracting from housing quality, enhances it by increasing residents' levels of independence and providing convenience and ease of use of dwelling spaces. For instance, in their review of LTH in the UK, Sopp and Wood (2001) note that most people who live in them regard the design features as an improvement on conventional dwellings (see also Bonnett, 1996; Carroll *et al.*, 1999). As one of the respondents to Sopp and Wood's (2001: 14) survey said: 'it's easy to get around the house – everything is accessible', while, for another, 'it's much easier to live with mobility problems'. Respondents to O'Brien *et al.*'s (2002: 60) survey of LTH in Northern

2.4 Octagon house design.

Ireland felt likewise, with one person noting that 'it makes it so much easier for my son to come and visit me. He's in a wheelchair and it was difficult in my last place where he couldn't access the toilet by himself.'

2.4 Conclusions

The testimonials presented by O'Brien *et al.* (2002) and others offer powerful insights into the bounded and barriered nature of much of the domestic environment (see also Allen *et al.*, 2002; Allen, 2004a). Such barriers, as the chapter has suggested, have to be understood in part with reference to the attitudes, values and practices of house builders, which, as part of the broader rationalities of real estate, are one of the sources of deficient design in dwellings in relation to the needs of disabled people. Builders' priorities revolve around the attainment of sales and profits targets, in which the provision of internal space and flexibility of use is limited by the use of standardized design packages. For builders, disabled people are part of a minority group that require specialized components of design which are costly to provide, and will detract from the sales potential of dwellings. Disabled people's demands, so builders claim, have the potential to disrupt tried and tested, hence profitable, systems of design and construction.

Such observations, regarding the potential effects of accessible design and/or legislation relating to access, are not necessarily borne out by the evidence (see also Chapters 5 and 6). A variety of studies suggest that the implementation of Part M, and accessibility guidelines more generally, will add little to design and construction costs, and may very well add to the use value of dwellings by enhancing their usability and/or livability (Carroll *et al.*, 1999; Peace and Holland, 2001; Sopp and Wood, 2001; Truesdale and Steinfeld, 2002). Likewise, there are many examples of well-designed dwellings incorporating accessible design features that do not detract, as some builders suggest, from individual (aesthetic) character or effect (see Steven Winter Associates, 1997). Indeed, the point made by builders, about accessible design being akin to 'institutional living' is more revealing about their lack of creative (design) imagination than it is about the alleged lack of design options in relation to designing for accessibility in dwellings.

A word of caution is that while such evidence seems convincing, much of it is based on single, small-scale studies, and while they are invaluable, what is missing are systematic long-term or longitudinal evaluations of the different claims made by the building industry in relation to regulatory control more generally, and Part M in particular (see also Chapter 5; Imrie and Hall, 2001a). Thus, when builders claim that Part M is likely to compromise aspects of aesthetic design quality and, as a consequence, reduce the marketability of dwellings, there is in fact little or no evidence, one way or the other, to provide measured comments on or assessments of this claim. The same point can be made in relation to a host of other objections and/or observations by builders about the effects of Part M, suggesting that there is a need for much more research into the nature and effects of regulatory control on the design and construction process.

What we do know is that the building industry is unlikely to respond to the access needs of disabled people unless required to by government. In particular, regulation to date, as the content of the next chapter makes clear, has not been strong enough, nor sufficiently well implemented or enforced, to achieve the quality of dwellings desired by disabled people. This does not mean that builders' responses to disabled people and their housing needs are necessarily predictable or inevitable. However, it does mean that seeking to push builders beyond minimum standards, to get them to think more about the usability and livability of dwellings, will require either a strengthening of legislation and/or the use of fiscal and other measures as incentives for them to respond to the challenges, as they see it, of inclusive design (see also Chapter 5). Even so, if legal rules do not transcend reductive conceptions of housing quality, as outlined in Chapter 1, then a legislative route to accessibility is likely to fail – a theme that I turn to in Chapter 3.

Further reading

Michael Ball and James Barlow have written more than most on the UK house-building industry, and their various writings are recommended. In particular, it is well worth while looking at Ball's (1983) important text which, in many respects, has stood the test of time. The papers by Ball (1996, 1998), Barlow (1999), Hooper (1999) and Nicol and Hooper (1999) are very good in providing insight into the dynamics of the speculative house-building industry. Mathew Carmona's (2001) book has an excellent chapter on the speculative house-building industry. In relation to the inter-relationships between speculative house-building processes and disability, little has been written bar the exceptions of Burns (2004), Imrie (2003a, 2004a) and Thomas (2004).

3 Housing quality, standards and the domestic environment

3.1 Introduction

While access regulations and codes are increasingly commonplace in relation to facilitating disabled people's entry to and use of public buildings, less has been achieved in relation to private (for sale) dwellings. This is due in large part to the market nature of the interrelationships between producers (builders) and consumers, in which the transaction, or sale of the dwelling, is conceived of as the expression of the free will or choices of both parties. Governments have been reluctant to intervene in such transactions, and have tended to provide voluntary guidelines relating to good practice. Since the late 1980s, however, legislation, most notably in England and Wales and the USA, is requiring builders to design and construct dwellings to minimum standards of accessibility. Thus, the Fair Housing Amendment Act (FHAA, 1988) in the USA, and Part M (DETR, 1999a) of the building regulations in England and Wales, represent the most far-reaching (if limited) legislative responses to the dwelling needs of disabled people.

This chapter explores the significance of contrasting legal and policy approaches in relation to responding to the needs of disabled people. The discussion will be placed in a broader exploratory framework showing, and seeking to explain, the significance of access rules, codes and regulations worldwide, with a particular focus on the United States and England and Wales. As the material indicates, statutes in relation to the provision of accessible housing are variable in form and content, and tend to be stronger in relation to social housing schemes or where government has a direct lever over the house-building process. However, the majority of policies are, as I will argue, what one might term 'degenerative' by virtue of the social construction of issues and target populations into 'deserving' and 'undeserving' groups (see Schneider and Ingram, 1997). In this respect, legal provisions such as Part M tend to mark disabled people out as 'special', and the provision of accessible design as a 'concession' that they ought to be grateful for.

The introduction of visitability standards for private dwellings is part of a broader raft of policies that are seeking to create contexts for citizens to take more responsibility for their lives. The FHAA in the USA, and Part M in England and Wales, are not aberrations; rather, they ought to be interpreted, I will argue, as part of the broader, purposive restructuring of welfare that has emerged from Western governments' emphasis on citizens 'rights and responsibilities' as a framework for political decision-making and action (Imrie and Raco, 2003). Here it is suggested that disabled people ought to take more responsibility for the conduct of their lives, in a context whereby government is committed to create, through rights legislation and other means, opportunity for such responsibilities to be exercised. In this respect, the political debates about disability tend to emphasize the costs to taxpayers of impairment, and the imperative for governments to reduce expenditure on disabled people by creating the social and economic contexts that permit them to become 'independent' and active citizens.

The chapter will also argue that the emerging policy frameworks are problematical for reducing issues about disability and access to dwellings to the attainment of minimal dimensional standards, as though technical responses, in and of themselves, have the capacity to create livable spaces. The technicist mentalities of government propagate a particular conception of housing quality that fails to recognize differences between different disabled people and their needs. The resultant standards appear to be no more able to produce the flexibility of design than those they are seeking to modify and/or replace. In part this is because the boundaries of permissible legislation are constrained, as already intimated, by governments wedded to the protection of builders' rights to self-determination (of the content of design and construction). This limits the extent to which standards can be extended, and does not address one of the sources of disabled people's inability to influence the design of dwellings: that is, their lack of power to control the actions and activities of both professional policy-makers and the corporate building sector (the focus of Chapter 7).

In developing these themes, I divide the chapter into three. First, I describe the broader social and political values and attitudes that shape countries' approaches to policy and practice in relation to disability and access to dwellings. In doing so, I evaluate the role of access legislation and/or directives in seeking to secure accessible dwellings in a range of countries. I develop the argument that the legal basis for securing access to housing is generally weak and ineffectual, with limited means of enforcement. Second, I explore the statutory environments in the USA and in England and Wales, and evaluate their strengths and weaknesses in seeking to regulate the attitudes and practices of house builders. I conclude by commenting on the possibilities, problems and issues in seeking to strengthen legal and non-legal (or voluntary) frameworks in order to facilitate disabled people's access to dwellings.

3.2 The right to habitation and the legal regulation of access

In Chapter 1, it was argued that dwellings that are inaccessible to and unusable by disabled people are an infringement of (dwelling) rights, or the right to habitation. As King (2003: 97) suggests, one ought to regard housing as 'the right that underpins all others in allowing human flourishing as it provides the freedom to be'. Such views are held by major international organizations, such as the United Nations (UN) and the World Health Organization (WHO). For instance, in 1948 Article 25 of the Universal Declaration of Human Rights said that 'everyone has the right to a standard of living adequate for the heath and well being of himself and his family, including food, clothing, housing and medical care and necessary social services'. Likewise, the UN's (1994: 2) draft international convention on housing rights notes that adequate housing is essential to freedom, dignity, equality, and security: 'everyone has a right to accessible housing'.[1] This right applies especially to 'those with special housing needs, including but not limited to mentally and physically disabled persons, the elderly, the terminally ill, HIV-positive individuals, persons with persistent medical problems and children'.

The report concludes, however, that 'the non-fulfilment of housing rights is a widespread and growing phenomenon and that no single country can claim to have satisfied in full their existing legal obligations arising out of the right to adequate housing' (United Nations, 1994: 1). This message was reinforced by a position paper at a UN (2001: 3) conference in 2001 that noted that the sentiments about access to adequate housing 'contained in international instruments have not been sufficiently reflected in national legislative and institutional frameworks'. The general situation is that while most countries have legal rules relating to accessibility in public buildings, there are few instances of legal regulation in relation to dwellings (Michailakis, 1997). This is particularly so in relation to the design of private (for sale) dwellings, in which governments, as Chapter 2 outlined, often seek to defend the building industry's autonomy, or what are argued to be builders' rights to determine much of the content of the design and construction process.

For instance, in Canada the Ontarians with Disabilities Act (2001), like legislation in most countries, does not apply to access to private (for sale) dwellings. Its content reflects the continuing strength of the Home Buyers Association (HBA, Canada), and the familiar refrain outlined by the President of the HBA's London Branch in Ontario, Paul Rawlings (2003: 1): 'demand is from a very small minority of those in the new home market . . . I wonder if it makes sense to legislate extra costs for generic solutions that may not address accessibility concerns adequately'. Likewise, in the USA federal policies towards access and dwellings exclude single (private) family homes for inclusion in legislation and, as Dunn (1997: 23) suggests, this reflects the anti-collectivist ideology which seeks to promote individual responsibility for social process and outcome, rather than government regulation and rule (see also section 3.2). Here the emphasis is on fostering disabled people's independence by means of self-provision, or individuals' adaptation of premises according to their (self-defined) needs.

The more common route taken by governments, in relation to the provision of accessible dwellings, is to encourage builders to take account of the needs of disabled people or to incorporate, where practicable, elements of accessible design into dwellings. Here, the onus is usually placed on the goodwill of builders to respond to voluntary codes. For instance, federal and state approaches to accessible dwellings in countries such as

Australia encourage voluntary compliance with access standards. One example is ResCode in the state of Victoria, which came into operation in August 2001 as a statewide planning policy, including provisions for access to multi-unit developments. Clause 55.05-1, entitled 'Accessibility', encourages the consideration of the needs of people with limited mobility in the design of developments. Likewise, in California in 2002 the state legislature passed a bill requiring the Department of Housing and Community Development to create guidelines for local governments on how new (single-family) homes could be built with universal design features. However, as Jeserich (2003: 1) notes, 'the guidelines are optional and do not mandate the building of any new accessible (single-family) housing'.

The dearth of appropriate national or federal legislation on accessible dwellings, in countries ranging from Canada to Australia and the USA, has led some state and local governments to develop their own initiatives, based on a range of legal measures and fiscal incentives (see also section 3.2 of this chapter). In parts of Australia, some local councils, directed by state building standards, have developed and implemented building regulations in relation to access to private (for sale) dwellings. For instance, in New South Wales (NSW) Willoughby Council requires new developments of more than nine dwellings to conform with the state regulation of one in nine new residential dwellings to be constructed to what is known as Class C of AS4299 – that is, an 'adaptable building standard' based on LTH criteria. Other authorities in NSW, such as Waverley and Ryde Councils, have followed suit by including a requirement in their development plans for multiple unit developments to adhere to the adaptability requirements of AS4299.

These directives are limited because, like most building standards elsewhere, they are characterized by exclusions and get-out clauses and, in particular, do not apply to a significant part of new construction, that is, single-family dwellings. This is the case in Norway, where the building regulations require an accessible entry and external approach to the common entrance of a building that comprises more than four dwellings (i.e. an apartment block or block of flats). However, toilets in all new dwellings, regardless of whether or not they are single-family or multiples, are supposed to be provided to cater for those with reduced mobility – although, as Christophersen (1995: 3) observes, 'this requirement has little practical effect and is usually overlooked'. Sweden is not dissimilar to Norway in that the Building Code of 1977 stipulates that there must be wheelchair access to all units in residential buildings of three storeys or more, including an accessible routeway from the pavement to the entrance of the building, accessible thresholds, and the provision of a lift. There is no requirement for single-family dwellings to be constructed to accessibility standards.

A minority of countries go further than this, in that their access regulations apply to most private (for sale) dwellings, including single-family types. For example, the extension of Denmark's building code to single-family homes in 1998 meant that for the first time dwellings other than those that are 'self built' have to be constructed to minimum levels of accessibility, including the provision of a no-step entrance. In 2001, the

Japanese government introduced a renewed welfare policy entitled the 'New Gold Plan', with a major emphasis on ageing-in-place. Regulations in the Plan require that all new housing, both public and private, should be built to universal design standards, for what has been characterized as 30 years of 'livability' (see Kose, 2000).[2] Some state and local governments in the USA, as the next section will amplify, require no-step entrances and other accessibility features into single-family homes, while (as previous chapters have suggested) Part M in England and Wales is perhaps the most far-reaching regulation worldwide in that it covers all types of private (for sale) dwellings.

While access legislation and/or building standards on accessibility to dwellings are still in their infancy, the quantity of regulation is much greater than 20 years ago. In part this reflects political pressure by disabled people's organizations to extend access regulations from non-residential to residential environments, but also governments' concerns to reduce welfare spending on the social and human problems created by inaccessible home environments (see Chapter 1). In particular, the various frameworks (both voluntary and legal) are based, I would contend, on what Woodhams and Corby (2003: 161) refer to as the 'liberal equal opportunity principle', in which fairness in the distribution of opportunity is 'necessary for every individual to have a reasonable chance of success and happiness'. Opportunities for self-enhancement and fulfilment are, however, not always equal, and the basis of legislation and/or building standards to remove physical barriers in dwellings and elsewhere is premised in part on the understanding that this action is necessary for disabled people to maximize their potential as human beings.

In this respect, the development of liberal conceptions of equality in relation to accessibility has shaped many policy responses in Western countries to the dwelling needs of disabled people. These range from 'special needs' programmes involving the provision of wheelchair and mobility housing to, more recently, 'people-centred' strategies characterized by supporting individuals in their existing homes, including, I would argue, Part M and the provisions of the FHAA.[3] The paramount example of the changing policy environment, in the UK, revolves around the 'Supporting People' programme, a policy initiative that, since April 2003, aims to deliver services to (so-called 'vulnerable') people in their homes, rather than moving them into care or institutional environments (see ODPM, 2001a; Oldman, 2002).[4] The initiative is indicative of a broader state agenda, not just in the UK, relating to the restructuring of welfare and governance, in which discourses of independent living, user involvement, control of services and, ultimately, the empowerment of individuals are to the fore.

This switch in emphasis, from 'special needs' to 'independent living', can be understood, in part, with reference to what Ellis (2000) refers to as the corporeal discourse of the independent body. As Ellis (2000) and others have suggested, since the late 1970s the relationships between state and citizen have been altered by a range of socio-economic and political changes, in particular the diminution of universal welfare and the emergence of a mixed economy of welfare increasingly targeted at specific bundles of demand. Physical impairment and frail bodies, as objects of welfare and support, became a target of new service cultures in the UK and elsewhere that sought to intervene 'no more than necessary to foster independence' (Department of Heath, 1989). The emphasis here was encouraging self-care in relation to bodily functions, and the development of independent bodies able to function as autonomous and self-activating economic agents.

The corporeal discourse of the independent body has been developed and extended by successive Labour administrations in the UK that, since May 1997, have sought to instil the importance of government responding to individuals' rights, within a context that emphasizes the responsibilities that have to be discharged by beneficiaries of government policies. The objective is to produce active citizens or, as Prime Minister Tony Blair (1997: 1) has argued: 'the basis of . . . modern civic society is an ethic of mutual responsibility or duty. It is something for something, a society where we play by the rules. You only take out what you put in. That's the bargain' (see also Imrie and Raco, 2003). For disabled people and others, this has meant increased emphasis by government on reducing individuals' dependence on welfare support by providing opportunities for job training through welfare-to-work schemes and other types of support to enhance employability.

Part M, the FHAA, rights legislations such as the Americans with Disabilities Act (ADA, 1991) in the USA and the Disability Discrimination Act (DDA) in the UK, and policies relating to the adaptation of dwellings, fit into this socio-political framework insofar that they seek to create contexts for disabled people to exercise their rights to access and movement and mobility, all of which are, arguably, prerequisites of active citizenry. Such prerequisites, so it is argued, provide a means for exercising self-responsibility, from facilitating the ease of use of the home for purposes of self-care and management, to providing the means of access to places of work and job opportunities (as the main source of welfare and social reproduction). This emphasis on consumer sovereignty and independent and active bodies is, however, limited and not necessarily empowering. Rather, as Heywood *et al.* (2002: 36) note, independent living is narrowly construed by government to mean not much more than 'living at home consuming minimum public resources and being supported by relatives'.

Others concur in noting that the facilitation of active or independent bodies is framed within a discourse that fails to break out of the medical mentalities that blame the victims for their plight (Dean, 1999; Dean, 2000; Ellis, 2000; Oldman, 2002). In particular, the FHAA, Part M and rights legislation more generally, revolve around dualistic categories that distinguish between active citizens (those who are capable and 'able') and targeted populations (those who are disadvantaged and at 'risk') who, as Dean (1999: 167) suggests, 'require intervention in the management of risk'. The targeted population is conceived of, in Dean's (1999: 167) terms, as a 'locus of vulnerability'; that is, 'deviant others' or individuals with personal bodily deficiencies that require working on, by professionals, legal systems, policy instruments, etc., in order to create the conditions for their (re) entry into the mainstream of normal society. Thus, the DDA (1995: sections 1, 2) suggests that disability is that which is not normal, or something that has a 'substantial and long term adverse effect on . . . ability to carry out normal day-to-day activities'.

These conceptions of disability are characterized by divisive social constructions (i.e. the able-bodied person and the disabled person) that, as Schneider and Ingram (1997: 102) suggest, are at the heart of what they term 'degenerative policy design'. Such policy design, in relation to access to dwellings, tends to reduce disabled people's identities to a type (i.e. the wheelchair user, the pitiful person, etc.), with little recognition of the intrinsic nature of impairment (i.e. that everyone has the capacity to be impaired or acquire an impairment), or understanding that disabled people (like all people) have fluid identities with capacity for change and development (see Barnes *et al.*, 1991; Dean, 2000). Posed in this way, the form and content of law and legal rule, in relation to access, dwellings and the built environment, may be more of a problem than a solution to the access needs of disabled people – a theme that I now discuss in relation to the FHAA and Part M of the building regulations.

3.3 Approaches to the regulation of accessibility in dwellings

Arguably, the two most developed legal frameworks in relation to access to private (for sale) dwellings are, at the time of writing, the FHAA in the USA and Part M of the building regulations in England and Wales. Whereas the former is a statute that seeks to prohibit discrimination on the basis of disability (and other ascribed social categories and status), the latter is a building regulation that is not based on or derived from rights legislation or, for that matter, any specific philosophical tradition. Both were born out of contexts characterized by builders' reluctance to follow voluntary guidelines and codes on accessible design, and disabled people's organizations winning, in part, the argument that lack of access to dwellings was unacceptable (see Imrie and Hall, 2001a). However, Part M and the FHAA, as we shall see, remain partial and weak responses to the dwelling needs of disabled people, reflecting in large part the dominance of corporate property interests in minimizing the scope of regulation in relation to the design and construction of dwellings.

In the USA in 1958, the American National Standards Institute (ANSI, 1958) called for the development of voluntary standards for the design of accessible buildings. This was translated into an accessible standard published in 1961 that described in detail the minimal features required to remove physical barriers preventing disabled people gaining access to buildings. It did not, however, lead to substantially more accessible buildings being constructed, nor did it incorporate dwellings into the standards.[5] Not until the passing of section 504 of the Rehabilitation Act in 1973 did dwellings come under the ambit of legal regulation in relation to accessible design (see Figure 3.1). Section 504 required recipients of federal funds, including affordable housing providers, to make a proportion of dwellings (i.e. no more than 5 per cent) in new or substantially rehabilitated multifamily units accessible to people with mobility, hearing and visual impairments. Public dwellings, or dwellings largely constructed out of public funds, were the principal targets of regulation; private (for sale) dwellings were exempt.

Section 504's limited scope was further reduced by dispute and debate

- Accessible doors that have a minimum clear opening of 32 inches (815 mm) with the door opening 90 degrees.
- Handle, pull, latch, lock and other operating devices on the entrance door that have a shape that is easy to grasp with one hand and does not require tight grasping, tight pinching, or twisting of the wrist to operate. This requirement only applies to the accessible entrance door.
- At least one accessible entrance. If a ramp is used, then the maximum slope is 1 : 12.
- At least one bathroom with (a) clear area to the right or left of the toilet; (b) architectural reinforcement to allow installation of grab bars (if not already installed); (c) removable cabinets beneath sinks; (d) shower spray unit with a hose at least 60 inches long.
- Kitchen that has clear floor space of at least 40 inches, or 60 inches if the kitchen is U-shaped.
- Other requirements relating to accessible cabinets, workspaces, sinks, appliances, etc.

3.1 The architectural elements of the Uniform Federal Accessibility Standards (504).

Source: Kochera (2002).

over its precise content and remit and, as observers have suggested, it was barely applied or enforced until the late 1980s (Toran, 1999; Kochera, 2002). In 1988 the FHAA was passed, and it stated that dwellings ready for occupancy from 13 March 1991 had to comply with certain access requirements (see Figure 3.2). While it specifies a series of lower access standards than 504, it covers more units and does not make a distinction,

3.2 The architectural elements of the FHAA.

(1) The provision of an accessible route on site from the point(s) of entry to each residential building with covered units, and to the public and common use areas, such as parking.

(2) The provision of accessible public and common use areas, including parking, mail boxes, community or recreational facilities.

(3) The fitting of usable doors that must have a 32-inch clear opening, and a minimal clear floor area on an accessible path of travel.

(4) The provision of an accessible route into and throughout each covered dwelling unit. All corridors and doorways must permit minimal access. The only exceptions are for some patios and decks, and for small sunken or raised functional areas (i.e. a sunken living room) where there is an alternative path of travel to other rooms.

(5) All light switches, outlets, thermostats, intercoms, door bells and other controls and outlets must be no higher than 48 inches nor lower than 12 inches from the floor.

(6) It is not a requirement to install grab bars, but reinforcement must be constructed inside the walls at the places where they may later be added (i.e. in the bathroom and/or WC).

(7) Kitchens and bathrooms must be usable. There must be a 30-inch by 48-inch clear floor space at the sink, oven and refrigerator. If the sink is located at the end of a U-shaped kitchen, it must be possible to roll under, or provide 60 inches in length to permit a parallel approach. In bathrooms, there must be a 30-inch by 48-inch clear floor space at the bath or shower and the toilet.

as does 504, between federally assisted and privately financed dwellings. Rather, it applies to both newly constructed and substantially renovated multifamily dwellings provided by private builders, private landlords and publicly assisted landlords, such as Public Housing Authorities (or social housing providers). FHAA requires builders constructing five or more owner-occupied dwelling units in buildings with one elevator or more to make all units accessible.[6] In buildings without an elevator, accessibility applies only to ground-floor units.

The FHAA and other rights legislation, such as the ADA (1991), reflected a context in which disabled people's lobbying against barriered build environments was beginning to change public and political opinion in favour of legislation to regulate builders' practices. However, the arguments for the FHAA, expounded by disabled people, politicians and other advocates, reinforced the view that the objective of barrier-freedom was the means to achieving broader (policy) objectives, such as independent and active disabled people contributing to their own welfare and economic well-being (see, for example, Gooding, 1994; Scott, 1994). In this respect, an economic rationality underpinned the FHAA, the ADA and related directives, which for Malleris (2000: 20) created a context for patterns of inclusive employment: 'when accessibility has been created at home it provides the base necessary for employment goals to be reached by those of us with disabilities'.

A similar tale, as recounted in Chapter 1, emerged from early attempts in England and Wales to develop access legislation in relation to dwellings. Until the early 1970s, disabled people, in Goldsmith's (1997: 349) terms, 'were not on the agenda', and were barely mentioned in influential postwar documents such as the Dudley and Parker Morris reports. Like regulation in the USA, private (for sale) dwellings were never considered a legitimate regulatory target in England and Wales or, as Goldsmith (1997: 349) notes, 'the idea that private sector house builders could contribute never surfaced'. Instead, formative attempts post-1970 to regulate for access focused on dwellings constructed by the public sector for rent. Borsay (1986: 73) refers to the 'snail like development' of these policies, which, for Wheeler (1982), were nothing more than modest, and made little inroad into the lack of accessible housing stock (for details, see Chapter 1; also, Milner and Madigan, 2001).

Rather, the pursuit of what Goldsmith (1997: 350) refers to as 'exhortation, encouragement, awards, and royal patronage' was favoured over statutory regulation in relation to private builders, and exemplified by the approach of the Prince of Wales Advisory Group on Disability (PWAGD). The PWAGD was set up in 1983, and comprised representatives from the house builders and the NHBC. It suggested that 'visitability' should be promoted, in which dwellings, public and private, would provide minimal access for disabled people. One of the original members of the PWAGD, Nancy Robertson (2001), recalled its formative meeting in which builders and some of their representatives expressed their opposition to accessible dwellings. As Robertson (2001) recalled:

we decided on various projects and the priority was to be housing, and first of all we had a meeting to which house builders, architects and all these were invited, and the Prince came and spoke briefly about making housing accessible for disabled people, and he was absolutely rubbished, you know . . .[7]

For Robertson (2001), the factor in pushing forward the agenda on accessible dwellings was that the builders' main representative on the PWAGD, the NHBC, 'felt there was some future in it . . . they were supportive and said to us, "We need regulation because our members are not going to do it unless they have regulation." ' Thus the emergence of Part M, in relation to dwellings, reflected (as previously mentioned) the failures of self-regulation, and house builders' antithetical responses to issues of housing quality in relation to specific consumers, such as disabled people (Imrie and Hall, 2001a; Milner and Madigan, 2001; P. Thomas 2004). As the Association of Building Engineers (1995: 6) said:

the house building industry has to date had ample opportunity to make these types of provisions available without the pressure of regulation. It has failed to do so and, sadly, it is felt will continue to ignore the needs of the disabled and an ageing population unless required to do so by statutory regulation.

The preferred route for regulation was to extend Part M of the building regulations from non-residential to residential buildings, and on 12 January 1995 the Department of the Environment (DoE, 1995) issued formal proposals to extend Part M to dwellings. In doing so, the DoE was rejecting the idea that the local planning system, including development control, ought to regulate for access in dwellings – although, as Planning Policy Guidance 3 (DoE, 1992: 3) stated, local planning authorities could, in a context of demonstrable local need, negotiate access on suitable sites but 'not seek to impose detailed standards'. This, then, left the way open for a revised Part M, and the proposed specifications for it were subject to comment and scrutiny by a variety of parties (see next section). What emerged was, so some suggest, a compromise in which LTH standards were rejected and visitability standards, applicable to all private (for sale) dwellings and incorporating a no-step entrance requirement, were accepted as reasonable by government (see Table I.1 in the Introduction).

However, how far do the FHAA and Part M of the building regulations provide an adequate (legal) context or basis for the provision of accessible dwellings? I address this question in two ways. First, I assess the claim that the directives on access to dwellings are limited in scope and ambition, and not likely to address issues relating to the sustainability of dwellings – that is, the creation of usable and livable places. In particular, I describe and evaluate some of the problems related to the enforcement of access regulation. Second, in a context of deficient national legislation and guidance on access to dwellings, coupled with problems of enforcement, some state and local governments in the USA and England and Wales have sought to use discretionary powers to secure higher standards of accessibility to dwellings. I describe some examples of this, and draw out the significance of such initiatives in seeking to create accessible housing for disabled people.

The scope of access regulation and standards

One of the key arguments presented in Chapter 1 suggested that the physical and technical nature of Part M, and other access codes and standards, may be at the expense of it conceiving of the interrelationships between disability and housing quality in terms of what Goodchild (1997: 46) calls 'the house as a home', or a place that carries real social and psychological meaning for its inhabitants (see also Mumford, 1966; Rapoport, 1977; Goodchild and Furbey, 1986; Papanek, 2000). Commentators, such as Papanek (2000) and Turner (1976), concur in noting that the development of design quality in housing ought to relate to and draw upon intangible and non-quantifiable variables, such as dwellers' sense of belonging, privacy, enjoyment, self-worth and well-being (see also Franklin, 2001). However, the FHAA and Part M have nothing to say about disabled people's expectations or experiences of the home, or of what they might want or expect from domestic habitation (other than to assume that they will want to visit dwellings and use a WC).

In this respect, disabled people and their organizations have noted that the FHAA and Part M are partial responses that do not address the issues of creating livable and usable spaces in dwellings (see, for example, Age Concern, 1995). As a respondent to the Department of Environment's (1995) draft consultation document on Part M said: 'the proposals have adopted a minimalist approach to the issue. The tone of the proposals is grudging. . .' (Bristol Churches Housing Association Ltd, 1995: 1). Others variously suggested that Part M would have 'little appeal' because it was 'excessively cautious . . . with little reference to the fact that accessible design benefits all' (Royal Association for Disability and Rehabilitation, RADAR, 1995: 1); 'the intention should be to enable independent living for disabled people . . . independence and dignity are primary requirements' (Disability Wales, 1995); and 'the aim should be not simply to make a part of each new dwelling accessible, but to make it possible to make the whole dwelling directly accessible so that liveability is the outcome' (Age Concern, 1995; see also Milner and Madigan, 2001).

In the USA, observations about the scope and relevance of the FHAA note that its effectiveness is limited by its lack of application to single-family dwellings that comprise most of the new build in any one year. However, comments about the FHAA are less critical regarding its broader principles and design criteria and more likely to take issue with procedural and technical matters, including compliance with and enforcement of the legislation.[8] For instance, the National President of the Paralysed Veterans of America suggested, in a letter to the Millennial Housing Commission, that the accessibility guidelines of the FHAA ought to provide more details about how to comply with its requirements (Fox, 2000). Others note that the FHAA, as a federal law, does not have to be incorporated into state or local building codes and, as some research suggests, this leads to a situation whereby local building inspectors, absorbed with the implementation of local codes and guidelines, rarely check how far the stipulations of the FHAA are being followed up on site by builders.

For some commentators, the FHAA is also conservative and unlikely to provide usable dwellings because it does not incorporate the full range of visitability criteria evident in Part M of the building regulations. Bausch (2000) refers to the FHAA as comprising 'adaptable' design criteria, which means that the dwelling provides minimum standards of access and potential, if need be, for later adaptation by the homeowner. The FHAA does not, therefore, provide the spaces for wholly independent use of dwellings, and places onus on individual actions, at a later date, to adapt the dwelling at potentially greater cost than if access features had been designed in at the outset (Imrie and Hall, 2001a; Truesdale and Steinfeld, 2002). Given this, the impetus in the USA is for the adoption of visitability criteria, not because they will provide a fully usable dwelling but more as a pragmatic political response, a staging post, which is, as Truesdale and Steinfeld (2002: 5) suggest, 'an important step toward making universal access to community life a reality'.

In contrast, most disabled people in England and Wales are unhappy with 'visitability' criteria as the basis for accessible design in relation to dwellings, and see it as falling far short of providing usable dwelling spaces (Imrie, 2004a). For instance, the Derbyshire Coalition of Disabled People (1995: 2) rejected the DoE's draft proposals for Part M because, as they said, it 'is based on the patronizing idea of visitability standards'. For the Coalition, Part M was not likely to reduce dependence on others for ease of use of dwellings, or to provide a significant enhancement of disabled people's quality of habitation. Carol Thomas (1995: 1), on behalf of 'Disability Wales', expressed similar sentiments in rejecting the idea of visitability because, as she said, 'we consider the intention should be to enable independent living for many disabled people'. This was the view of most organizations, with Age Concern (McEwan, 1995: 1) suggesting that 'the aim should be not simply to make a part of each new dwelling accessible, but to make the whole dwelling accessible'.

This apparent insensitivity to the specificities of disability, impairment and livability is, however, not surprising given that, as Franklin (2001: 83) suggests, government directives and advice about housing quality construct it as 'relatively unproblematic, objectifying it in terms of specifications, standards, measurement and dimensions'. For instance, the FHAA and Part M objectify the disabled body as, primarily, comprising a physiology with impaired mobility, in which a wheelchair is required to facilitate movement, mobility and access (Imrie and Hall, 2001a; Imrie, 2003a). This guides the prime objective of the regulation – that is, to provide a 'fit' between the dimensions of a wheelchair and specific technical dimensions of the dwelling. The effect of this is to reduce issues about design quality, in relation to disability and housing, to a specific form of impairment (i.e. that related to restrictions of physical movement and mobility) and to achieving the technical dimensions relating to an inanimate object (i.e. a wheelchair).

The impairment-specific nature of the draft proposals for Part M was commented on by a range of disabled people's organizations (see also Figure 3.3). For instance, a representative from RADAR (1995: 1) noted that the orientation of design in the draft proposals towards wheelchair users meant that there was 'little reference to the fact that accessible design benefits everyone'. Others concurred and, as the access officer for Norwich City Council commented: 'the proposals do not go far enough in

3.3 Observations about Part M of the
Building Regulations.

Comment about Part M	Organization
'There is no mention of windows in the document . . . being able to open and shut windows is important.'	Association of County Councils
'People with mobility impairments ought reasonably to be able to gain access to their gardens without assistance.'	Kent Access Forum
'The lift size is too small.'	Disability Wales
'Access to rear gardens or amenity areas is not catered for.'	Rushmoor District Council
'The proposals ignore the benefits which more comprehensively improved access would have for people who experience periodic, progressive, or less severe mobility problems.'	Bristol Churches Housing Association Ltd
'The inclusion in the document of stepped ramps and stepped footpaths . . . is extraordinary. Stepped ramps in particular would cause problems for people with HIV who have impaired vision and loss of balance.'	Bristol Churches Housing Association Ltd
'Your proposals are misguided in some respects . . . it seems a mistake to make extensions and material alterations exempt; this means that a valuable opportunity to improve an existing building may be lost.'	City of London Access Group
'It is quite ridiculous that in this day and age in an advanced technological society lifts are not compulsory for all dwellings over ground level. We are actually building many three and four storey blocks of flats in this Borough without lifts thereby perpetuating the problems of the elderly, carers with babies, etc.'	Ken Mathieson, Access Officer, London Borough of Hammersmith

Source: Department of the Environment (1995).

addressing the needs of people with more severe impairments who would need more space and facilities than those set out in the draft document' (Forrest, 1995: 1).[9] Likewise, Thomas (1995: 1) suggested that 'the access requirements of people with sight and hearing impairments should be given more consideration'. Such observations are not dissimilar to those about the FHAA, and comments about the Fair Housing Accessibility Guidelines (Department of Housing in Urban Development, HUD, 1991: 3) noted that they 'were biased toward wheelchair users, and that the Department has erroneously assumed that the elderly and the physically disabled have similar needs'.

The conflation of ageing with disability in the FHAA is, however, overshadowed by it, like Part M, being wedded to a medical conception of disability in which, as the FHAA (1988: 2) states, disability is a 'physical or mental impairment that substantially limits one or more of such person's major life activities'. Likewise, Part M (DETR, 1999a: 5) notes that a disabled person is characterized by 'an impairment which limits their ability to walk or which requires them to use a wheelchair for mobility . . . or impaired hearing or sight'. In both instances the definition is problematical, because it draws attention to the impairment as the limitation on a person's use of the environment and ascribes it (i.e. impairment) with causal or determinant status. This conceptual term of reference, as many observers note, has the potential to 'blame the victims' for their plight, such as their inability to use dwellings, and is likely to see the remedy for inaccessible dwellings to rest more in individuals accommodating or adjusting themselves to the design than for builders to provide appropriate design in the first place.

Not surprisingly, the FHAA and Part M are characterized by exemptions and get-out clauses that serve to reduce builders' commitment to inclusive design, or design that provides usable dwellings.[10] Such exemptions revolve around the stipulation, as stated in Part M, that 'reasonable provision' has to be provided to give disabled people access to buildings, including housing (DETR, 1999a: 5). While the notion of reasonableness requires builders to meet the requirements of Part M, it provides scope for interpretation about how precisely the requirement, from one plot to another, will be met. One of the more problematical exemptions relates to builders being permitted to provide ambulant stairways, not ramps, in contexts where 'the topography is such that the route from the point of access to the entrance has a plot gradient exceeding 1 in 15' (DETR, 1999a: 26). For Rose (1995: 1), however, 'any exemptions, relating to steepness of slopes . . . would be open to abuse', because builders could choose not to level or reduce the gradients on site, and in some instances could even increase them (see Chapters 5 and 6).

The stipulations of reasonableness in the FHAA are more far-reaching than Part M in that they potentially provide builders with greater latitude to side-step the legislation. Thus, reasonable provision of access, according to the FHAA, is that which does not impose a 'fundamental alteration' to a programme, and does not impose 'an undue financial burden' on the builder. As Kochera (2002) and others note, this has led to endless debates about what constitutes the basis of 'reasonable provision', a matter not facilitated by the lack of clear design guidance about the technical standards that have to be attained to satisfy the requirements of the FHAA. Similar observations have been made about Part M and, as material in Chapters 5 and 6 will show, there is some confusion by both builders and building control officers about what constitutes a satisfactory or reasonable response to the design requirements of Part M. This appears to be because the design guidance document provides some scope for interpretation, or use of alternate ways to achieve the requirements of the regulation.

Enforcement and the significance of local discretion and policy

While the scope of access legislation needs to be broadened to provide the legal basis for attaining usable domestic environments, the lack of compliance with, or enforcement of, the FHAA and, to a lesser extent, Part M poses serious problems in securing even the minimal standards of accessibility in dwellings. In the USA context, Stephen-Kaye (1997: 204) notes that 'housing policies developed as a result of these statutes have been inconsistent and difficult to enforce'. For instance, section 504 was passed in 1973, yet the Department of Housing In Urban Development (HUD) did not begin to implement it until 1988. As Price (2003) suggested, 'It took fifteen years for the implementing regulations, at least for HUD, so that's an excellent example of the problems that we have with regulation and enforcement. They're practically non-existent.' Likewise, the National Council on Disability (NCD, 1994) reviewed the entire enforcement history of HUD, both under 504 and the FHAA, and, as Price (2003) argued, 'they found that there was next to no enforcement, there was a real dearth of enforcement'.

This dearth is widespread throughout the USA, with Leonnig (2001) recounting the situation in Washington, DC in which the Housing Authority has never complied with the 1973 Rehabilitation Act's accessibility requirements, including making 5 per cent of its 10,460 apartments accessible for use by disabled people.[11] The situation is no better elsewhere, with Gold (2000) noting that out of nearly 7,000 public housing units in Philadelphia only 22 are accessible, when, under section 504's 5 per cent rule, 350 accessible dwellings ought to have been constructed. As Gold (2000: 1) says, the lack of accessible units in the city has led to 'wheelchair users living in inaccessible third floor apartments and people who use walkers having to crawl up and down stairs'. Similar observations have been made in relation to the FHAA, with Toran (1999: 13) noting that its compliance procedures 'have generally been fairly weak'. For instance, the Memphis Center for Independent Living (2001) conducted an access audit that found more than 1,700 barriers in 26 apartment complexes required to comply with the FHAA.

Some observers have suggested that the procedural and administrative requirements of the FHAA render it less than effective, and even counter to its original purpose (Toran, 1999). Any complaint against a builder is made to HUD and may be pursued as a civil action in a state or federal court. These procedures are lengthy and, as Toran (1999: 10) notes, by the time a complaint has come to HUD, the building has often been constructed and is unlikely to be retrofitted.[12] Likewise, Galster (1991, 1999) suggests that the effectiveness of the FHA is limited because for it to be activated, victims have to recognize, first and foremost, that their rights have been violated. For Galster this is a fundamental flaw of the legislation, because many victims of unfair treatment might not recognize it as such or, if they do, may not possess the necessary resources, material and otherwise, to pursue a complaint. Galster (1991) notes that much more needs to be done than just informing potential victims of their rights; rather, the onus must be placed on producers or providers of services to demonstrate use of, and compliance with, non-discriminatory practices (although, see arguments in Chapter 8).

The enforcement of Part M in England and Wales is not subject to rights legislation like the FHAA, but rather depends on building control officers' willingness to exercise their enforcement powers, through the context of the Building Act, where transgressions of the regulation are brought to their notice. There are, however, few if any systematic studies of compliance with, or the enforcement of, Part M of the building regulations in relation to dwellings, although anecdotal information suggests that the interpretation and application of the regulation by builders and building control officers has been variable and inconsistent (see Chapters 5 and 6; Imrie, 2004a). Such inconsistency is a function, in part, of a complexity of conjoined factors, ranging from the purposive evasion by builders with compliance, to building control officers' inability to police (for reasons of resource) builders' responses to the legislation (see Chapter 6). Enforcement problems of this type, and the limitations of the legislation more generally, have, however, met with some response.

In particular, the limitations of the FHAA and Part M of the building regulations have encouraged some state and local governments to 'go it alone', by pursuing policies and programmes that seek to attain standards of accessibility in excess of the national statutory minima. The existence of variations in local policy responses to federal or national access legislation is indicative of, in part, what Bagguley et al. (1990) refer to as the determinate nature of local political environments. By this, Bagguley et al. (1990) suggest that the operation of local political and institutional systems is not wholly determined by central or federal direction; rather, local political systems are characterized by some autonomy from the centre, in which there is capacity to determine local social and political process and outcomes (see Imrie, 2000a). Such outcomes are, so Bagguley et al. (1990: 12), suggest, conditioned by a range of place-specific social relations, including the 'material, political, and cultural capacities of different potential actors', or the resources which are available to different individuals and/or groups to realize their (political) interests.

An example of the potency of local state or municipal responses to the building industry is provided by Derby City Council in England, who in 1988 made it clear that the council would seek to negotiate with builders over the provision of dwellings to visitability standards (Derby City Council, 1988). While nothing was written into the local plan, members' support for planners' use of section 106 of the planning legislation, which permits local planning authorities to enter into a legal agreement with developers over the content of development schemes, provided the political support and means to secure accessible dwellings. As the access officer noted, 'the word got out that builders were likely to have difficulties getting planning permission for proposed schemes unless they complied with requests for dwellings to be constructed to visitability standards' (Watts, 2002). What was critical to the success of Derby City Council's approach was, however, their ownership of much of the developable land in the city. This enabled them to attach conditions to its use when selling it on to developers.

Other authorities in England and Wales have also regarded Part M as 'too little, too late', and were, prior to the inception of the regulation,

requiring builders to construct dwellings to visitability (or even LTH) standards. The main mechanism for securing access in this way has been
through the local planning framework, by stipulating either in the local
plan or supplementary planning guidance (SPG), as in the case of London
(see Figure 3.4), that dwellings ought to be constructed to specified levels
of accessibility. For instance, the London Borough of Harrow's draft
Unitary Development Plan identified the need for a supply of LTH, and
noted that the 'provision of housing that accommodates various stages of
the human life cycle and different circumstances can contribute to a stable
and sustainable community' (London Borough of Harrow, 2002: 172). The
access officer for Harrow suggested that 'developers already provide LTH
here and we have been very successful with this, and we expect more and
more of this' (Kashmiri, 2003).

Similar local responses have emerged in the USA given that, as previously intimated, more than two-thirds of dwellings built in recent years are
single family and fall outside the scope of the FHAA. Several state and
local governments have responded by introducing ordinances requiring
access in single-family dwellings, and by using a range of fiscal and other

3.4 Lifetime homes and supplementary
planning guidance: the case of the Greater
London Plan.

Policies have been included throughout the London Plan (published February
2004) to promote social inclusion and to help eliminate discrimination. This Supplementary Planning Guidance (SPG) provides detailed advice and guidance on
the policies which promote an inclusive environment in London. SPG does not
form part of the statutory plan: only the policies in the London Plan have the
status that the GLA Act 1999 provides in considering planning applications.
However, SPG can be taken into account as a further material consideration so
has weight as a formal supplement to the London Plan. Twenty-eight implementation points should assist boroughs when reviewing their Unitary Development
Plans and development control practices and procedures and when assessing
planning applications...

...It is much more cost effective to build new homes that are generally accessible to a wide range of people, than to build homes that are not future-proof,
so become inappropriate to our changing needs. The government recognized
this in 1999 by extending the requirements of Part M of the building regulations
1991 to include housing ... These minimum standards still, however, fall short
of making the home easily accessible for all our changing housing needs...

...**SPG Implementation Point 12: Lifetime Homes:** The mayor will and boroughs should seek to ensure that all residential units in new housing developments are designed to Lifetime Home standards. These standards should be
applied to all new housing, including conversions and refurbishments, and
including blocks of flats, for both social and private sector housing, and should
cater for a varying number of occupants...

...Planning applicants should be asked to provide an Access Statement which
sets out the approach taken in both the external and internal environment to
deliver accessible homes and the opportunities and constraints of each proposal.
Where elements of the scheme are unable to meet the full lifetime home standards solutions introduced to overcome the constraint should be explained in the
Access Statement...

Source: Greater London Authority (2004).

incentives to encourage builders to provide accessible domestic environments. For instance, in 1992 an ordinance was passed in the city of Atlanta that required single-family dwellings constructed with any type of subsidy from the city government to incorporate visitability features. The ordinance was the result of lobbying by a local organization called Concrete Change (www.concretechange.com) which, in the words of its founder, Eleanor Smith (2003), campaigns against inaccessible dwellings because it is 'unacceptable that new homes continue to be built with basic barriers – unacceptable, given how easy it is to build basic access in the great majority of new homes, coupled with the harshness lack of access inflicts on so many people's lives' (see also Figure 3.5).

Others have followed the Atlanta ordinance, although, as in Atlanta, most do not require no-step entrances, and are applicable only to builders in receipt of subsidies from the municipality (see Figure 3.6).[13] The range of requirements does not differ greatly between the municipalities, although the Urbana ordinance requires the provision of non-slip surfaces on the accessible route to the dwelling (Kochera, 2002). A different approach to these municipalities has emerged in the state of Vermont, where since 2001 legislation has required builders of non-subsidized single and multi-family dwellings to incorporate some visitability features (Kochera, 2002). However, no-step entrances are exempt, along with customized houses built by the owner for personal use. The Vermont statute requires the distribution of a pamphlet to builders outlining the advantages of providing a no-step entrance, but it is difficult to see how this can do much to change builders' practices and attitudes towards disabled people's needs.

In contrast, from 1999 to 2002 the municipality of Bolingbrook, near Chicago, secured a range of no-step single-family dwellings through voluntary agreement with builders (Bannister, 2003). This occurred because of the understanding that the mayor and the local political system, including a strong disability lobby, were unwilling to let builders be given building permits to construct to less than a visitability standard that included a no step feature (see Chapter 7 for further details of this case). The voluntary approach was superseded by a building code in November 2003 that requires, by law, all unsubsidized privately constructed dwellings to incorporate visitability standards, including no-step entrances. The approach in Bolingbrook, however, remains one of the few exceptions in a context whereby the spirit and intent of visitability legislation, at the municipal level, is so shot through with exemptions and get-out clauses that it is rendered less than effective in creating useful and usable dwelling environments for disabled people.[14]

3.4 Conclusions

One interpretation of access legislation, suggested by arguments in the chapter, is that it represents no more than the state's restructuring of welfare provision and support, and the emergence of a mixed economy of welfare. In a context of the dismantling of state welfare, in which the provision of welfare goods and services is increasingly originating from private sector organizations, governments are encouraging citizens to develop themselves as self-reliant and active individuals, with the means to exercise

A legal or statutory approach is not the only way to secure good access in dwellings. While most builders choose not to incorporate accessible design into the construction of new dwellings, there are some exceptions. One example relates to Maple Court Development that comprises 48 apartments. It is situated in the city of Naperville, 30 miles west of Chicago. It was constructed by Maple Court Development Inc and opened on 6 September 1996. The development has 20 barrier-free apartments that are designed to meet the needs of disabled people, particularly people with mobility impairments and those who are dependent on the use of a wheelchair. The development cost $4.6 million and rental levels for barrier-free apartments are set at 'fair levels' in recognition of the lower than average incomes that most disabled people have.

The range of access features and related dimensions far exceed what is required under the FHAA, and in many respects Maple Court is state of the art in relation to accessible design. Kitchen cabinets and tabletops are lower than normal to permit ease of reach and use by people sitting in a wheelchair. There are seats in shower units and door handles are designed to be easy to grasp and use. All switches and meters are visible and reachable. Bathroom walls will support grab bars, and doors are 3 ft in width and open automatically. Carpets in public areas provide grip for ease of movement of wheelchairs and windows are set at heights that provide ease of vision from a sitting position.

The developer and owner of Maple Court Development, William Malleris said: 'my goal is to create an integrated environment, where you have people with and without disabilities' (quoted in Finley, 1997: 1). For Malleris, it is important to get away from the old stereotyping, so creating integration not segregation. As a wheelchair user, Malleris (2000: 21) feels that 'I, and others in my situation, should not be blocked from obtaining needed accessible housing or being forced to sacrifice this because of the non-knowledge of developers.' He has brought his personal experience to bear upon accessibility issues in that much of his working life has been as a developer and/or builder.

As Malleris explained: 'I've been able to help the movement and the cause by pushing, and being from the private sector, I can come at things differently compared to others from the advocacy side, or from the governmental side. I'm in the private sector. I have my own business; I'm on my own. So by being in the business I am able to share a private entrepreneurial perspective that brings a whole different level of credibility.' In describing his interactions with the National Home Builders, Malleris recounted one encounter with this organization:

> They just don't see beyond the forest. I told the leader of the local National Home Builders, 'Until you're sitting in this chair and you can't get into the bathroom, when you're sitting in your own bowel movement, that's when you're going to find out what life's all about. And you'll look at yourself in the mirror twenty years from now, it may not happen now, it may not happen, maybe when you're ninety-five years of age you're going to be sitting here, and I want you to remember everything that you're doing.' And you know what, he couldn't look at me at all.

William Malleris is using Maple Court as a demonstration project of what can be achieved within the context of the commercial objectives of builders. Part of his mission is training developers in the principles that underpin the design and construction of the scheme. As Malleris, in interview, said: 'developers come here and spend a day here and I go through a load of issues about how to use accessible design as well as financing, and putting the whole package together. As a developer, I'm able to bring people, city officials and other people here, to show them what works. And that's besides doing the training and the site visits and the presentations.'

3.5 Maple Court Development, Naperville, USA.

3.6 Summary of local ordinances and state laws for visitability in selected places in the USA.

Visitability criteria	Atlanta 1992	Austin 1998	Urbana 2000	Georgia 2000	Minnesota 2001	Texas 1999
Entrance to homes	At least one no-step entrance on accessible route; minimum 32" opening	At least one no-step entrance on accessible route; minimum opening 32"	At least one no-step entrance on accessible route; minimum opening 32"	At least one no-step entrance on accessible route; minimum opening 36" (yields at least 32" opening)	At least one no-step entrance; 32" clear width door opening	At least one no-step entrance on accessible route; minimum door opening 36" (yields at least 32" opening)
Interior doors	All interior doors minimum 32" opening and lever handles	All interior doors on first floor* to be a minimum of 30" opening and lever handles	All doors or openings minimum 32"	All interior doors on first floor minimum 32" opening	All doorways 32" clear width	All interior doors on first floor minimum 32" opening
Accessible route	36"-wide level route provided through main floor of unit	36"-wide level route provided through main floor of unit	Corridors shall be at least 36" wide	36"-wide level hallways on first floor		36"-wide level hallways on first floor
Bathroom walls	To be reinforced	First-floor bathroom walls to be reinforced	To be reinforced	First-floor bathroom walls to be reinforced		First-floor bathroom walls to be reinforced
Light switches, thermostat, electrical outlets, electrical panel	Maximum 48" height; minimum 15" height	For first floor, maximum 42" height; minimum 18" height	Maximum 48" height; minimum 15" height	For first floor, maximum 48" height, minimum 15" height		For first floor, maximum 48" height, minimum 15" height
Miscellaneous			Additional requirements for accessible route to the home regarding landing, non-slip surfaces and slope	Electrical box must be inside building on the first floor	There must be at least a one-half bathroom on the main level	Electrical box must be inside building on the first floor
Waiver	Through Commissioner of Department of Housing if topographical conditions make compliance impossible	Through the building official if topographical conditions render compliance an undue hardship	Where site conditions or other restrictions warrant, the Building Code Board of Appeal may recommend waiver, which must be granted by the City Council		Minnesota Housing Finance Agency may waive no-step entrance if site conditions make it impractical. One-half bathroom and no-step entrance may be waived if it reduces the affordability for targeted population	

*In the USA, the first floor in dwellings is equivalent to the ground floor in UK dwellings.

Source: adapted from Kochera (2002: 12).

self-care and choice of lifestyle. No longer is it permissible for individuals to live off welfare; rather, the objective of the state is to encourage individuals to exercise their rights, but only if certain responsibilities are discharged. In this respect, access law and legislation is supposed to be part of an emergent enabling culture insofar as it seeks to promote a context (i.e. accessible dwellings) in which disabled people can exercise degrees of self-determination and activity commensurate with the objectives of governments' promotion of the self-reliant citizen.

However, legal directives and regulations on physical access in private (for sale) housing are usually weak and difficult to enforce, often ineffective, and in many countries non-existent. Thus in the USA the FHAA does not cover much new build, and evidence on its implementation suggests that builders are able to sidestep many of its provisions. In England and Wales the situation is not dissimilar, and most builders find Part M easy to achieve and will admit that it is not providing that much for disabled people (see also the arguments in Chapter 5). This is because law and legal principle, in relation to physical access to housing, revolves around the propagation of voluntary codes and actions, underpinned by the minimal regulation of the building industry. It is assumed, by politicians and others, that market mechanisms rather then legal directives are best able to secure the quality of design that is necessary to produce habitable housing environments.

The contents of Part M and the FHAA are regarded by some as no solution to the dwelling needs of disabled people because they perpetuate, at best, a technical, standards-based conception of housing quality, or one that reduces conceptions of (housing) quality to the attainment of dimensional measures. This means that the legislation is not likely to change, in any dramatic sense, the quality of habitation for disabled people. There is also a question mark about the relevance of legislation, such as the FHAA, which does not apply to single-family dwellings and which, like Part M, promotes a concept (such as visitability) that fails to recognize the importance of providing design to encourage the occupation and use of dwelling space. When combined with the legislations' understanding of disability as a medical condition and problem, requiring in large part individuals to adapt and change, then the legal route, as presently construed, is not helpful in seeking to secure habitable dwelling environments for disabled people.

Further reading

A good introduction to debates about disability and law is Gooding (1994). There are very few texts and/or journal articles that describe access legislation and related policies and programmes in different countries. A superficial overview, although a useful starting point, of access legislation in different countries is provided by Michailakis (1997). The publication by the United Nations (1995) of *Promotion of Non Handicapping Physical Environments for Disabled Persons: Case Studies*, UN, New York, is one of the better publications although it suffers for its brevity of treatment of the subject matter. The theme of government and active citizenship is well covered in the excellent book by Dean (1999). Ellis (2000a, 2000b) discusses this subject matter in relation to conceptions of the body.

PART II
SECURING ACCESSIBLE HOMES

4 'Ideal homes'
Disabled people's experiences of domestic design

4.1 Introduction

> Empowerment is often found in the details of the mundane world. It comes from controlling access to personal space, from being able to alter one's environment and select one's daily routine, and from having personal space that reflects and upholds one's identity and interests.
>
> (Ridgway *et al.*, 1994)

A person's mental and physical well-being is related to many circumstances, not the least of which is the quality of their housing and home environment. An important part of such quality is physical design and layout, and how far it enables the ease of people's mobility and movement around the dwelling and the use of different rooms and their facilities. As previous chapters have outlined, the design of housing is often not well suited to the needs of disabled people, particularly for those with mobility impairments and/or those who are dependent on the use of a wheelchair (Borsay, 1986; Karn and Sheridan, 1994; Heywood *et al.*, 2002). Harrison and Davis (2001: 115), for instance, note that the poor physical design of housing can prevent self-management of impairments, 'and may exacerbate a condition'. Likewise, Sharma's (2002) study of families with disabled children notes that housing often lacks space for the storage of specialist equipment (like wheelchairs).

Such studies, amongst others, seem to indicate that disabled people's domestic experiences are potentially at odds with the (ideal) conception of the home as a haven, or a place of privacy, security, independence and control. In part this is because design conceptions, in relation to floor plans and allocation of functions to specific spaces, do not conceive of impairment, disease and illness as part of domestic habitation or being. The impaired body is rarely imagined or drawn into domestic design and the production of housing or buildings more generally (see Imrie and Hall, 2001a; Imrie, 2003a). This is unsurprising given that representations of idealized domestic life revolve around what Hockey (1999) refers to as positively perceived values, such as companionship and freedom, but tend to exclude, even deny, other aspects of domestic life, such as disease, impairment and dying. This reflects a broader problem with debates about the meaning of the home, and housing studies more generally, in which, as the Introduction to this book suggested, the impaired body is rarely a subject of comment and analysis.

In seeking to redress this, I divide the chapter into three. First, I outline in brief some of the broader debates about the meaning of the home, and suggest that these are far from helpful in enabling a coherent understanding of disabled people's experiences of domestic environments. Second, I refer to testimonies from interviews with disabled people that highlight some of the paradoxes and problems of idealized conceptions of the home that hinge in part on little or no recognition of impaired corporeality as a potential part of home life.[1] I conclude by developing the idea that there is an urgent need to 'corporealize' the meaning of the home, in which conceptions of domestic life become underpinned by an understanding of the interactions between a person's bodily or physiological condition and their patterns of behaviour in the domestic environment.

4.2 Seeking to embody the meaning of the home

It has been well established in housing studies that the home is one of the fundamental places that gives shape and meaning to people's everyday lives (Rakoff, 1977; Saunders and Williams, 1988; Saunders, 1989, 1990; Gurney, 1990; Dupuis and Thorns, 1996). A burgeoning literature has, in various ways, explored the social, health and psychological effects of the home (Allan and Crow, 1989; Hopton and Hunt, 1996; Madigan and Munro, 1999; Gilman, 2002). For instance, Sixsmith and Sixsmith (1991) note that the home is a symbol of oneself or a powerful extension of the psyche. It is a context for social and mental well-being or, as Lewin (2001) suggests, a place to engender social, psychological and cultural security. For others, the home is the focus for personal control and a place that permits people to fashion it in their own image (Saunders, 1990). In this sense, the domestic setting is, for Lewin (2001), a mirror of personal views and values (see also Cooper, 1995).

Gilman's (1903, reprinted 2002: 3) seminal text suggests that the home ideally should offer a combination of rest, peace, quiet, comfort and health, and be a place for personal expression. Indeed, throughout the twentieth century the home has been counterpoised to work, as a place of retreat, social stability and domestic bliss far from the travails of everyday life (see, for example, arguments in Rakoff, 1977; Saunders, 1990). From builders' marketing brochures that seek to sell the dream of the ideal home to television programmes about selling a place in the sun, the home is popularly portrayed as the focus of convivial social relationships and a source of human contentment. It is, first and foremost, a place for family interaction and the setting for personal seclusion and intimate behaviour free from public comment or restraint. The home is also the setting for the development of personal values, and patterns of socialization and social reproduction more generally.

These characterizations of the home, however, do little to reveal the complexity of the cross-cutting variables that imbue domestic space with meaning. Saunders and Williams (1988) and Saunders (1989, 1990) have been accredited with (re)igniting debates in housing studies about the meaning of the home that, in part, have gone some way to identifying such complexity and in fleshing out, empirically, what Lewin (2001) refers to as the home as a composite concept (see also Allan and Crow, 1989; Chapman and Hockey, 1999). For Saunders and Williams (1988) the meaning of the home is not fixed but varies, potentially, between different household members, especially in terms of gender and age, and between households, especially in relation to differences in social class. They also suggest that people's experiences of, and meanings attributed to, the home may differ according to geographical context or setting.

Such studies indicate that the meaning of the home is unstable and transitory. Gilman (2002: 5) anticipated as much when, writing in 1903, she noted that 'this power of home-influence we cannot fail to see, but we have bowed to it in blind idolatry as one of unmixed beneficence'. For Gilman (2002: 8), despite the prevailing wisdom that homes were 'perfect and quite above suspicion', the home was a potential source of repression. In particular, she referred to women's' exclusive confinement to the home as leading to 'mental myopia' in which the individual was made into 'less of a person'. Likewise, a range of feminist writers has sought to deconstruct ideal images of the home by suggesting that the home, for some women, is a place of captivity and isolation (McDowell, 1983; Allan, 1985). It is, as Goldsack (1999: 121) notes, 'less of a castle, and more of a cage'. Others note that the home is as much about the focus for the drudgery of domestic work as for personal pleasure, and a place of fear where, potentially, domestic violence takes place.

While these and related studies have done much to destabilize popular representations of the home, they tend to refer to abstract categories (e.g. gender, ethnicity, etc.) that rarely relate to or reveal how specific bodily or physiological phenomena interact with housing to produce personal experiences of, and generate particular meanings about, the home (although, for exceptions, see the excellent writings of Gurney, 2000, and undated). Indeed, I concur with Gurney (1990), who notes that it is problematical to explain the meaning of the home with reference only to generalized categories, such as class, income or tenure. Rather, for Gurney, the significance of the home is influenced by different personal experiences. Foremost, I would contend, it relates to the body in that, as Twigg (2002: 436) comments, the body is a necessary condition of life inasmuch that 'social life cannot proceed without this physiological substratum' (see also Shilling, 1993; Ellis, 2000a, 2000b; Crossley, 2001).

Others concur in noting that the body is the most significant referent of a person or, as Merleau-Ponty (1962: 150) notes, 'I am not in front of my body, I am in it, or rather I am it'. For Merleau-Ponty (1963: 5), the 'body is not in space like things; it inhabits or haunts space . . . through it we have access to space'. Here the body, as a sensory and physiological entity, is constitutive of space or, as Lefebvre (1991: 174) comments, 'the most basic places and spatial indicators are first of all qualified by the body'. Physiological substratum is also core to domestic life in that the home is the focus for the care of the body, including washing, dressing, grooming and preparation for entry to the world beyond the front door. The physical design of housing is 'thoroughly embodied' in that each part of the domestic environment can be thought of as a 'body zone', or where particular bodily functions, both physical and mental, are attended to. Thus the bathroom is the place for washing the body, while the bedroom is the place for physical and mental recuperation.

While such functional demarcations are neither inevitable nor unchangeable, they are part of a broader, and powerful, social and cultural encoding of what constitutes appropriate domestic space and their legitimate (bodily) uses. Such encoding, however, rarely relates to impairment, or to bodies that may require an integration of rooms and/or functions, or more flexible forms of domestic design. In particular, disabled people often experience the home as a series of 'disembodied spaces' or places that are designed in ways that are rarely attentive to their physiological and bodily needs and functions. Thus interactions between features of bodily physiology, such as muscle wasting, and domestic design, such as heavy doors, can combine to demarcate domestic spaces that are off limits to (particular types of) impaired bodies. For Hockey (1999: 108), such embodied experiences, in which people are excluded from participation 'in the performance of home as idealized', is to undermine a view of home as a sanctuary or 'place of secure retreat'.

Insights into disabled people's experiences of and meanings associated with the home, ought to proceed, however, by rejecting reductive conceptions of disability and impairment. Thus, the body is neither a naturalistic organic entity unaffected by socialization, nor a socialized entity unaffected by physiology. Rather, the body and its interactions with domestic space reflect a complex conjoining of physiological and social and cultural relations to produce specific, person-centred meanings of the home. For instance, doorsteps have long been part of the aesthetic décor of housing, and reflect values about what constitutes appropriate design (see Milner and Madigan, 2001). However, for wheelchair users steps prevent ease of entry to homes. In such instances, the experience and potential meaning of the home as a form of embodied encounter is influenced by the interplay between physiological matter (i.e. the absence of use of limbs) and those social and cultural relations that give rise to and legitimate particular design features (i.e. steps).

In this sense, the chapter makes the plea for an embodied understanding of the meaning of the home that, in the context of impairment, does not seek to explain such meanings purely in terms of biological phenomena (i.e. the medical condition causes the experience and determines the meaning), or in terms that assert the primacy of social phenomena over biology (i.e. the organic or biological condition is irrelevant in the construction of people's experiences of, and associated meanings derived from, the home) (see also Oldman and Beresford, 2000; Allen, 2004a). Given these caveats, I now turn to an exploration of the multiple meanings of the home in relation to the experiences of people who are dependent, for most part, on the use of wheelchairs.

4.3 Disability, domestic design and the home environment

In investigating disabled people's feelings about disability and domestic design, two research methods were adopted (see also Appendix 1). First, two focus groups were held in October 2002 with members of a disabled persons' user group located in a south coast conurbation. This was followed, over the course of the next five months, by interviews with twenty individuals living in three different towns. Each person was contacted through the context of an intermediary, or gatekeeper. Thus in one place the chair of the local access group permitted me to give a lecture about my research to the group, and to leave my contact details for individuals to contact me if they wished to talk with me at a later date. In contrast, in the other places I approached the chairs of user groups and they posted out my details to their membership inviting them to contact me if they were willing to talk about aspects of disability and domestic design.[2]

Interviews normally occurred in the subject's home, and were usually two to three hours in length. They covered a wide range of themes relating to individuals' life histories and, especially, their experiences of the home. Respondents talked about the various places that they had lived in, and how parts of their domestic lives were affected by the onset of impairment. In particular, respondents were asked to articulate how the meaning of their home had been transformed, if at all, by the interaction between impairment and the physical design of their dwellings. The conversations were taped and transcribed, and copies of testimonials were returned for comment to each individual. The subjects are all individuals with various mobility impairments, ranging from those with problems of balance due to the early onset of Parkinson's disease to individuals with advanced stages of multiple sclerosis that render them dependent, for some of the time, on a wheelchair.

The respondents lived in a mixture of different types of places including flats (five respondents), detached homes (four), institutional care settings (three), and terraced and semi-detached houses (eight). The mix of tenures was evenly divided between those occupying social (eight) and owner-occupied (nine) dwellings. Because the sample was 'self-selecting' and derived from access groups, the respondents were knowledgeable about design issues and were usually forthright in their opinions. Their membership of an access group meant that most were aware of the need to campaign politically to try and change the processes underpinning the production of disabling built environments. Most of the respondents, from their standpoint, had thought through the issues relating to design, disability and domesticity, and were able to articulate different ways in which they felt society should change. In a modest way, the transcripts are able to 'give voice' to the politicized knowledge of the respondents (see Millen, 1997 and Letherby, 2002 for an outline of these issues).

In describing and evaluating the research material, I divide the discussion into three. First, I develop and evaluate the argument that the design of home environments interacts with impairment to produce, more often than not, a series of disembodied spaces that are rarely sensitized to the needs of disabled people. Rather, such spaces, so some claim, lead to what Leder (1990) terms 'corporeal dys-appearance' (see also Paterson and Hughes, 1999). Second, I consider how far, and in what ways, dominant representations of the ideal home (such as privacy, security and sanctuary) accord with disabled people's experiences of their homes. Finally, I develop the argument that disabled people are not necessarily passive victims of insensitive domestic design but, depending on social, personal and material resources, are able to influence aspects of the design and usability of the home environment (see also Allen *et al.*, 2002).

Corporeal dys-appearance and privation in the home

The physical design of housing tends to reflect a particular conception of corporeality based around a body that is not characterized by impairment, disease and illness (Hockey, 1999). For instance, most kitchen units in homes are provided as a standardized package in which tabletop and cupboard heights are reachable only by an upright person. People who are dependent on a wheelchair, or whose mobility is such that they have to hold onto a support structure to stabilize themselves, often find it impossible to use their kitchen unless it is adapted to meet their needs (see Figure 4.1). Thus, as Ann recounted about her kitchen before it was adapted:

> It was too high, I couldn't have used the wheelchair, the cupboards were too high, the cooker was completely unusable, I would leave the thing on and oh, it just went on and on and on . . . As a mum it totally demoralized me.

The design of most housing is also underpinned by values that rarely relate to or incorporate the needs of wheelchair users. Some respondents were angry that their homes were short of space to permit them ease of movement from one room to another, or even within rooms. For John, his bedroom is an apt example of where design values have been applied without relating to impairment. As he recalled:

> there are some basic assumptions. I'm just talking about a very simple basic thing, like there is no way on this earth that my wheelchair can go to the other side of my bed. It doesn't matter what you do; you can't configure the bedroom any other way, so the assumption must be that I'm not going to make my bed, that I don't need to get to the other side of the room.

John is unable to get access to the bedroom window and, consequently, cannot open the window to air the room. He said that 'it's obviously assumed that I don't need to open my window'.

Others commented on the lack of space as the most important factor in preventing them from getting access to rooms and living as they please in their homes (see also Oldman and Beresford, 2000; Percival, 2002). As Carol said:

> the kitchen is really very small and when you're manoeuvring a wheelchair you do need a bit of space. You can hardly get your furniture in the lounge and you have to eat in it. It's things like this, and I'm thinking to myself, you've got a life and you want to lead your life and this isn't really helping you.

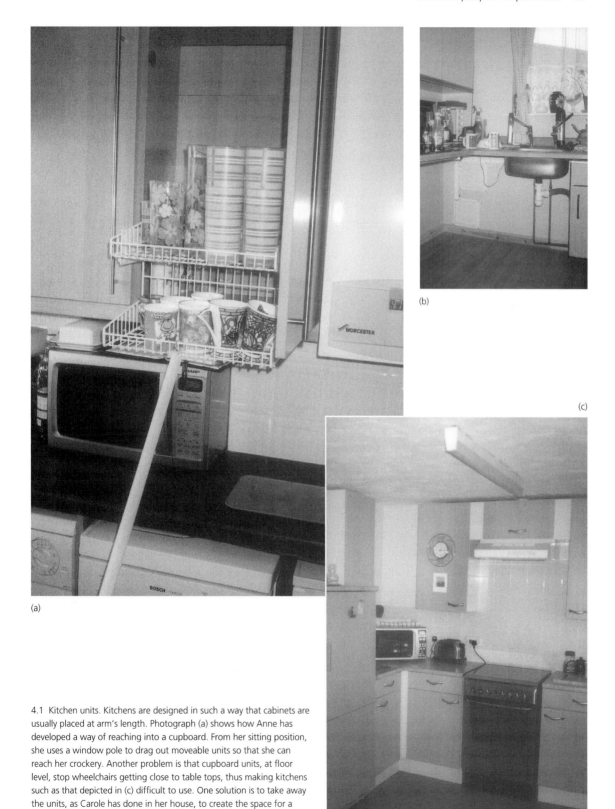

(a)

(b)

(c)

4.1 Kitchen units. Kitchens are designed in such a way that cabinets are usually placed at arm's length. Photograph (a) shows how Anne has developed a way of reaching into a cupboard. From her sitting position, she uses a window pole to drag out moveable units so that she can reach her crockery. Another problem is that cupboard units, at floor level, stop wheelchairs getting close to table tops, thus making kitchens such as that depicted in (c) difficult to use. One solution is to take away the units, as Carole has done in her house, to create the space for a wheelchair to pull up close to work surfaces (b).

Similarly, Janet was unhappy with the shortage of space in her WC which, she felt, compromised the quality of her life:

> if my loo had been built eighteen inches longer it would've meant I could've got my whole wheelchair in, but as it is I can't use it with the wheelchair . . . I have to leave the door open, and it just brings it home to you about what you can't do in your own home.

Such examples serve to illustrate what Leder (1990: 84) refers to as the 'dys-appearing' body or where, as he suggests, 'the body appears as a thematic focus of attention but precisely in a dys-state' (see also Paterson and Hughes, 1999). What Leder (1990) is inferring is that in everyday life, consciousness of the body, either by oneself or by others, is minimal or non-existent. That is, the body has more or less disappeared from consciousness. It only reappears, explicitly, in a context of pain, disease or bodily dysfunction. Its reappearance is characterized by encounters with the embodied norms of everyday life, or those that are reflective of, primarily, non-impaired forms of carnality. Such norms serve to reproduce a world in the image of non-impaired bodies, with the consequence that, in Paterson and Hughes' (1999: 603) terms, the impaired body is experienced 'as-alien-being-in-the-world'.

This characterization was recognized and understood by a number of respondents, who said that aspects of design quality in their homes are not sensitized to the needs of impaired bodies. For instance, Clare referred to the poor quality of internal walls that prevented her erecting a stair lift: 'it didn't even have a solid wall to put the stair lift in, you know, it was only like chipboard or something . . . I've had to live down here because of this'. Jim was also frustrated because he was unable to reach a lot of things in his (council-owned) home, and could only see the sky out of his windows. In noting this, he highlighted a common observation of respondents about window levels being too high to see outside, and that window design 'is just done for people who can stand up, not for me'. Carol felt that a similar situation in her home was akin to cutting off part of her life, 'because it's nice to be able to look out and see what's happening'.

These experiences are illustrative of what is not embodied in the design of housing – that is, bodily difference and, in particular, impairment. Grosz (2001), in referring to sexual difference, suggests that part of the problem is that designers foreclose on the question of sexual difference and do not sensitize design to the sexualized nature of embodiment in the built environment; consequentially buildings, in Grosz's (2001) interpretation, are phallocentric. So too in relation to impairment, in which the interactions between many disabled people and the design of housing is akin to an absent presence. The body is simultaneously there but not there, characterized by material practices (i.e. moving from room to room, bathing, etc.) that draw attention to 'out-of-place' bodies, or bodies unable to operate wholly in environments characterized by the embodied norms of society.

Such embodied norms rarely recognize the intrinsic nature of impairment to the human condition, and were highlighted by respondents in relation to the separation of functions by floor levels. In particular, the spatial separation of the bathroom and toilet (upstairs) from daily living functions (downstairs) is premised on a walking and mobile person. For Elaine, the deterioration of her leg muscles restricted her to downstairs, with the consequence that she had difficulties bathing. As she said:

> when we moved in here four years ago my husband had to shower me in the back garden with a hosepipe, because I couldn't get upstairs and there wasn't even a shower downstairs; we put that in ourselves.

Likewise, a traumatic experience for Heather in her former home made her realize that upstairs was no longer feasible for her to use. As she recalled:

> it was difficult to use the house. The stairs was twisting and I had fallen down the stairs . . . I'd lost my balance, and I injured my ribs really bad. I was shouting out for help and my family didn't wake up [laughs] and I was in the most awful pain for a long time . . . after that, I never went upstairs again.

The best that respondents felt they could get was partial access to, and use of, some rooms. Thus even when a house has supposedly been designed to facilitate ease of use by wheelchair users, aspects of design do not always work well. For instance, Pete's house was, in his words, 'purpose built around me and it works'. However, he admitted that 'I'm not independent in it, I can't pull my own curtains, and I can't get into all the corners of my house, at all'. As Pete suggested:

> there's still parts of it I will never use where other people will be able to use their homes, so it depends again on what you mean. Can I fully function within my house? Well, I can get in and out and my care could be provided within that facility, etc., but no, I can't use my home in the way I still think I would be able to, given the sort of facilities within it that are available to be put in.

In this respect, much of Pete's house is indicative of disembodied spaces, or places that are not habitable in the present circumstances.

For most respondents, living in the home is achieved by accepting and adapting to the standards of design that reflect the primacy of non-impaired bodies. While respondents often expressed anger about this, they felt that there were few options open to them. For instance, Joe commented on the unfairness of imposing on him domestic design that tended to amplify and draw attention to his impairment: 'if I try and use that room then it only shows up that my body isn't up to it . . . it's not me though, it's the lack of space in there'. However, he felt he had no option but to compromise, although he felt it was all one-sided in that disabled people are the ones who have to take what is on offer. As he said: 'you compromise all the time. I hear people all the time saying "It's good, I can get by, I make do, I'm quite happy." I don't hear that from temporarily able-bodied people. They're not saying that about their homes.'

The feelings of disembodiment in the home were, more often than not, related to design details or the micro-architecture of the house (see also

Imrie, 2000b). Thus it was often the subtle aspects of the design of the home environment that caused most problems. For instance, John referred to the fitting of an electric window to permit ease of opening of windows by the use of remote control. However, as he said:

> I mean, my electric window is beautiful, wonderful, but the switch is on the pelmet [laughter] and out of reach. It's like when they fitted it they didn't look at me or ask me if it was OK. They just did it.

Likewise, Ann, until recently, was unable to transport food around the house due to a slight gradient in the floor:

> this floor level in here was two inches lower than the hall. So I couldn't bring food in and out, I wouldn't have been able to have used a tray because everything was going to slop . . . the detail was very minute and you couldn't see it, but it was very major to me.

Impairment and destabilizing the meaning of the home

Binns and Mars (1984: 664) suggest that the ideal of the home as sanctuary is undermined in circumstances where the home environment becomes 'the product of withdrawal from wider social networks'. Indeed, for some respondents broader social, attitudinal and environmental circumstances, beyond the immediate confines of their home, had led them to 'stay at home' and rarely venture beyond the front door. For instance, Harry recounted demeaning reactions from 'friends' concerning his inability to access, unaided, stepped thresholds into their homes:

> they think I'm being awkward . . . it's not as friendly an atmosphere as what it used to be, when I was up and walking . . . people say I'm seeking attention or whatever. They're wrong about that [laughs].

For Harry, it has become easier not to visit friends or to expose himself to possible ridicule or suggestions that he's 'putting it on'. Rather, as Harry said, 'I spend most time indoors, and it feels like I'm confined to quarters'.

In other instances, social interactions have been curtailed or have stopped altogether. As Harry noted, 'I don't get invited to some of the parties any more, as they've got to lift me into the house'. Such situations have also prompted Harry to withdraw 'voluntarily' from most social engagements because, as he said, 'it means I've got to rush back here just to use the toilet'. Others also recalled how their lives have become 'home-bound' because they cannot get into friends' homes. As Ann said:

> well, obviously you can't get into them. There isn't really a home that I can get into. Obviously I can get into Mum's, but as for anywhere else, it's not, you know, there isn't anyone that I can actually go and visit.

Likewise, Carol's recent dependence on using a wheelchair has changed, in part, her patterns of mobility. She is less likely to go outside the home to visit people. As she said:

I can't go and visit my sister. Three steps up to her front door, to start with. My mum's the same. I can't go to my hairdresser to get my hair done. She has to come to me, for the same problem, access to her house.

Others recounted similar tales of how the onset of impairment led to a form of entrapment in housing circumstances that were socially and psychologically damaging. For instance, John was more or less confined to his house for six months awaiting adaptations to be carried out by the local authority. During this period he was unable to get out of the front door unaided, and, as he said:

it's no good saying to me 'Oh yes, John. Oh, we know you've got MS, but we'll get the house sorted out in six months' time.' By that time the damage is done, you know, you're stuck indoors, you're not going out, you don't want to come out, you've lost your confidence.

For John, his confinement to the home had significant social and personal consequences. As he explained:

if you're stuck indoors for a month, six weeks, a month, it's very hard to start getting back out, when you used to go round the pub and meet your mates or walk out in the garden and see people walking down the street. That confidence goes and that's part of the trouble, once it goes it takes twice as long to get it back.

For John and other respondents the home had become the place of confinement and, far from being a haven, was, in part, a signifier of a life that had been lost. Their testimonials confirm, in part, Allan and Crow's (1989: 4) observation that the experience of privacy in the home is not always positive and that it can 'signify deprivation as well as advantage'. Ann amplified this point:

it makes friendships and relationships very difficult, because they always have to come to me, you know, you accept things, you know that things are going to change or they have changed and I've just accepted them really. It is just part of life now. Which is why it makes it all the more, sometimes it makes it harder because I have always had this vision that I would be out and about and doing, and now I'm not, it's not going to happen.

Likewise, Elaine said that because of her weakening muscles, and physical impediments on the pavement and the lack of access into the local shops, she had stopped going out. For her, 'it all stops at the garden gate'.

Others recalled the loss of independence and personal control in their home due to interactions between impairment and physical design. The effect, for some, was the onset of a series of social and psychological traumas. As Trish explained:

I used to live in a two-up and two-down house and then I got an impairment that made me dependent on a wheelchair. I couldn't get upstairs and I was reduced to living downstairs. The sanitary conditions were awful and I was depressed and could see no way out and my living situation was not supporting my needs.

For Trish, the home became associated with a complete loss of independence and the performance of personal acts in degrading situations. As she said:

my husband used to carry me upstairs and there were so many practical issues. He had to get my dresses from upstairs and I had to use a bucket for a toilet and I had to be bathed on towels downstairs in the living room. The experience made me realize that the correlation between psychological and physical states should not be underestimated.

For others too, the home was less a place of independence and more a context in which things had to be done for them. Thus everyday household activities became, with the onset of impairment, more or less impossible to do without some assistance. For instance, Judith, who lives with her parents, now depends on her mother to cook for her because the kitchen tabletops and cooker are too high for her to reach. Cupboard and storage space are beyond reach, and the practical implications for Judith are such that she is unable to gain easy access to stored foodstuff: 'if I want a packet of noodle soup I can't get it, it's up there. So I've got to go, "Dad, can you pass me that, can you pass me that?"' Her father added that 'there's got to be somebody in there, if nobody's in the house she's had it you know'. If her parents are away for the weekend, Judith has recourse to a microwave machine or the oven: 'I'd just live off jacket potatoes and cheese in the microwave, or fish and chips in the oven'.

Moreover, the idea that the home might provide for personal privacy is not always the case. For instance, Ann is constrained in using her downstairs WC because there is no guarantee that she can use it without being seen by another family member. Although she lives on her own, family members and a carer come and go without warning and they have a key to the front door. As Ann explained:

I can't take the wheelchair in, I have to stand, I can't close the door as the chair blocks it and the front door's there and everyone in the family has a key, so I mean, it's not ideal and anyone could come in at any time.

Others felt that the design of their homes was such that they would never be able to easily function as private individuals. As Carol suggested:

I always get the feeling that they purposely built these places not always for somebody who lives on their own but for somebody who lives with somebody, so they don't do it all, or don't have a life, quite frankly.

Such experiences were, for these respondents, destabilizing and left them feeling that they had little control over circumstances. This, then, suggests that the nature of privacy in the home is never stable or guaranteed and, as Allan and Crow (1989: 3) suggest, 'an individual's ability to secure some degree of privacy is conditional'. Likewise, the idea of the home as a retreat, haven or place of sanctuary and security is not always borne out, particularly in a context where a deteriorating body requires third-party care and attention. For instance, some respondents felt that care staff were 'invasive' and made them feel uncomfortable and insecure. Ann recalled that it was difficult to find good carers locally because of high demand and the unpopularity of the job. While she praised the good ones that had cared for her in the past, recent experiences had been a problem. As she said: 'the ones I've had recently have been indifferent to me, they just saw the wheels and this thick person that's not got a brain'.

For Ann, these individuals were akin to having a stranger come into the home and then treat it in whatever way without permission:

> you had those that were literally there to earn some money and would sit here for three hours, and I couldn't get them to move, they just didn't want to do the work . . . they just did as they pleased, used my phone, cooker, the lot, and I would dread them coming.

Jim recalled similar situations with relatives who took it on themselves to come around unannounced purportedly to help out. Jim did not recognize his home as his haven because, as he said, 'I was always on edge, either waiting for them to turn up or for them to leave and sometimes they'd be here all day and just do as they pleased . . . it didn't matter what I'd say to them'. In such circumstances, the home, for Jim, felt like a place where he could not exercise much autonomy or control, or close the door on outsiders.

Insecurity was also felt by those who said that they had attracted negative comment when outside, and did not want to draw attention to the fact that an impaired person lived in the house. For Harry: 'you want to blend in and not reveal that you can't walk. It makes you a target'. Others concurred, and some respondents were wary about fitting a ramp up to their front door for fear of it labelling them as 'defective' and 'different'. As Carol said:

> I mean, I want to be able to live in my home but I don't want it to be screaming at anybody that walks in, to be inhibited because a disabled person lives here. That's the other thing, you know. I'm very, very conscious of this because one of my sons particularly found it very, very difficult to come to terms with it, and I don't want it screaming 'Oh dear, this poor woman lives on her own, she's in a wheelchair.'

This, then, illustrates in part the point by Saunders and Williams (1988), that the external physical features of the house convey subtle shades of meaning and act as signifiers to the outside world.

Resisting domestic design and generating usable spaces

The social model of disability has tended to dominate research and writing on issues about disability and the built environment (Oliver, 1990; Gleeson, 1998). It posits that the design and layout of particular physical objects, such as steps or street furniture, is the primary source or determinant of a person's disability. Thus insensitive design, based on values that do not recognize disabled people as users of buildings, creates physical barriers that prevent ease of mobility and access. This perspective, while not without merit, tends to conceive of individuals as 'victims' of circumstances beyond their control, in which they are oppressed by social and environmental factors. Impairment and physiology is more or less disregarded as having little role to play in determining disabled people's experiences of the environment. In Allen's (2000) terms, the human body is treated potentially as a 'physiological dope', without agency or the capacity to ameliorate or circumvent the 'given' conditions of existence.

In concurring with Allen (2000), I suggest that disabled people are not passive victims of insensitive design, nor necessarily resigned to dependence on others to facilitate aspects of their home lives. Far from it: the experiences of disabled people in this study and elsewhere, illustrate the capacity to generate usable spaces out of the social and physical impediments that are placed in their way (Oldman and Beresford, 2000; Hawkesworth, 2001; Allen *et al.*, 2002; Heywood *et al.*, 2002; Percival, 2002). For instance, Allen *et al.* (2002: 65) note that parents of vision-impaired children do not necessarily see them as victims of the built environment. This is because most are able to construct what Allen *et al.* (2002) refer to as 'memory maps' or guides of their home and neighbourhood environment that permit them to navigate, with relative ease, from one space to another.

For Harry, for example, the development of Parkinson's disease has led to a reappraisal of how best to use the house. As he said, 'well, I don't use upstairs often . . . there's no way I can actually do the stairs'. Harry did what many do, by moving downstairs permanently. He set about changing the layout, taking out doors, installing external ramps front and rear, removing the carpet, installing a new shower unit and fitting lever taps. Anything he needs to use in the kitchen has 'been brought down to ground level' and, as Harry said, 'it's like a new home now, set up easily for me to use'. Judith's parents did likewise by building an extension on the ground floor that serves as an ensuite bedroom for their daughter (see Figure 4.2). It gives her ease of access out through the back door of the house. As Judith's father said: 'it's been quite a major civil engineering task to adapt this house . . . she has an accessible way in and her own place to do as she wants'.

The strategies deployed by respondents were in part dependent on income and social class. For respondents on low incomes, and living in council or housing association property, it was often a struggle to get things changed (see Heywood *et al.*, 2002). As Jenny observed:

if you've got no income and Social Services are making the alterations for you, you will have had a fight that's probably gone on three or four years to get it, and the chance of you succeeding again getting it if you move to another house is not very high, so you never want to move, you stay where you are.

4.2 Getting out of the house. The photograph shows Judith at the back door of her home at the top of a purpose-built ramp. It has a shallow slope that makes it easy for her to get in and out of the house from the street without any need for assistance.

Others concurred in expressing their frustration with delays in getting adaptations done. As Stan noted:

> this is one of the arguments I've had with Social Services for years and years and years. If you need handrails and a ramp, or a toilet adapted, you need it quickly ... you know, when you're disabled you need help quickly.

In contrast, those with higher incomes, and who owned their home, had more choice about how and when to adapt the domestic environment. Jenny expressed a common view: 'If you're middle class and you can afford to do it in the manner that I have, and you've got an income, you're earning money ... then you do it.' Jenny's income had given her the means to install a state-of-the-art kitchen and knock-down internal walls to create more space. For Jenny, what was important was not a singular or generalizable approach to adapting her home. Rather, as she said:

> you want to bespoke what is done very precisely for yourself. You won't really want somebody to say 'Here's a wheelchair ramp, you make do with that.'

In this regard, Jenny had spent thousands of pounds in changing internal layout and creating the sort of spaces that would permit her access to, and use of, all the rooms in the house.

Respondents, regardless of income or tenure, were able to rearrange layout by, primarily, 'clearing up the clutter' and making space to facilitate ease of movement and use of rooms (see Figure 4.3). Jenny moved into her house when she could walk and furnished it throughout. As she said: 'the house was designed for no more than a walking disabled person ... and now it's inconvenient for me'. However, her more-or-less constant use of a wheelchair now means that 'if I wanted to get into a room I had to push chairs out of the way to get to the far wall ... there was furniture everywhere'. For Jenny, the solution was to sell the furniture, or, as she said: 'I've just chucked everything out and we're now in a situation where there's not even any chairs for anybody to sit on'. Others have done similar things, and Heather, living in housing association property, 'got rid of the big furniture and put up grab rails everywhere'.

Like Heather, other respondents have changed aspects of the micro-architecture of their homes that had previously made a big difference to their mobility around the home. For Carol, the floor surface had to be changed when she became dependent on a wheelchair. As she said: 'I had carpet everywhere when I first moved in as I could still walk although not very well. Because when you're able to walk your feet skid, and you need carpet.' However, the carpet had prevented ease of movement of her wheelchair, and so she ripped it up to reveal wooden floors which she restored. Likewise, Jim persuaded the local authority to provide a grant to adapt the downstairs toilet door so that it now slides open and permits easier access than was hitherto the case. However, it was a struggle to get this: 'it's a big issue, apparently you're not supposed to have a sliding door in a bathroom, don't ask me why, that's what I was told'.

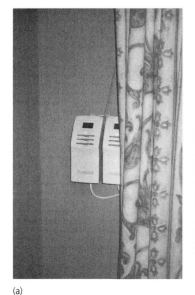

(a)

(b)

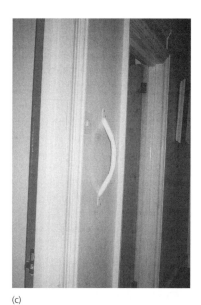

(c)

4.3 Making changes to the micro architecture of the house. Most of the respondents were able to make a range of important adaptations to their houses, thus creating more livable environments. For instance, photograph (a) shows Colin's electronic system that opens and closes the curtains; a remote control device, hand held, is used to operate the system. Likewise, as depicted in (b), Colin's front door is opened by means of a remote control system. In (c), grab rails have been fitted by Helen to provide her with the means to walk around the house, while, as shown in (d) she has fitted lever taps on her kitchen sink to facilitate ease of grip and use.

(d)

Adapting and/or the reorganization of the physical layout of domestic space are not the only means for disabled people to exercise some control over the use of the home environment. Some research suggests that energy-saving strategies are part of the daily routine of people with particular types of impairment (Rubinstein, 1989; Oldman and Beresford, 2000; Percival, 2002). For Carol, home life has always revolved around preserving her bodily energy and organizing tasks in ways that enable her to get through the day. As she commented:

What you're doing is you're parcelling up energy when you're disabled. I've been doing this since I was seven. You know how much energy you've got for the day and you know what you're using on each of the tasks, and there's a whole list of tasks that you're buggered if you're going to waste any time on. One is washing up, eating is another one. When you're really tired you do not cook. You stand at the work top, you stand at the fridge and you eat, you know, a bit of cheese and a tomato and that's it.

Jenny followed a similar routine and was able to use her income to hire people to do some of the basic household chores. As she said:

when I moved into my house there was no question of me not having a cleaner for a few hours a week, just to do things like the floors and the dusting and the washing, she did my washing. And she does the ironing, which was the critical thing, the sheets and the ironing; I'll do the other things.

For most respondents, the need to think ahead is paramount because of the knowledge that bodily deterioration will necessitate different ways of using the home. Jenny bought her present house when she was able to walk but knew that, in time, she would be dependent on a wheelchair to get around. As she explained:

I bought the house because it was very flat. I was actually going round saying to my relatives 'Oh, this will do for a wheelchair.' And they were going 'Don't be stupid, you'll never go in a wheelchair.' And I always sort of knew my limitations; I knew it was on the cards.

Carol, who lives in council-owned property, pre-empted a move to more suitable accommodation by discovering an empty mobility house near to where she lived. As she said: 'I had a tip-off that it was empty, got in touch with the council, told them what I needed, and now a year later they've gutted it and made it up to what I need.'

However, such behaviour and/or actions appear to be no more than 'little victories' in a context whereby the design of most homes remains resistant to the needs of impaired bodies. Indeed, respondents were of the view that the only way to (re)claim domestic space for impairment is if professional experts, such as builders, architects and occupational therapists, respond to experiential information and guidance provided by disabled people themselves (see also Chapter 7; Turner, 1976; Imrie and Hall, 2001a). However, too often, as Jim said, 'the assumption, I presume, is that you've got no skill or knowledge that would actually have been of value to the person putting in your door'. Others concurred, with Jane expressing her frustration at the attitudes of the builders who had adapted her house: 'that's the interesting assumption about disabled people, isn't it, we obviously have got nothing to contribute back'.

4.4 Conclusions

The testimonials in this chapter suggest that there are tensions between ideal conceptions of the home and the material, lived, domestic realities of disabled people. While aspects of the home may well provide for privacy, sanctuary, security and other aspects of 'ideal' domestic habitation, such provisions are always conditional, contingent, never secure, and likely to be challenged by (amongst other things) the onset and development of bodily impairment. However, explorations of the meaning of the home, and housing studies more generally, rarely consider the body and impairment and its interactions with domestic space. This is curious, because impairment is a significant and intrinsic condition of human existence and can affect anyone at any time (see Zola, 1989; Bickenbach, 1993; Marks, 1999; Imrie, 2004b). In this sense, a person's feelings about and experiences of the home cannot be dissociated from their corporeality, or the organic matter and material of the body.

Indeed, dominant representations of the meaning of the home, propagated by builders, architects and others, are underpinned by specific conceptions of embodied domestic spaces that do little to acknowledge the possibilities of bodily impairment as part of domestic habitation (see, for instance, Hockey, 1999; Imrie and Hall, 2001a; Milner and Madigan, 2001; Imrie, 2003c). Such representations revolve around the home as part of the ideal of family life, in which non-impaired bodies, with relative independence of movement and mobility, are paramount. The dominance of non-impaired carnality is reflected in physical design that, as the testimonials suggested, rarely includes the fixtures, fittings or spaces to enable the ease of use of domestic spaces by disabled people. Rather, such spaces, for many disabled people, are potentially disembodying in the sense that they deny the presence or possibility of bodily impairment, and as a consequence are likely to reduce the quality of their home life.

The interaction between domestic design and impairment produces a complexity of bodily experiences that ought to be the basis for the development of debates about the nature and substance of housing quality. However, too often debates about housing quality are about physical design and technical standards *per se*, in abstraction from bodily, or organic, form and function (see also Harrison, 2004). Such debates, as material in previous chapters has suggested, are themselves 'disembodied' in failing to refer to or specify the human context or content that comprises domestic habitation. An example of this is Part M of the building regulations that, as outlined in the Introduction to this book, requires builders to construct new housing to minimum standards of accessibility to facilitate ease of entry for wheelchair users. The regulations are deficient because the standards refer to disabled people in abstract and generalized terms, such as 'people who have an impairment which limits their ability to walk' (Department of the Environment, Transport and the Regions, 1999a: 5).

Such definitions reduce corporeal complexity to something that is limited, even fixed, in type and scope, and that can be accommodated within a narrow range of physical or technical responses. However, as the data in this chapter indicate, bodily impairment is neither fixed nor static: nor is it something that acquires meaning or function independent from social context or setting. Rather, as respondents noted, their home lives revolved around resolving issues relating to functioning in restrictive spaces, in contexts whereby bodily changes, particularly organic deterioration, were manifest realities. Housing quality, then, cannot be understood or defined separately from an understanding of the interactions between organic matter and the domestic setting, of which physical design is a component part. This should be one focus for seeking to develop an approach to housing studies that recognizes the importance of embodiment in influencing people's experiences of, and meanings attributed to, the home.

Further reading

There is an extensive and interesting literature on debates relating to people's complex interactions with the home. The text by Gilman (1903, reprinted 2002) is a classic. The debate about the meaning of the home is summarized and explored in the very good book by Chapman and Hockey (1999). Readers should acquaint themselves with the important papers by Saunders (1988), Saunders and Williams (1989) and Gurney (1990, 2000). On the theme of the body, an excellent introduction is Chris Shilling's (1993) book, but readers should then look at Merleau-Ponty (1962, 1963), Grosz (2001) and Twigg (2002).

Case study

Domestic lives – Jenny, Elaine and Toni

Jenny

Jenny is a 'self-made person' who for many years ran her own employment agency. She moved into her first (owner-occupied) house at the age of 35 years, and used her savings and income to make her 'ordinary little Victorian house' into an accessible and habitable home. As she said:

> I pulled up the electrics to waist high on the wall before I moved in . . . I put in a handrail on either side of the stairs and I put rails on the steps up to the front door. I dropped the work surfaces a bit to my height and I put in a new kitchen to suit me.

After three years of struggling to get up the stairs, Jenny had a lift installed:

> I couldn't carry things upstairs, to take a cup of tea upstairs you have to put a cup on a stair one at a time and pull yourself up another step . . . it was so boring and trying to get clean sheets upstairs . . .

Her awareness of the limitations of the design of housing was heightened by visits to her brothers' houses, which did not have downstairs WCs. As Jenny recalled: 'as soon as I wanted to go to the loo I had to say "sorry I'm going now" [laughs] because there was no way I could go to the loo'. She was able to overcome this problem, in part, by the purchase of a specially adapted van that contains a WC or, as Jenny said:

> one of the reasons I bought the van in the way I did and spent the sort of money I have on it, is because I've got a loo in the back, so I had to get around visiting people by taking my loo with me in my van.

As Jenny acknowledged, not everyone could do this, or, as she said: 'that is the response of somebody who's taken their own life in their hands, and is earning some money'.

Jenny moved to her present place, a detached house located in rural West Sussex, after much deliberation about its potential for future adaptation to meet her needs. She was aware that her degenerative condition was likely to require her to use a wheelchair some time in the future. As she recalled:

> I was actually going round saying to my relatives 'Oh, this will do for a wheelchair.' And they were going 'Don't be stupid, you'll never go in a wheelchair.' And I always sort of knew my limitations; I knew it was on the cards.

For Jenny, the house was everything she felt she would need at a later stage and, as she observed:

> when I looked at that bathroom when I first looked at the house I thought 'Wow, a wheelchair would easily go in there and spin round and go from one side to the other.' I have to say this that I knew I'd be able to make this work, stay living in it, I knew I'd be able to stay living in it.

An important part of Jenny's independence in her house is related to the installation of a customized designed kitchen. As Jenny said, 'when I came here I moved in with my boyfriend and he was perfectly normal, so in fact we had a perfectly normal kitchen put in here because he liked cooking so he took over the catering'. Jenny now lives alone and a re-designed kitchen became imperative but, as she recalled,

4.4 Jenny's kitchen.

it was difficult to get any company to design and construct her a kitchen because she did not want cupboards or the usual fixtures. As she explained:

I wanted under the surface free for my knees and that meant they weren't going to make any real money, because they make their money out of prefabricated units and selling them on expensively but making them cheap ... so I'd have taken most of the profit away.

Four companies declined to construct a kitchen for Jenny and, as she recalled, 'they just said they were very busy but it was because I was in a wheelchair'.

An accessible domestic space

Jenny's kitchen (Figure 4.4) is customized to her needs. It permits her to get her knees under the work surfaces and close to food preparation areas. All fixtures are easy to reach and designed around the dimensions of her wheelchair. She can also reach the window and let fresh air into her home. As Jenny explained, the design and layout of the kitchen is to minimize her movement and create ease of access to facilities such as the cooker and sink:

a kitchen company helped me with it, and the guy was really quite careful. He came up with the idea of putting a separate vegetable sink here, which I hadn't thought of, so that I could do vegetables and put them straight into the pot, because one of the difficult things with a wheelchair is the constantly drying your hands to use the hand control, and you're sort of travelling along with dripping things, you know. And he just said 'Well, you can do your cooking here, you've got a waste disposal here, and you don't have to move any of it.'

One of the main adjustments to the house made by Jenny is to ensure that electrical and gas meters, sockets and fuse boxes are accessible to her. The

biggest problem for her has been stretching up to reach the fuse boxes and, as Jenny said: 'the fuse boxes are costing a fortune to move, you know, by the time I've finished I will have spent well over three thousand adjusting the electrics'. In addition, the meters were located outside the house and, as Jenny noted:

I've had to bring indoors the main meter for the house, I've brought it in here. This is the old scullery which I've decided not to change because I've set the house up to eliminate me needing to come in here, but they're all here, there's the meter ... I've moved all the meters so that I can get at them when a breaker goes.

Elaine

In contrast to Jenny, Elaine lives in a former council-owned property that she and her husband purchased because, as Elaine said, 'we wanted a bit more control over what we can change in the house'. The new house is better than her previous place because, as she noted: 'it didn't even have a solid wall to put a stair lift in, it was like chipboard or something'. Her present home has a stair lift, but she finds it difficult to move around in her wheelchair from one downstairs room to another because 'all the doors in this house are very hard to get through'. However, the house is a vast improvement on her previous circumstances, in which the kitchen was too small for her to get into and the WC was tiny: 'I did actually fall in there and I was behind the door and my husband couldn't get in.'

They moved into the house partly because there was an outdoor loo that Elaine could get access to. However, her condition has worsened over the last year or so and Elaine finds it more or less impossible to get access to the downstairs toilet because, as Figure 4.5 shows, it involves her having to negotiate a large step:

there's a handrail, to help me get down the step. So I have to sort of

4.5 The step at the back door.

manoeuvre, because my right side's not as good as it used to be ... and I can just about reach, you know, sort of tilt over and grab the wall and shuffle round.

For Elaine's husband, the manoeuvre is too hazardous: 'if she tries to get in here it's like dangerous, like with a Zimmer, so my heart's in my mouth, is she going to fall'. The kitchen is also poorly designed, with tabletops too high to reach and the sink unit impossible for Elaine to use; in effect, the kitchen has more or less become off limits to her.

The purchase of the house means that Elaine is eligible for a disability facilities grant (DFG), and she is awaiting work to extend her kitchen and put in a downstairs bathroom that will permit her to live downstairs independently of assistance from her husband. The main reason for the changes is because it is difficult for Elaine to get up to the first-floor level more than once a day. Even with the stair lift, Elaine's condition is such that, as her husband explained:

she might get up, maybe once, maybe down then she'd be totally knackered and she wouldn't be able to move properly. But even some days I just wouldn't let her attempt that, even if that stair lift wasn't there.

For Elaine, the motivation for the changes is to reduce, first and foremost, the burden on her husband, and as she explained: 'I've got MS and my husband's had a bypass, so it's not very suitable for him to lift me now.'

Much of the design of the house does not permit Elaine to gain easy access from the sitting room to the dining room, or into the kitchen, especially if she has to use her wheelchair. As Elaine said, 'I can get through this door, but that's got a sharp turn from the hallway, so hopefully the builders are going to extend that door a bit so I can turn the wheelchair.' The changes will also permit Elaine to use the kitchen, and as she said: 'we'll extend the kitchen a little bit so I can get into

it, because I don't cook now'. This will make a difference to Elaine because, while she feels she will not be able to cook, she wants a kitchen where she will be able to get her wheelchair under the worktops. For Elaine, this will allow her to reach utensils and food and, as she said, 'to make myself a cup of tea and a sandwich'.

Toni

Toni lives in a one-bedroomed council flat that was originally constructed to provide wheelchair access. It has since been adapted by her to meet most of her needs and, as she said, 'To be honest, it's not as if I'm going to move again in five years' time, you know, this is it as far as I'm concerned.' Her situation reflects a broader trend amongst disabled people; that is, to remain *in situ* rather than to move around if they have found suitable accommodation. For instance, Jenny felt that her present home would be her last: 'somebody like me will spend a lot of money on slowly making their home reasonable, they're never going to move. The money it costs is so enormous.' Elaine and her husband felt likewise and, as Elaine said, 'it will be difficult to find anything else to match my needs, so we have to stay here'.

Toni has had a series of moves because previous housing did not cater particularly well for her needs and made it difficult for her mother to cope. As Toni explained:

we did in fact move about four or five times just because they were either not suitable or were up a flight of stairs and it was very difficult for my mum back then to cope with, she had three kids under five, one of whom was me.

As Toni recalled, 'my mum had to do a lot of lifting and it was too much for her, and she hurt her back a few times trying to carry me'. The family eventually moved to Bracknell, where there was a surplus of wheelchair and mobility homes, and, as Toni said: 'we ended

(a)

(b)

4.6 (a) Toni sitting near to the back door that leads into a small garden. The door is opened by electronic controls. (b) The sitting door is much wider than prescribed for under Part M.

up with a wheelchair-accessible house, so we were very lucky really'.

After moving away to college Toni came back to Bracknell and lived in a bedsit. It was provided by a housing association, and was adapted to meet most of her needs. However, as Toni said: 'I didn't see that as my long-term housing and never have, so I always was determined to be independent in the end, so this was always in my focus.' For Toni, the bedsit felt like temporary accommodation and it lacked privacy and home comforts. She felt unsettled and sometimes unhappy in the place. As she said: 'there was literally a bedroom and living space in one, and you had a shared kitchen, laundry, and you know, shared facilities, like the lounge. So it wasn't really for me.' There was a lack of privacy in this place and limited control over what one could do, or, as Toni said, 'you never had any chance of living a private life there and you couldn't make it into your home'.

Because of the shared facilities she had no choice but to mix with other people that she did not have much in common with:

> I have to say, the hostel wasn't right for me and I felt I was suffering as a result. You know, I just felt that, with all due respect, not everyone was on the same wavelength as me, so I found it quite an oppressive atmosphere.

To try and rectify this situation, Toni made daily enquiries to the council about alternative property that did not achieve much. As she explained, this situation led her to write 'to my MP in the end and I said "Could you put a bit of pressure on the council because they don't seem to be trying very hard to find me somewhere?" And lo and behold, within a couple of months of me writing they phoned up and said this was available.'

After moving in Toni set about redesigning the flat, and she was provided with scope to influence the architect and to request the removal of internal walls and the repositioning of fixtures and fittings (Figure 4.6). As she said:

there were two internal doorways so I asked them to move this one out completely because I didn't need it, and they also had a radiator along this wall, I think it was, and I asked them to take that out and relocate it elsewhere in the bungalow, so yeah, they did do a lot.

In addition, Toni requested, and was provided with, level access into and out of the front and rear doors, so providing her with access to the garden; the builders 'also put an electric door on the front, and an electric door on the back'. Much of the building work was directed by Toni:

> my dad built the whole kitchen, the council didn't touch the kitchen, because we wanted to build it around me when I was sitting in it, so he literally had me sitting in there for two days saying 'Where do you want this? Where do you want that?'

Summary

Toni, Elaine and Jenny's experiences show different housing circumstances, and contrasts in the ways in which they lead their lives. For Jenny, her financial independence has made it possible for her to redesign much of her house. An important point made by her is that she feels designers need to be responsive to the specific needs of individuals, and not just apply a series of prescriptive design standards. As she said: 'somebody like me is not really going to be helped by anything designers do, because all our impairments want different levels of slope or wider, narrower or different types of doorways'. While Toni and Elaine have less financial scope than Jenny to make changes to the design of their homes, in both cases the provision of specific adaptations has been vital in facilitating some independence – although for Elaine it is unclear how far she will be given sufficient DFG funds to make her house into a much more usable environment.

5 House builders, disability and the design of dwellings

5.1 Introduction

> Part M has nothing to do with quality because if it were it would be a very different regulation. If you were doing it properly you would do so much more. So, is it really about housing quality?
>
> (From an interview with a builder)

Disabled people's experiences of seeking to create a habitable environment within the context of the dwelling provide insights into the interactions between impairment and design as a context for the perpetuation of disability. As the previous chapter indicated, the design of most dwellings does not permit their ease of use by disabled people – a point that is usually lost on most builders and building professionals, who rarely design or construct dwellings with the needs of disabled people in mind (see also Chapter 7). Rather, as earlier chapters have suggested, builders and their design and construction teams tend to (re)produce design and building processes that make few concessions to individual, bespoke, bodily needs, and they rarely depart from the construction of tried and tested house-types. Instead, the rationalities of real estate, as outlined in Chapter 2, encourage builders to minimize innovation in design and to construct dwellings for consumers who are understood by builders to exhibit similar tastes and requirements in relation to the form and functioning of domestic environments.

Such assumptions lie at the root of the reaction by government, outlined in Chapter 3, which led to Part M of the building regulations being extended to incorporate new (private for sale) dwellings in October 1999, with the likelihood of it being extended further from 2007 to incorporate LTH standards. As previous chapters have suggested, the requirement for builders to construct dwellings to Part M standards has been controversial, and builders have been reluctant to incorporate into their house-types what they regard as the regulation's 'disproportionate response'. However, despite much hyperbole and rhetoric concerning builders' feelings about and reactions to the needs of disabled people, there have been few studies of house builders' understanding of and attitudes towards disabled people and their dwelling needs (although, for exceptions, see Burns, 2004; P. Thomas, 2004). This is particularly so in relation to Part M, in which there has been little critical scrutiny or investigation of the ways in which builders are responding to, and implementing, the regulation, and with what effects on the building process.

In seeking to rectify this, and develop some understanding of house builders' reactions and responses to the needs of disabled people, this chapter describes and evaluates builders' reactions and responses to Part M of the building regulations. A range of themes will be discussed, including house builders' attitudes towards and understanding of the housing needs and aspirations of disabled people; builders' interpretations and understanding of Part M; the impact of the regulation on the design of house-types, production costs and markets; and the relevance of Part M in addressing the design needs of disabled people. I divide the chapter into two. First, referring to information from a telephone and postal survey, and follow-up interview data, the impact and implications of Part M on the design and construction of new housing is assessed. Second, I discuss different ways in which housing policy ought to address the concerns of house builders in relation to Part M while simultaneously addressing the as yet unmet needs of disabled people for good-quality, accessible housing.

5.2 House builders' responses to the needs of disabled people

In investigating house builders' attitudes and responses towards Part M and disabled people's housing needs and aspirations, a postal survey of a 5 per cent sample of house builders operating in England and Wales was undertaken between November 2001 and February 2002. The results include a mixture of both quantitative and qualitative responses (and respondents often added their written opinions or testimonies to a range of open-ended questions). In addition, data in the chapter draw on telephone interviews with house builders (and building control officers), and face-to-face interviews with builders; these latter interviews with builders provided the opportunity for the collection of documentary materials, and other information related to site visits (see Appendix 1 for full details of the research methods that were used to generate the data for this chapter).

In discussing the material collected from the research, I divide the discussion into three. Using telephone survey data, the next section describes how far builders, between October 1999 and December 2002, were constructing new dwellings to the requirements of Part M or, alternatively, were circumventing aspects of the regulation. The following section refers to data from the postal survey, and data gathered from follow-up interviews with builders, to evaluate the contrasting ways in which house builders have reacted and responded to Part M. The data suggest that there is little to support some of the original fears expressed by the HBF and some house builders about the potentially deleterious effects of Part M on the industry. Rather, most builders grudgingly accept the regulation and their testimonies suggest that its effects on them have been minor. Then, in a subsequent section, I discuss some of the conceptual and practical problems and limitations of Part M, including what some builders see as its half-hearted approach to redressing disabled people's physical access to housing.

Constructing new dwellings to Part M standards

As already intimated, since 25 October 1999 Part M of the building regulations has required new housing to be constructed to minimum standards of access. However, there is evidence to suggest that some builders submitted applications for building control consent prior to the deadline date, in the hope of being able to circumvent the new standard. In particular, a tactic deployed by many builders in the lead up to Part M was to submit applications without any plans or details. Building control officers tended to reject these applications, although once in the system applications were deemed to be on deposit. This meant that builders had up to three years in which to re-submit the application and, by providing full details, be accepted under the old, pre-Part M standards. Some observers note that this means that much new stock is still being constructed (at the time of writing) to pre-Part M standards (see, for example, King, 1998a, 1998b).

To halt what was seen as an abuse by most observers outside of the building industry, a six-month period (between 25 October 1999 and 1 April 2000) was brought in by the Department of the Environment, Transport and the Regions in which builders had to supply the full plans and details, and these had to be approved without condition. If the plan was rejected and re-submitted within a three-year period, then it could only be accepted under the new (Part M) regulation. However, despite this, anecdotal and other evidence suggests that some builders were able to circumvent the new standard and have been building substantial proportions of new housing to pre-part M standards. For instance, one large-volume builder that I interviewed claimed that 60 per cent of the housing that they constructed in 2002 was to pre-Part M standards, largely due to consent obtained prior to 25 October 1999 (Imrie, 2003a).

A Building Control Surveyor (BCS), interviewed by me in June 2002, recalled the haste with which builders were trying to get building consent before the deadline for Part M. In one instance, a builder submitted an application for 432 dwellings. As the BCS said:

> I know that Barratts put in an approved application for the full 432 over at the hospital site, days before Part M was coming in, and as a consequence that's gone through and they're all being built without Part M applicable. And it's a huge site.

This was unusual behaviour for builders, who tend to divide sites into 'development phases' and apply for building control consent 'phase by phase' rather than for the whole site at one time. As the BCS noted:

> we were wondering, 'Why is this in so quick?' You know, why is it? And of course, all of them, they've put the lot in, when normally they do a bit and a bit, but the whole site came in and we thought, well, we know why that is, we knew straight away it was to avoid Part M.

The BCS estimated that Barratts would be constructing on this site until well into 2005.

Beyond such evidence, there is little information about the proportions of Part M compliant to pre-part M housing that have been built, or that are presently under construction. While estimating the numbers and proportions of new housing constructed to Part M standards is fraught with difficulties, respondents to the telephone survey did provide a range of indicative data. As Figure 5.1 shows, the sample of builders (in the telephone survey) included 25 who had constructed in excess of 1,000 dwellings over the study period. For 27 of the sample, more than 80 per cent of their build, as Table 5.1 indicates, was in the form of houses. In total, the sample was responsible for the construction of 154,394 housing units, representing 39.3 per cent (392,400 units) of all dwellings built in England and Wales between October 1999 and December 2002 (see NHBC, 2001, 2002). The respondents estimated that of the 154,394 units that they constructed over the study period, 124,987 (80.9 per cent) were houses and 29,407 (19.1 per cent) were flats (see Table 5.1). Of the total numbers of units constructed, builders estimated that 105,790 (68 per cent) were built to be in full compliance with Part M standards.

Not surprisingly, more builders were constructing to the standard towards the end of the study period than at the beginning. For instance,

5.1 Proportion of housing units built, October 1999 to December 2002.

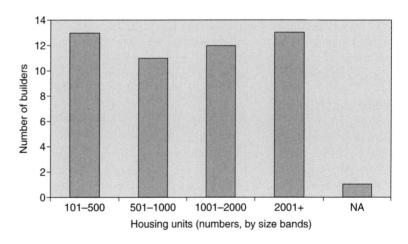

Table 5.1 Proportion (%) of units, by type, constructed by builders, October 1999 to December 2002.

Units (%)	Houses Number of builders (%)	Flats Number of builders (%)
<50	7 (14)	39 (78)
50–70	3 (6)	2 (4)
71–80	9 (18)	2 (4)
81–90	6 (12)	2 (4)
91–100	21 (42)	1 (2)
NA	4 (8)	4 (8)
Total	50 (100)	50 (100)

Source: Author's telephone survey, 2003.

Figure 5.2 shows the change in relative proportions of units not constructed to Part M in the period from October 1999 to December 2002. Thus, in the period from October 1999 to December 1999, 24 builders said that they had constructed no dwellings to Part M standards. Between January and December 2000, only four builders said that they had constructed no dwellings to Part M standards, a figure that had declined to a single builder between January and December 2002. As a builder said, 'the number of sites that we had with pre-Part M consent are drying up, and I can't think of any now where we are actually building to the old standards'. Others concurred and, as another builder commented: 'we tried very hard to push through consents before the regulation came in, but most of the officers we dealt with were wise to it'.

Other data confirm the trend towards increasing levels of incorporation of Part M into the construction of new dwellings. For instance, Figure 5.3 indicates that only five firms were constructing all of their housing to Part M standards in the period from October to December 1999, and each of these was constructing less than 50 dwellings to the standard (refer also to Table A, Appendix 3). Between January and December 2000, however,

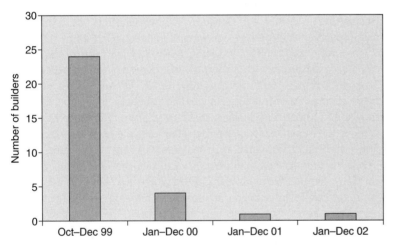

5.2 Number of builders that did not construct any buildings to Part M, October 1999 to December 2002.
Source: Author's telephone survey, 2003.

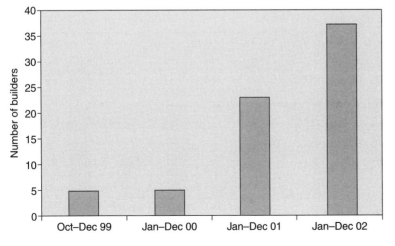

5.3 Number of builders constructing all units to Part M standards, October 1999 to December 2002.
Source: Author's telephone survey, 2003.

five builders were constructing all of their dwellings to the standard, and a further eight were constructing between 75 and 99 per cent of their stock to Part M of the building regulations (refer also to Table B, Appendix 3 for details). This trend continued, and between January and December 2001, 23 of the sample constructed all their dwellings to the standard, a figure that had risen to 37 for the period January to December 2002 (see Tables C and D, Appendix 3).

However, as Figure 5.4 shows, some builders have, since October 1999, been constructing a proportion of dwellings without incorporating Part M standards. Thus, nine (18 per cent) builders said that less than 40 per cent of their stock was constructed to Part M standards in the period from October 1999 to December 2002. At one extreme is a builder who has constructed 265 units since October 1999, of which only 10 per cent (26) have conformed to the regulation. As he said, 'we've only just started doing it'. Others justified their record as one of seeking 'to beat the system' or, as one builder said, 'to be honest, before that date we rushed things through to get the applications in'. Another noted that 'I think you'll find a lot of the bigger companies scraped in before the new standards'. Likewise, a volume builder said that 'on Part M we had three or four sites where we got the foundations in as quickly as possible; we knew it was coming' – a sentiment echoed by another, who said 'we crammed as many approvals in as possible; we weren't trapped by Part M'.

In contrast, as Figure 5.4 indicates, twelve (24 per cent) of the sample companies constructed all or most of their dwellings to Part M standards between October 1999 and December 2002. Typically, these were the larger companies, operating regionally and nationally. Indeed, as Table 5.2 shows, 36 (72 per cent) builders constructed at least 50 per cent of their stock to the requirements of the regulation over the study period. For one firm, which had constructed all of their units to Part M standards, 'we try to pre-empt regulations . . . it's our policy to keep standards high'. Another company said that 'we try to think ahead when new standards are coming in to difficulties in adapting to new requirements'. Likewise, another respondent noted that 'it was easy to incorporate the regulation and we decided to do it from day one'. For another builder, 'it was the right thing to do, and we wanted to change sooner rather than later, sort out the suppliers, and get everyone to understand what was required'.

5.4 Proportion of units built in Part M standards, October 1999 to December 2002.
Source: Author's telephone survey, 2003.

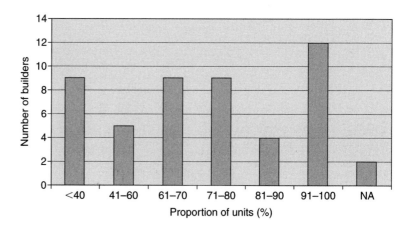

Number of units built	Less than 25%	26–50%	51–75%	76–100%	NA	Total
<500	2	1	5	4	1	13
501–1,000	–	2	4	5	–	11
1,001–2,000	2	3	4	3	–	12
2,000+	–	1	6	5	1	13
NA	–	–	–	–	1	1
Total	4	7	19	17	3	50

Table 5.2 Proportions (%) of housing units constructed to Part M standards, October 1999 to December 2002.

Source: Author's telephone survey, 2003.

At the time of the (telephone) interviews, most respondents were either constructing housing units or were awaiting the start of construction on sites with building control consent. Of the respondents 36 (72 per cent) stated that housing units presently being built, or to be built, would all be constructed to Part M standards. Five respondents provided no answer or had no information. The remaining nine builders were still constructing parts of their stock to pre-Part M standards for a mixture of reasons. For instance, one builder said that 'I have a few sites and they're all on steeply sloping sites, so it won't be possible to build any of these with level or ramped access'. For another, 'we've got the next two phases of this site with pre-part M consent, and we're building them all with doorsteps ... that's about 500 houses over the next couple of years or so'. In contrast, a builder of one-off, commissioned dwellings was keen to resist all aspects of the regulation: 'If I have my way, I'll never build a house without a doorstep.'

Disability, regulation and builders' responses to Part M

The viewpoint expressed at the end of the last section is indicative of many builders' ignorance of and lack of empathy with disabled people. In seeking to understand further house builders' attitudes and values in relation to disabled people and Part M, a postal survey and follow-up interviews were carried out with builders (see Appendix 1 for details). As Tables 5.3 and 5.4 show, postal survey responses were received from all parts of the house-building industry. Imrie and Hall (2001b) suggest that property developers' definitions of disability and disabled people show a limited notion of what disability is, or, alternatively, a broad-based conception relating to an exclusive set of (usually) mobility impairments. House

	Number of respondents (%)
National house builder	12 (5.7)
Regional house builder	39 (18.6)
Local house builder	159 (75.7)
Total	210 (100.0)

Table 5.3 Type of organization.

Source: Author's postal survey.

Table 5.4 Numbers of housing units produced annually by the sample.

Number of housing units	Number of respondents (%)
1–100	175 (83.3)
101–500	24 (11.4)
501–1,000	7 (3.3)
More than 1,000	4 (1.9)

Source: Author's postal survey.

builders are no exception in referring to disability in partial terms. As a builder's testimonial to the postal survey noted: ' "disabled" in inverted commas, just covers such a magnitude of problems, but as a developer, and I probably speak for most of the company, disablement means legs. Wheelchairs.' Others concurred: 'I think of wheelchairs and movement, but we never have to deal with disabled people so it's not an issue.'

A number of respondents, albeit a minority, felt that the building industry is ignorant of and unresponsive to disabled people, and is unlikely to provide for disabled people unless regulated by government. One builder admitted that 'I'd never thought about disabled people before Part M and hadn't got a clue about what they might want from a house ... Part M has made us focus on this'. Others felt that disabled people had as much right as anyone else to a choice of house. As one builder said, 'we need to provide choice for disabled people, this is the crux of the matter'. Some builders lamented the decline in space standards: 'we'd gone too far prior to Part M, and I think what Part M did was to produce minimum sizes that are useful for everyone, not just disabled people'. Others concurred: 'I think the cloakrooms had got far too small for the able-bodied ... I mean, you'd got the situation where I think the smallest one I ever saw was less than a metre. Pretty small [laughter] that, actually.'

However, the majority of postal survey respondents (132 or 62.8 per cent) were not satisfied with Part M and felt that the regulation is out of proportion to the scale of the problem. As one builder said, 'we already do more than enough for disabled people' (see Table 5.5). For others, the regulation reflects partisan and political interests: 'where does one start – the most ill thought out legislation in my memory'. Others feel that Part M is the 'thin end of the wedge' or, as a respondent said: 'there's lots of inconvenience with Part M and next it will be Braille doors and wall paper for the blind and lights for the deaf'. One builder expressed a typical viewpoint:

Table 5.5 Should house builders provide more accessible dwellings for disabled people?*

	Number of respondents (%)
Yes	33 (15.7)
No	86 (41.0)
They already provide a sufficient supply of accessible dwellings	88 (41.9)

*There were three non-responses to this question.
Source: Author's postal survey.

I mean, the initial reaction was throw your arms in the air and shout with horror because it was a case of, well, this is going to cost six hundred pounds per house, it's going to throw the costs of the infrastructure out of the window, we won't be able to develop the site ... but it's like everything, you absorb it. You know, you realize that it's not that bad when you come to do it.

Nearly half the sample, as Table 5.6 shows, believes that Part M has added to development costs. As a builder said, 'it's costing us more now than before we had this regulation ... valuations increase due to the additional downstairs toilet, but not as much as the cost of providing it'. Others agreed, with one builder noting:

we aren't able to quantify it. It does cost more, but not an alarming amount more. Not so much more that we would think 'My God. This is too expensive to do.' We have accommodated it within all the structure prices.

This reaction was more common than not, with builders asserting that Part M 'had cost them' but being unable to provide unequivocal and quantifiable evidence of a rise in building and construction costs. Indeed, others were less certain of the cost implications of Part M, and as a builder said, 'I don't think anyone has really ever sat down and said, "Part M on this site is costing us".'

Most respondents feel that the regulation is squeezing out starter homes and leading to the loss of house-types aimed at first-time buyers. As one builder suggested, 'we had a range of two or three small house-types that were very popular, and they just went by the board, basically, and we had to commission three new standard house-types' (see Table 5.7). He acknowledged that the new house-types were more expensive than the previous variety, and concluded that 'regulations inevitably cost the consumer more and we can't afford to stay in the starter market'.

	Number of respondents (%)
Very significantly	17 (8.1)
Significantly	84 (40.0)
An insignificant increase	86 (41.0)
No real increase	23 (10.9)

Table 5.6 Has the implementation of Part M added to your development costs?

Source: Author's postal survey.

	Number of respondents (%)
Significant changes	54 (25.7)
Some changes	95 (45.2)
Few changes	54 (25.7)
No changes	7 (3.3)

Table 5.7 Have you had to change house designs to comply with Part M?

Source: Author's postal survey.

Some builders feel that Part M is more likely to restrict disabled people's access to housing than to facilitate it, by contributing to the removal of more affordable starter homes from the market. As a builder (somewhat condescendingly) said: 'because of the earning potential of disabled people, and their lack of ability to actually get onto the housing market, we've not helped them, I believe, by Part M, because we've removed the first rung of the ladder'.

The attribution of Part M to the (alleged) collapse of starter homes is questionable. There is some evidence that starter homes were beginning to be reduced towards the end of the 1990s, independently of any impact of Part M. As one builder suggested: 'I think there was a general shift, within the industry at that point, to chase where the profit was. And the profit wasn't in one- and small two-bed units, the profit was moving up-market.' For others, the stimulus to move out of the starter market was less to do with Part M and more with changes in land and construction costs. Thus, as another builder noted: 'land is too expensive ... it is the rising cost of land that led most developers to refocus and move away from starter homes'. As the builder explained, 'we were being pushed up the value-added chain by changes in land and operating costs, and you get more back for your investment by constructing for the middle to upper end of the market ... we felt there was no other way to go'.

Builders also feel that Part M may be contributing to a reduction of space standards in particular parts of the dwelling. A range of respondents suggested that Part M had focused their attention on re-designing floor plans to operate, as one put it, 'cost effectively'. For this builder, the rationale remains one of providing 'the maximum accommodation within the smallest floor or land take or floor plan'. Thus, as another builder explained: 'you lose it in the other rooms. It's usually to the detriment of the kitchen or the lounge on the ground floor'. Another builder concurred in noting that the new house-types are 'about the same floor area, gross floor area, but certain rooms have been compromised as a result internally'. Some feel that this is to the detriment of housing quality or, as a builder said, 'some of the quality has gone with Part M, as we're squeezing everywhere else in the house to make it fit'.

Although complying with Part M, as Table 5.8 suggests, is not too difficult for builders, some have experienced difficulties in achieving part of the requirements. For instance, one builder felt that 'there should be the removal of the ramp requirements where the depth of the frontage does not allow construction at a set gradient in a straight line between door and footpath'. Some feel that Part M is creating new design problems and faults. As a builder said: 'the contours of sites and frontages pose serious problems and there will be long-term problems with damp ingress'. Others agreed in noting that damp ingress and water penetration was likely with ramped access and accessible thresholds. As a builder noted, 'we are concerned about the long-term implications of paths at damp proof course [dpc] level'. Others had experienced difficulties in preventing leakage through the front door: one builder suggested, 'in some instances we have produced accessible thresholds to double doors and these always seem to leak' (see Figure 5.5).

	1 No. (%)	2 No. (%)	3 No. (%)	4 No. (%)
A level or ramped approach to the house which is at least 900 mm wide	15 (7.1)	50 (23.8)	94 (44.8)	51 (24.3)
An accessible threshold at the entrance to the house	42 (20.0)	70 (33.3)	57 (27.1)	41 (19.6)
An entrance door which provides a minimum clear opening of 775 mm	88 (41.9)	82 (39.0)	30 (14.3)	10 (4.8)
A toilet in the entrance storey which wheelchair users can access	18 (8.6)	72 (34.3)	73 (34.8)	47 (22.3)
Corridors and hallways in the entrance storey sufficiently wide to allow circulation by a wheelchair user	36 (17.1)	76 (36.2)	70 (33.3)	28 (13.3)
No change of level on the entrance storey using steps, apart from on steeply sloping plots	26 (12.4)	73 (34.8)	83 (39.5)	28 (13.3)
Switches and sockets sited between 450 mm and 1,200 mm from the floor	141 (67.1)	49 (23.3)	11 (5.2)	9 (4.3)

Table 5.8 Complying with the requirements of Part M.

1 = Easy to comply with in all dwelling-types and sites
2 = Easy to comply with in most dwelling-types and sites
3 = Not easy to comply with in some dwelling-types and sites
4 = Difficult to comply with in most instances.
Source: Author's postal survey.

For some builders, developing design solutions to Part M is, as one builder said, 'a matter of trial and error'. Many were unhappy about the lack of technical guidance contained in Part M's guidance notes, the Approved Document (AD). Thus, for one builder: 'the AD is just theoretical and doesn't relate to reality and the site conditions we have to deal with'. Others concurred: 'with Part M there was nobody that could offer technical solutions to the requirements. I think most of us in the drawing office felt that it was an imposing document with no solutions offered.' Builders are also loath to share ideas between each other: 'there's no sharing, in the last few years we've employed extra technicians in my department, and whenever they've joined I've robbed their ideas from their previous companies to see what they're doing'. This behaviour reflects the intense competition in house building and the lack of what Barlow (1999) terms 'proprietorial innovation, or the sharing of ideas across the industry. As some builders admitted, the absence of collaboration may well inhibit the flow of knowledge and access to technologies and products in relation to accessible design.

5.5 Potential design faults with Part M. Photographs (a) and (b) depict sloping, ramped surfaces cutting across damp proof courses. Builders are concerned that such features will lead to damp penetration. Builders suggest that the absence of a step will permit rainwater to enter under the door, although there is not much evidence, to date, of this occurring. (a) is poorly constructed and may well lead to problems, although this is less likely in (b), where more care and attention has been paid. Photograph (c) shows an accessible threshold with a run-off grill to drain away rainwater.

(a)

(b)

(c)

Such perceived problems are making little or no difference to the saleability of houses (see Table 5.9). As one builder said, 'Part M has never been detrimental to a sale but it has raised eyebrows'. Another builder felt that 'Part M does not enhance saleability' but conceded that 'we are still selling houses, as the customer has no choice'. Others agreed, and a builder commented that 'although purchasers do not want Part M in their houses, they have no choice in the matter'. Most respondents feel that Part M is irrelevant as a sales feature when set beside other considerations. For one builder: 'we do not want to draw people's attention to entrance ramps, as they require naff detailing. Wider doors, who cares? Clients are interested in oak finishing, not door widths.' For some builders, sales have been affected by the regulation. For one builder, specializing in quality constructions in conservation areas, the saleability is affected 'mainly because of the surface required for the access ramps, which can spoil the

	Number of respondents (%)
Improving the saleability of houses	4 (1.9)
Reducing the saleability of houses	35 (16.7)
Making no difference	171 (81.4)

Table 5.9 Impact of Part M on the saleability of houses.

Source: Author's postal survey.

conservation nature of our site . . . the access level is often out of character with our designs'.

As Table 5.10 shows, a minority of builders (72 or 34.2 per cent) said that customers are satisfied with Part M designed houses. For one builder, 'it's giving rise in some instances to more spacious accommodation', while, for another, 'people seem to like the accessible entrance and also the plugs higher and light switches lower'. Others suggested that the general population was benefiting from some Part M features: 'wider ground-floor doors and corridors is a benefit anyway'. Another third (69 respondents) said that customers were less than satisfied or dissatisfied with Part M designed houses. As a builder noted: 'I get the impression from my customers that it's all irritating and features like split levels are much preferred, and sockets much less obtrusively positioned.' For another, 'we have had many requests to change the ramp after occupation.' Small builders are particularly affected in situations where a one-off client commissions the house. Thus, for one builder: 'most of the houses we build are for one-off customers . . . they feel that Part M is an infringement of their rights'.

Some conceptual and practical limitations of Part M and its implementation

Part M draws attention to disabled people as a 'special needs' group that is to be accommodated through the building regulations. The AD only makes references to wheelchair users and ambulant impaired people, and the impression is conveyed, perhaps unwittingly, that Part M has relevance to those with particular impairments. This is problematical, because it deflects attention from the universal nature of impairment and treats it as discrete or something that is static and confined to a specific population (Zola, 1989). Not surprisingly, Part M does little to challenge, and indeed reaffirms, the reductive conceptions of disability held by most builders. For

	Number of respondents (%)
Very satisfied	3 (1.4)
More than satisfied	2 (1.0)
Satisfied	72 (34.3)
Less than satisfied	41 (19.5)
Unsatisfied	28 (13.3)
I don't know	64 (30.5)

Table 5.10 Are customers satisfied with Part M designed housing?

Source: Author's postal survey.

Milner and Madigan (2001) and others, such understanding of disability reflects the dominance of disablist discourses within housing policy, or where policy-makers' attention is focused first and foremost on redressing bodily and/or mental incompetence (Barnes, 1991).

The reductionist nature of Part M is, however, evident to some builders. As a builder said: 'it only helps people in wheelchairs, or people with ambulant problems, it doesn't help any other disability. I mean, how does that help a blind person get into the house?' For another: 'what about those who are impaired in other ways than physical? . . . adaptations could be made for them too'. Others were critical of the impairment-specific nature of Part M, and its potential to be demeaning by drawing attention to a person's functional incapacities: 'the regulation makes them stick out, and there is no need for disabled people to feel that they are being treated any differently from able-bodied individuals'. Another builder felt likewise in noting that the regulation has the potential to embarrass disabled people: 'impairments vary, and those to whom we have talked are embarrassed by special provisions – they feel patronized by the present legislation'.

A number of builders, albeit a minority, pointed out that Part M does little to address the diverse needs of disabled people and ends up by satisfying no one party. As a builder said: 'they put off the able-bodied and don't address the real problems of actually living in a house by a disabled person – go the whole way in a small number of houses and not at all in the others'. For another: 'we find Part M insufficiently developed; it is a general procedure where we have found that impairments are specific to the individual and they need their specific requirements designed into the house'. Some builders said that the dimensions laid out in the AD lead to less than satisfactory outcomes. Thus, as a builder noted: 'the narrow toilets have such tiny wash basins in order to comply that you can only wash one hand at a time'. For another, 'if a disabled person is looking for a new house they will need a lot more specialized equipment than is provided by Part M'.

Most builders, however, tend to reproduce the reductive sentiments of Part M and, as a consequence, feel that the market for accessible housing is either small or insignificant (see Table 5.11). As a respondent commented, 'the market for disabled people is so small it's (Part M) not worth it'. Others said that they rarely saw disabled people or, as a builder noted, 'in 26 years of house building I have never sold one unit to a disabled person'. Not surprisingly, 173 (82.3 per cent) respondents said that they do not draw attention to Part M design features in the marketing of their

Table 5.11 How big is the market for accessible housing?

	Number of respondents (%)
Very large	3 (1.4)
Large	5 (2.4)
Not very large	41 (19.5)
Small	88 (41.9)
Negligible	66 (31.4)
I don't know	7 (3.3)

Source: Author's postal survey.

housing. As a builder said: 'the size of the market is such as to not warrant any focus ... it is not a marketable asset to the properties'. Such views are, however, based primarily on anecdotal evidence, in that 193 (92 per cent) respondents said that they do no market research on the housing needs and aspirations of disabled people. As a builder commented: 'we can sell anything, so why do market research?'

Builders are in no position to comment on the housing needs and aspirations of disabled people, yet they assume that disabled people are not worth responding to because they rarely see them or have enquiries from them. For Wheeler (1982), the problem is that builders view their target market as a homogeneous group of self-reliant and independent consumers who, in the words of one respondent, 'can take or leave what we provide, they can always go elsewhere' (see Borsay, 1986). However, as some research suggests, the pre-conditions for disabled people to choose are not always present (i.e. the lack of income, the absence of accessible dwellings, etc.), and more often than not, as discussed in Chapter 2, their housing needs are unheard or not articulated (Morris, 1990; Imrie and Hall, 2001a). In this respect I concur with Barlow (1999: 39), who suggests that 'mechanisms for identifying unarticulated needs ... need to be improved'.

The implementation of Part M is not straightforward, nor assured, and builders are aware of (their) failures to adhere to the regulation. On-site understanding and implementation is a problem for most, or, as one builder said: 'I wouldn't say it's second nature, because the people on site still miss the most important parts of it, and we have to keep banging it home to them.' For another, 'the typical ground worker wouldn't know Part M if it jumped up and hit 'em between the eyes, to be honest. They may look at something and think, "That's silly. Why on earth are they doing this?"' Inconsistent interpretation and enforcement of Part M by building control officers was also cited as a factor leading to different design solutions from one site to the next. As a builder said, 'currently the AD is only a guide and you get asked to do different things from one building control officer to the next ... there seems to be no consistent standard'. One respondent was particularly aggrieved:

> you can work to the same rule, to the *diktat* of the document, and one inspector will have a determination. You go to another authority, think-ing that the determination's the same, and this other building inspector will say, 'Well, no. I don't agree with that, this is the way I want it doing.' And you think 'Well, I've now got to change my detail to absorb the policy required by A, you know, when B has already given me his policy agreement' ... it drives us nuts.

Respondents highlighted differences between the quality of decision-making of local authority officers and private sector Approved Inspectors appointed by the NHBC. Builders can choose to use either a public or private sector inspectorate for building control matters (see also Chapter 6). As a builder suggested: 'the view from site managers is that the NHBC doesn't inspect as well as local authorities'. For another: 'our site managers complain that the NHBC are hardly around to inspect and are nowhere near as efficient as local authority officers ... the problem is that the NHBC, as a national organization, is remote from local points of reference'. Thus, as a builder commented: 'I guess it's because the local authority knows their patch. NHBC take a broad view and they don't get as involved. They're supposed to inspect at various stages but they don't seem to do this.' The implication, then, for mobility-impaired people, is that the extent to which housing is Part M compliant will depend, in part, on the particular control system in use.

Building control does not operate in isolation from broader regulatory frameworks, and this, for some builders, is a source of confusion in relation to officers' decisions concerning Part M. In particular, some builders expressed confusion about the interrelationships between Part M and other planning and building regulations. In one instance, a builder's application to construct housing along a sea front and close to a sea defence wall led the local authority to issue a waiver of Part M (see Figure 5.6). This was on the advice of the Environment Agency that the floors of the dwellings ought to be constructed at least 60 cm higher than the ground or site level on which they were being built. The objective was to ensure protection against flooding and the possible break of the sea defences. However, as the builder said, 'we could have found a solution to suit all, so I sometimes wonder how serious local authorities are about Part M.

5.6 Boathouse Development Ltd, Jaywick Sands, Essex. Phelen Construction Ltd constructed eighteen seafront apartments in 2003 in Jaywick Sands, a small coastal settlement near Clacton-on-Sea in Essex. The site is located in a place that has suffered from several floods due to high tides and/or storm waters breaching the sea defences. The area remains at risk from flooding. The development incorporates design features that are not dissimilar to those found in most town houses. The two-bedroom apartments are positioned on the first and second floors of the development, and they have a ground-floor garage with a connecting door into a utility room and common stairway up to the principal entrances. The design of the scheme effectively excludes wheelchair users and other mobility impaired people from ease of access to the dwellings. However, this design was a requirement of The Environment Agency in order to minimize the impact of future flooding on residences.

They provided us with a letter within a day to say they wouldn't impose the regulation on us.'

Some builders also highlighted what they perceive as a potential conflict of policy between recent government directives on housing densities and the content of Part M. For instance, Planning Policy Guidance 3 (DETR, 1999b) is encouraging local authorities to direct developers to increase housing densities to a minimum of 30 units per hectare. As Groves (2002) notes, this has led to a noticeable increase in three-storey housing and flat units and, as a builder said, 'whereas it would have been unique for us to develop a three-storey house, now it's become the norm'. For Groves (2002), the design of these units often includes no habitable room at ground-floor level, with living quarters often positioned on the first floor above a garage. As a builder said, 'how are we supposed to follow PPG3 and also Part M? . . . we can't easily make the new units accessible'. Others also noted on how PPG3 housing is designed to fit tightly onto sites (see Figure 5.7) and, as one builder said: 'it means that houses have to come close to the footpath and we can't easily get ramped access up to the principal entrance'.

PPG3 is encouraging what some builders perceive as a new starter homes market in the form of flats rather than houses (see Figure 5.8). As a builder remarked: 'the whole urban renaissance message is pushing us towards higher densities and you're almost saying to the starter end of the market, "We can provide you with accommodation but what we can't provide you with is the traditional garden and frontage space."' Builders are also unlikely to provide lifts to enable mobility-impaired people to access the upper floors of flatted developments. As one builder said: 'well, you know, we'd rather not put a lift in, we'd rather put an ambulant stair in . . . we would find a way of accommodating the £15,000 for a three-storey lift within the infrastructure of the cost of the work. It's no problem.' However, as he admitted, the company would not provide a lift unless required by law to do so: 'We will have far more people walking away from that because there's no lift to the third floor. But then again, is it a problem, because we know they will sell? The third floor will sell quicker than the ground floor. We know it will.'

When asked if they design beyond Part M by constructing housing to lifetime homes or other standards, 158 (75 per cent) respondents said that they never or rarely did so (see Table 5.12). Those that did exceed Part M did so only in partnership schemes with housing associations, where a higher specification is mandatory. The rationale for not exceeding Part M

Table 5.12 Do you design beyond the requirements of Part M?

	Number of respondents (%)
Always	8 (3.8)
Sometimes	42 (20.0)
Rarely	60 (28.6)
Never	100 (47.6)

Source: Author's postal survey

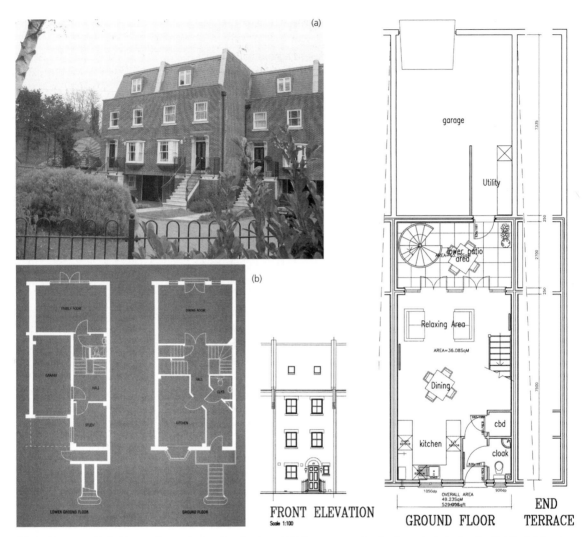

5.7 Seeking to provide livable space in town houses. The directives of PPG3, are encouraging developers to design housing that fits tightly onto the street. A typical design is that by Fairclough Homes, at Kingswood Place in Weybridge, Surrey (a). Here, the ground floor is a misnomer in that it is raised well off the ground and only accessible by climbing up an external stairway to the principal entrance. The only way that a wheelchair user can gain access to the dwelling is through a connecting door from the garage into the lower ground floor. However, once inside the dwelling a wheelchair user is effectively confined to the lower ground floor. A WC is provided that conforms to Part M and there is sufficient space to convert rooms into living spaces, such as a bedroom and dining area. However, kitchen and cooking facilities are not provided.

In contrast, some house builders are constructing town houses that provide a greater range of facilities that cater for livability rather than just visitability. For instance, Copthorn Homes have recently completed a scheme in Peckham, South London, comprising a mixture of flats and three-storey town houses (b). As the illustrations indicate, the ground floor of the town houses provide wheelchair access from the garage into a patio area, which is connected, through two sets of double doors, to an area that is open plan. This features a sitting room, dining area and kitchen. There is a separate WC and a stairway leading to the first floor. The ground floor is spacious and provides for ease of wheelchair movement, while the provision of a kitchen makes it into a much more livable space than most town house designs.

The problems of town house design are also contentious in California, where, in May 2003, State Senator Martha Escutia, of Norwalk, sponsored a measure, SB 1025, to close loopholes in the Fair Employment Act that allow developers to build townhouses without accessible features (see Jeserich, 2003). The Housing Rights Center (HRC), on behalf a wheelchair user, lodged a complaint against the Olson Company, which was building inaccessible town houses in Pasadena. The company responded by saying that the homes have no ground floor or elevators, exempting them from fair housing laws. It was correct. HRC suspects other developers are also exploiting the loophole, and these new developments are called 'Walks' because a potential buyer has to walk to enter the homes. Senator Escutia's bill (SB1025) requires 10 per cent of new town houses, of four or more units, to incorporate accessible features into the ground floor, to accommodate people with mobility and hearing impairments. The measure passed its first committee hearing in June 2003.

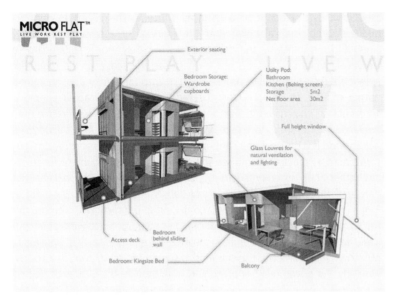

5.8 The micro flat. The effects of PPG3 and other factors have encouraged a dramatic rise in the numbers of flats being constructed in the UK. Indeed, in 2002, for the first time ever, more flats than houses were constructed (NHBC, 2002). An example is the micro flat, or a dwelling about 250 square ft in size, although with ceilings of up to 3.5 yards in height. The rationale for the micro flat is to provide relatively inexpensive accommodation in inner city locations or in places where there is an absence of affordable dwellings for first-time buyers. Stuart Piercy, the architect of the micro flat, notes that the design is based in part on caravan and yacht technology, so everything is designed to stack away neatly and to be slightly smaller than normal. However, it is not likely to provide sufficient space for ease of access of wheelchairs, or their use within the confines of the flat.

was explained by one builder: 'as with all construction decisions, conformity with the regulations is either conform to a satisfactory standard or exceed it and pay the price. Now, fundamentally we're down to profit.' Others were openly hostile to any suggestion that Part M should be extended to incorporate other standards. For one respondent, 'access should not be law' and there ought to be 'a reversal of policy'. For others, 'it should be a code rather than mandatory' and 'Part M is an unnecessary imposition and should be deleted . . . it should be abandoned – making everyone provide "slightly" appropriate housing is daft'.

5.3 Conclusions

The evidence from house builders suggests that the impact of Part M on the operational market and other aspects of house building has been insignificant. While the original proposals for Part M were received with hostility from some house builders and their organizations, the reality of the regulation is that it has been more or less absorbed, with minimal disruption, into the day-to-day operations of the house-building industry. Indeed, some house builders said that Part M was fast becoming an accepted benchmark that the industry would be reluctant to pull back from. This, though, has more to do with cost considerations than a commitment to enhancement of quality of space standards and access for disabled people in new housing. As a builder said: 'if you got rid of Part M now, I honestly don't believe that there would be a huge number of builders reducing corridor widths and cloakrooms . . . I mean, we're all set up for Part M now so it would just cost more to go back'.

Such comments are revealing, in part, of the limits of the regulation, particularly as a benchmark for assuring access for all disabled people to, and their use of, new dwellings. Indeed, builders' comments indicate that Part M draws attention to a specific category of the housing market, mobility-impaired people, and in doing so (re)produces the view that the regulation is a response to a minority concern. This serves to reinforce builders' problematical belief that the market for accessible housing is small and insignificant, and consequentially barely worth responding to. However, while builders are not keen to see the scope of the regulation extended, their testimonies provide insights into the partial and incomplete nature of Part M. In particular, the regulation treats disabled people as second-class citizens in denying them their rights to live within new housing. Part M seeks to create 'visitable' housing, but, as a builder said, 'what good is a house if you can't get upstairs to the bedroom?'

While most builders would see this comment as an argument for revoking rather than extending Part M, it clearly highlights the half-hearted nature of the regulation that seems to satisfy no single party. For builders, Part M is, as one respondent said, 'confusing and difficult to interpret, and full of contradictions'. The regulation appears to conflict with other policies, such as PPG3, and it is inconsistently interpreted and applied by building control officers. The situation is something of an irony in a context whereby the government is preaching, mantra-like, the virtues of 'joined-up policy'. For disabled people, far from Part M representing a significant breakthrough, it is a continuation of the 'timid policies' of the last 30 years (Borsay, 1986). Such policies have rarely been underpinned by an articulated ethical position about society's responsibilities towards disabled people, and governments have refused to recognize that there is an infringement of human liberties by denying disabled people rights to access.

Legislation in relation to access tends to be weak because of legal frameworks that are designed to educate and persuade, rather than coerce. These frameworks are underpinned by codes of practice which seek to maintain governments' commitment to ensure that access requirements do not impose 'unnecessary burdens' on employers, commerce and related interests (Department of Employment, 1990: 16). While Part M is broadly a continuation of this lineage, it is an attempt, albeit limited, to intercede in and respond to debates about sustainable housing policies, such as the intergenerational capacities of lifetime homes. This provides possibilities for the future of the regulation, but only if the terms of debate are shifted to incorporate explicitly a moral and ethical dimension that draws on a language of rights in seeking to define the nature of housing quality in relation to (disabled) people's housing needs; and a political agenda that seeks to challenge and transform the voluntaristic ethos of access, and related, legislative and policy programmes.

Further reading

There are few papers or writings about the relationships between builders and disabled people. Two of the best pieces are the papers by Burns (2004) and Thomas (2004). Readers should also look at the unpublished PhD thesis by Nicky Burns (2002) that provides a very full account of disabled people's experiences in seeking to get access to owner occupation. In relation to disability and the development process more generally, readers should consult Imrie and Hall (2001a).

Case study
Constructing accessible dwellings on
sloping sites

One of the main clauses of Part M in England and Wales, and the FHAA in the USA, permits builders to avoid providing level and/or ramped access where the steepness of the site or the plot exceeds a gradient of 1 in 15. As Part M (DETR, 1999a: 26) states: 'if the topography is such that the route from the point of access to the entrance has a plot gradient exceeding 1 in 15, the requirement will be satisfied if a stepped approach is provided'. There is evidence that some builders are constructing what are called ambulant steps as an alternative to ramped access. Crest Nicolson, a volume UK builder, is (at the time of writing) finishing construction of 800 dwellings on a site in Sussex, South East England. Figure 5.9 shows some examples of the mixture of design solutions that have been used on the site. The project manager noted that the ambulant steps are a 'nonsense', because 'there's no way anyone in a wheelchair will get up there so there seems no point in having to do this'. As he said, 'we considered levelling this part of the site, but it would have detracted from what we want to be selling to the customer'.

A level or ramped approach at least 900 mm wide is, according to both builders and building control officers, the most difficult standard to achieve, and most respondents suggested that compromises are often the outcome. As a building control officer interviewed by me said, 'we have a lot of impractical situations with topography, it's difficult terrain here and sometimes there have to be exceptions made'. However, the evidence suggests that there is much variety in how parties interpret the standard and how, subsequently, it is achieved, whatever the nature of the topography (see also Chapter 6). Much depends on builders' attitudes and willingness to respond to the challenge of constructing level and/or ramped access in situations where topography might well permit them to construct steps. For instance, Figure 5.10 shows two contrasting dwellings built on different sites characterized by sloping topography. The angle of slope is more or less the same on both sites, and the same local authority building control department adjudicated both schemes.

The house with steps (Figure 5.10a) was built by a builder who refused to construct a level or ramped approach throughout because, as he said, 'the angle of slope was too great and the frontages were too close to the road . . . we could never achieve access here'. He further noted that 'the architect had looked at the site but quickly dismissed ramped access as being impossible to achieve'. The builder suggested that 'it would have cost a lot more to excavate the site to level it, and the elevation provides us with a marketing angle

5.9 Design 'solutions', including ambulant steps.

(a)

(b)

5.10 Sites characterized by sloping topography.

which we didn't want to lose, it's a nice feature of the site'. In contrast, the other builder decided to overcome the problem by raising the level of the road to counter the angle of slope and, in some instances, by a sloping driveway levelled off near the entrance to the principal entrance (Figure 5.10b). As the project manager said: 'we did not see the slope as a problem or much of an issue, and we were happy to comply with Part M, it was a straightforward engineering solution . . . it's important to provide for everyone, and it wasn't a big deal to do this'.

These examples reveal that attitudinal and value or cultural differences between builders are important in influencing how regulations such as Part M are interpreted and implemented. Not surprisingly, there is much variation between builders' approaches to access on sloping sites. For instance, Figure 5.11 shows that change in gradient can have an effect on builders' perception of their ability to achieve level or ramped access. In this example, the builder has raised the pavement area to reduce the significance of the changing levels (Figure 5.11a); however, the response was insufficient to prevent the insertion of steps in the properties towards the top end of the slope. In contrast, the same builder, on what is a steeper site, has achieved ramped access to all the dwellings (Figure 5.11b). The issue is, why is there a difference between the two sites? The answer to this is not clear because, as the builder said: 'the project managers on the sites were told to make all the houses accessible, but I guess it was done like this for practical reasons . . . probably to do with the site constraints that had to be dealt with on a plot-by-plot basis'.

(a)

(b)

5.11 Achieving level or ramped access.

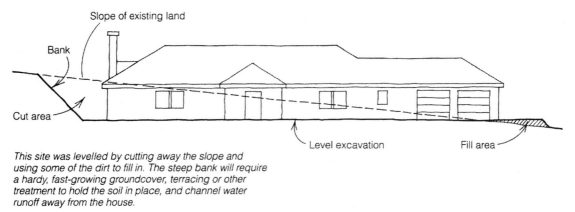

This site was levelled by cutting away the slope and using some of the dirt to fill in. The steep bank will require a hardy, fast-growing groundcover, terracing or other treatment to hold the soil in place, and channel water runoff away from the house.

(a)

A level entrance is an important element of accessible design. Even if the site slopes, sometimes this goal can be achieved simply by changing the house's design or orientation to the site.

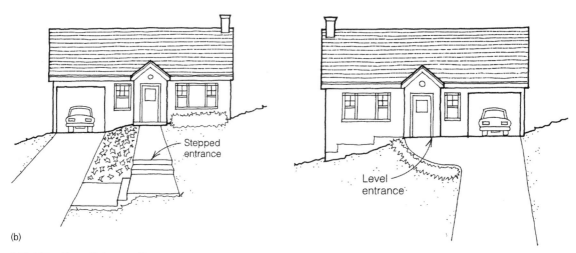

(b)

5.12 (a) Levelling a site by excavation;
(b) orienting the house on the site.

Some studies show that there is a range of ways in which plots can be prepared, and dwellings aligned or sited, that do not require the use of a stepped approach (see Steven Winter Associates, 1993; Goldsmith, 1997). Steven Winter Associates (1997) conducted research into the feasibility of constructing dwellings on sloping sites to visitability standards and, as Figure 5.12 shows, different options are possible. For instance, Figure 5.12(a) shows a dwelling in which the site was levelled by cutting away the slope and using some of the dirt to fill in. The steep bank created by the excavation will require, as Steven Winter Associates (1993: 44) suggest, 'a hardy, fast-growing groundcover, terracing or other treatment to hold the soil in place and channel water runoff away from the house...'.

In Figure 5.12(b), a house across a slope, the usual solution is to provide steps between the different levels, particularly from the driveway and garage area to the principal entrance. A simple solution, however, is to ensure that the driveway and garage are located on the high side of the slope so that the car does the climbing and the entrance to the house is level. One example of such design is in the City of Decatur near Atlanta, USA, where a number of dwellings have been constructed on steeply sloping plots

(a)   (b)

5.13 (a) The front part of the house is set on a steep slope and accessed by a series of steps. However, the driveway is engineered up to the back of the building and once out of the motor vehicle there is ramped access through the back entrance of the house (b).

without the use of a stepped approach to all or part of the dwelling. For instance, Figure 5.13 shows an example of where the driveway for a motor vehicle is effectively the ramped access to the level part of the driveway in front of the entrances to the dwellings. The expectation here is that disabled people will drive to the level portion of the driveway, and from there gain access to the dwelling. Eleanor Smith, a local campaigner for accessible dwellings in Atlanta, noted in interview that 'it's a good demonstration of what can be done, and we only wish all builders would think of this'.

Figure 5.14 shows a variation on this design. While the houses are located on a steeply sloping site overlooking a valley, access has been provided by designing the road to the rear of them at a level that permits level access from the edge of the road to the back entrances of the dwellings. The use of gradient in this way permits the reten-tion of the elevation. The houses were constructed in this way due to the polit-ical leverage that politicians in Decatur City Council were able to exercise over the builder. The dwellings are aimed at low- to middle-income owner occupiers,

and the developer's costs were partly subsidized by the city council. Ordinar-ily, such housing does not have to be constructed to visitability standards if the builder does not receive any federal or state funding. However, as Eleanor Brown said, 'the city council received a phone call from us to tell them that a development was imminent and to find out if there was any chance of getting some basic access designed in . . . it's not usual for this to occur, but the Head of the City Housing Department was persuaded'.

Such examples are instructive for practices in England and Wales, where builders and building control officers rarely seek to use the driveway as a means of overcoming the problems of sloping sites. However, paragraph 6.8 of Approved Document M (DETR, 1999a: 25) provides encouragement and advice on doing this or, as it states:

the driveway itself could be designed as the approach from the pavement or footpath or may be the place where visitors park. In such cases, a level or ramped approach may be possible from the car parking space, particu-larly on steeply sloping plots.

5.14 Providing level access to the back entrance.

However, interviewees tended to suggest that this option was rarely pursued, and as a building control officer noted:

I think there is perhaps not as much awareness as there should be about that bit in the building regulations that tells you about where you can get out of a car next to an entrance. So you can still build on a bit of a hillside, as long as you can get your vehicle up there and get out of your vehicle next to the entrance, you can still have a level access . . . but it isn't done much.

In part, this is because some builders baulk at the idea of having to excavate sites to provide level access owing to their perception that the process will be expensive. As one builder said, 'the costs for disposing of construction waste in landfill sites are very expensive, and we try our best to avoid this option'. Other builders felt likewise and, as another respondent commented:

And I'm sure that there is probably a big cost when, if you've got a slope up to the front door rather than a few flights of steps up a bank and then a flat bit and then maybe some more steps, you know. If you've got to cut that out and take it away from the site, then that is a very expensive exercise . . . since the controls on carting it

away have been tightened up, all the prices have gone up phenomenally for that, for carrying it away. And that could be a very expensive part of it. Probably more so than all these damp proof courses, and bits and pieces.

For Steven Winter Associates (1997: 44), however, the provision by builders of level entry and access ought to be the priority, and they suggest that the use of ramps might be regarded as a failure of the design process because they are 'often added on to houses because the siting, orientation and foundation planning . . . were not done'. They also suggest that ramps still present problems for some people, and that they are 'not as safe as level products . . .' In interview, a disabled person said that 'I still walk a bit, and I prefer steps to ramps because I'm less likely to fall over . . . I can't easily walk up or down slopes, even shallow ones'. Some ramped approaches to dwellings, such as those in Figure 5.15, are a potential danger to wheelchair users by not providing a physical barrier to prevent the possibilities of a wheelchair running off or over the ramp. Figure 5.15 illustrates a range of designs that, as one officer described, 'are potential traps for the unwary and could cause injury . . . it makes a good case for making all entrances as level as possible'.

5.15 Potentially dangerous ramps.

6 The regulation of the house-building industry

6.1 Introduction

I think it's like everything, I mean, regulations *per se*, whatever, you can only do so much, and people's lifestyles are so different and so specific that it's difficult to know if there is a generalized sort of design or building standards that can actually accommodate those things.

(From an interview with a building control officer)

The advent of New Labour to power in the UK in 1997 signalled an apparent change in public policy with regard to the development of design quality in the built environment. The White Paper on the future of towns and cities in England (DETR, 2000a: 43) notes that 'poor quality design and layouts and poor building practices' are partly to blame for the creation of 'poor quality places'. It suggests that 'we need design and planning policies that promote a better quality environment' and which encourage the construction of 'good quality buildings' (DETR, 2000a: 43). The government argues that quality in the built environment can be enhanced by recourse to (amongst other things) the reform of planning policies and procedures, the enhancement of the design skills of planners, designers and developers, and 'improvements to the quality of construction' (DETR, 2000a: 53; see also Urban Task Force, 1999; Carmona, 2001). Such measures, in combination, are, so the White Paper alleges, core to the renaissance of towns and cities.

In relation to the development of the design quality of housing, government has sought to extend and enhance the role of legal directives through the use of particular instruments, such as the building regulations. For instance, recent amendments to Part E of the building regulations in England and Wales require house builders to provide higher standards of sound insulation in housing. In addition, a hitherto neglected aspect of housing quality, disabled people's access to dwellings, is being addressed, so government claim, by Part M of the building regulations (see also Chapter 3). As the Urban White Paper suggests, Part M, amongst other building regulations, will 'play a key part in assuring the safety and quality of the urban environment' (DETR, 2000a: 53). This regulation, like all others, is based on the understanding that housing quality can be attained by recourse to technical and prescriptive behaviour that, as Rowe (1993: 289) suggests, provides 'fundamental guidance for housing design activity but without predetermining the entire character of the final form'.

In exploring the role and relevance of the building regulations as a means of enhancing housing quality for disabled people, I divide the chapter into three. I begin by briefly outlining debates about the interrelationships between housing quality and standards, and the role and significance of the building regulations as a means of achieving quality in housing design. Then, referring to a postal survey of and interviews with local authority building control officers, I provide an evaluation of the role and relevance of Part M and document the contrasting ways in which the regulation is being interpreted and applied. The evidence suggests that there is some confusion about the logic and *raison d'être* of Part M, and often diverse, sometimes problematical, interpretations by officers of its provisions. I conclude by discussing how best disabled people's needs in relation to physical access to and use of housing can be addressed over and beyond the application of Part M or building regulations more generally.

6.2 Standards, regulation and housing quality

Part M is a departure from the premise, widely held by previous governments, that government has no right to interfere in influencing the quality of consumer goods such as housing (see Goodchild and Furbey, 1986; Goodchild, 1997; Carmona, 2001; Franklin, 2001). For instance, circular 22/80, issued by a Conservative government, noted that 'functional requirements within a development are for the most part a matter for developers and their customers' (DoE, 1980, paragraph 5). Likewise, in the early 1990s the publication of PPG3 reinforced a more or less carbon copy message, that the 'functional requirements within a development are for the most part a matter for the marketing judgements of developers, in the light of their assessment of their customers' requirements' (DoE, 1992, paragraph 6). In contrast, Part M sets out, as the Introduction to the book and Chapter 1 outlined, design criteria that specify aspects of the functioning of housing, such as the use of particular rooms (like the WC).

Such directives are indicative, in part, of what Hunt and Wickham (1994) characterize as broader societal changes in which legal regulation becomes more deeply ingrained as one component of social relations and institutions (see also Foucault, 1977; Cruikshank, 1999; Dean, 1999). Thus for Foucault (1977), the rule, or regulatory basis of society, is seen as the prerequisite for the foundation of social order, or that which produces social interaction that is a prerequisite of existence; only the rule, so some argue, can control human conduct (see also Rowe, 1993; Bentley, 1999; Hill, 1999). This observation reflects, in part, enlightenment or Western thinking, which suggests that rules are part of what Max Weber (1947) calls 'traditional action' – that is, practices carried out under the influences of custom and habit which seek to control human conduct (see also Bierstedt, 1970).

In relation to the design and construction of the built environment, the (dominance of the) rule is particularly evident as part of the policies and practices of building regulation and control (Wright, 1983; Goodchild and Furbey, 1986). Bentley (1999: 60) regards building regulations, and the control system more generally, as a manifestation of a (long-term) process of the embedding of design ideas in which, as he suggests, certain form-types, or conceptions of what is appropriate design, 'become institutional-ized as deep types within the overall social system'. For Bentley (1999), 'deep types' are categories of places and spaces, what he terms – 'grasp-able structures' – and they provide a frame of reference that enables people to make sense of their surroundings. Such types become part of what Bentley (1999: 60) refers to as the 'unspoken structure of assump-tions' that, once enshrined in and supported by legal rule and conduct, are resistant to change.

The 'structure of assumptions' that underpins most building rules and regulations is, for Rowe (1993), problematical, because of its insensitivity to cultural variations, and predilection towards what Rowe (1993: 58) terms 'human biological similarity' based around measures of central tend-ency (see also Chapter 1). For Rowe (1993), the emergent building stand-ards of the twentieth century were based on generic characterizations of the building user and/or occupant and the imposition of the norm, or what Canguilhem (1991: 239) refers to as that which draws its meaning 'from the fact of the existence, outside itself, of what does not meet the require-ment it serves' (see also Chapter 1). Aligned to and derived from the techno-management paradigm that, at the turn of the nineteenth century, was seeking to propagate what Rowe (1993: 57) terms the 'scientific cer-tainty to overcome cultures of tradition', the value-bases and practices of building regulation and control encouraged the development of concepts of housing quality defined primarily, as outlined in Chapter 1, in terms of the attainment of physical structure.

Franklin (2001: 82) suggests that, because of the dominance of tech-nical and physical criteria in underpinning the form and content of the building regulations, or those things that are measurable as quantities, the practices of regulation are likely to avoid anything 'which is potentially too subjective'. King (1996, 2003) makes similar observations in questioning how far technical regulatory regimes, such as the building control system, are able to achieve 'dwelling', given that dwelling 'does not exist as an object separated from our subjectivity' (King, 1996: 162; see also the argu-ments in Chapter 1). For Franklin (2001), a possible response to King's observation is that the evolution of building regulation, based on physical standards and control, reflects a concern less with broader values about how one 'ought to live' than with the prosaic and mundane application of (relatively fixed) technical criteria of building form and function which are, so Franklin (2001) suggests, accessible and easy for regulators, builders and others to comprehend.

This suggests that recourse to building regulations or codes as a primary means of securing housing or design quality may well be a partial and problematical response (Karn and Sheridan, 1994; Goodchild, 1997; Carmona, 2001). For instance, Goodchild and Furbey (1986: 80) also note that 'such controls are negative devices which can only prevent dwellings with certain characteristics being built'. It is also suggested that the minimum design standards of the building regulations tend to be confused with optimal or best standards, when in reality they represent what Wylde *et al.* (1994: 248) refer to as the 'least acceptable solution' (see also Goodchild and Furbey, 1986; Karn and Sheridan, 1994; Carmona, 2001). Rowe (1993: 259) also suggests that while regulations provide prescriptive guidance up to minimum standards of design, they 'offer no guidance to building activities well above the standard' and, as a consequence, might encourage builders to construct to the standards rather than above them.

These and related observations suggest that Part M, and the building regulations more generally, may not necessarily be the best route to achieving housing quality (in its broadest sense) for disabled people. However, aside from partisan opinion and anecdotal reports of the effects of Part M on domestic design, there is little or no systematic information about or insights into the ways in which the regulation is being interpreted and applied by building control officers, and with what effects on the design of new housing. It is to this that the chapter now turns, in which I seek to develop the observation by Wright (1983: 125) that while building control is concerned with the implementation of technical standards and building dimensions, it is 'far from being confined to technicalities of buildings'.

6.3 Seeking to secure access to housing through the context of Part M

As intimated in the previous section, despite some observers' comments about the limitations of the building regulations and other regulatory mechanisms in influencing housing quality, there is little evidence about how far, and in what ways, Part M is able to enhance the quality of new dwellings for disabled people. In seeking to redress this, the rest of the chapter describes and evaluates the contrasting attitudes and practices of local authority building control officers in relation to their understanding, interpretation and application of Part M. The data are based primarily on a postal questionnaire that was sent to chief building control officers in local authorities in England and Wales, in the period from December 2001 to April 2002 (see Appendix 1 for details of the survey). In order to corroborate some of the views of respondents, interviews were also held with fifteen officers working for a variety of local authorities (see Appendix 1). This generated a range of additional data, including site plans, drawings, photographs of Part M design features, and oral testimonies of the interviewees.

I divide the discussion into three. First, I describe and evaluate officers' views and feelings about the role and relevance of Part M. As the data suggest, most officers regard the regulation as partial and incomplete, and insufficient as a means of securing quality housing environments for disabled people. Second, I discuss officers' views about the problems in interpreting aspects of Part M, and in seeking to ensure that builders respond to the regulation in a satisfactory manner. Given the ambiguity of aspects of the regulation, it is not surprising that the data indicate an absence of uniformity of interpretation of the regulation, with the consequence of different types of design solutions. Moreover, the evidence suggests that while most builders conform to Part M, there are various applications and, sometimes, evasion of the regulation. I conclude by considering how far officers are able and willing to enforce the regulation, and to persuade builders to construct housing beyond the requirements of Part M.

The role and relevance of Part M

The procedures and practices of building control in England and Wales seek to regulate the construction of buildings in the interests of public health and safety. The advent of the building regulations was in response to issues about drainage, fire hazard, rights to light and unstable structures. They comprise a series of technical or functional requirements that buildings must adhere to, and government regards them as basic performance standards. These range from rules about the supply of adequate systems of foul water and surface water drainage, to the specification of standards so that buildings can safely carry the loads expected to be placed on them. Such standards are discharged through the context of prescribed behaviour by regulators, or what Eward (1990: 141) refers to as a 'rule of judgement and a means of producing that rule' (see also Foucault, 1977). In this sense, the practices of building control tend to be regarded by practitioners as no more than the application of rules and procedures, or a mode of regulation, in the pursuit of technical norms.

Such conduct is not bereft of value judgement or bias, and, as the data indicate, officers' general antipathy towards Part M and issues about disability and access is not unconnected to the origins of building control. As one officer said, 'Part M is not high on the list of health and safety priorities', while for another, 'Part M isn't mainstream health and safety . . . it's difficult to attach the same importance to it as other regulations'. This was a common response, with respondents noting that Part M is seen as one of the less significant building regulations. For instance, one officer suggested that, 'I've got to be honest, in terms of you know, building control, access is by no means our main concern. Our biggest concerns are the building structure and fire precautions, and Part M forms one of the other half dozen sort of middling regulations.' Some, albeit a minority, were grudging about the amount of time and effort that it takes to administer Part M. As one officer commented: 'never before has a building regulation requirement demanded so much resource to control'.[1]

However, officers generally accept that the use of the building control system to respond to the access needs of disabled people is 'a good thing'. As one officer said, 'it's important to have a house you can get into and out of easily, and that should be the point and purpose of the building regulations'. Others concurred, and another respondent noted that 'it has to be a part of our job, what's the point if people can't get into their home?' Most officers were equivocal when asked about their feelings in relation to the adequacy of Part M in securing access to housing. As Table 6.1 shows, postal survey respondents tended to feel that Part M is an adequate regulation with shortcomings. For one officer, Part M has 'laudable aims but too many loop-holes', while for another the regulation 'seems to be neither a full answer or no answer to the needs of disabled people. It appears to be a token gesture by government.' Others were

Table 6.1 Officers' attitudes towards Part M.

	Nos. (%)
A comprehensive regulation with no shortcomings	3 (1.28)
A good regulation, albeit with some shortcomings	83 (35.47)
An adequate regulation with shortcomings	118 (50.42)
An inadequate regulation with many shortcomings	22 (9.40)
A poor regulation	8 (3.42)

$n = 234$
Source: Author's survey, 2002.

unimpressed by the final version of Part M, or, as an officer said, 'between the consultation document and printing the regulation, someone lost their nerve'.

This observation is apt in relation to what officers perceive to be the limited scope of the regulation, particularly the failure of Part M to address issues about living in a dwelling. As an officer stated, 'it needs some tinkering so that we don't end up with the ludicrous situations where you can just get in the front door and that's it'. Such views were common, and reflect officers' concerns that the regulation is not able to address disabled people's use of dwelling space. For instance, as one officer said, there is a 'need to provide for disabled people to live in the property rather than to merely visit . . . the basis of the regulation should be on occupation rather than visitability'. For another officer, Part M is 'too narrowly confined, you apply it only to a principal entrance storey, I'd like to see that application extended to other areas where disabled people can gain access'. This point was particularly evident in relation to specific house-types, such as town houses, where living quarters tend to be on first floors and above. Thus, as one officer stated:

And I think the definition, you see, principal entrance storey, not necessarily principal living storey, is a big problem with Part M. So your principal entrance may well be out of the car and in through that door up the stairs to your lounge and kitchen, and a ground floor might be just utility and toilet. This is common in town houses around here. So a disabled person can get to utility and toilet facilities, that's your principal entrance, but they can't get to living areas.

Others expressed the view that the government should 'make the regulation fully inclusive' or, as one officer commented, it 'does not cover items such as door opening force, future adaptations, stair lifts, and access to upper floors'. The regulation is also perceived as problematic because, as one officer suggested, 'it only covers the obvious impairments . . . and does not fully meet the needs of all'. Thus Part M does little to ensure that the provision of 'fittings can be easily used by people with grip and strength difficulties', while 'there's little in the regulation about vision-impaired people, the deaf, and other types of impairments, so it's half-hearted stuff'. For another, 'it doesn't take into account blindness, it doesn't . . . so it's very limited in its approach. And you know, you're thinking we're designing properties for all, but you're not.' As an officer suggested, 'it touches the surface of the needs of disabled people . . . it identifies the problem but doesn't do a lot more'.

However, officers were sympathetic with builders in noting that the regulation is, potentially, restrictive on builders and consumer choice and ought to provide more scope for flexibility. Most postal survey respondents (175 or 75 per cent) said that the majority of builders are unhappy with the provisions of Part M and, not surprisingly, very few exceed the regulation (see Table 6.2). Respondents feel that Part M is problematical because it requires builders to construct dwellings to standards for which, it is alleged, there is a limited demand: 'access arrangements should be at the option of the individual', while, for another respondent, 'why do three-storey houses have to conform when surely a disabled person would not purchase it?' Others concurred in variously suggesting that 'the blanket regulation for all dwellings is overkill', and that 'it imposes in certain areas . . . I mean, the argument I get thrown at me every time I go on site is the fact it's only strictly applicable to 1 per cent of the population'. Likewise, another officer noted that 'I think there's a lot of alterations taking place in buildings for a relatively small number of people'.

These observations indicate, in part, officers' ignorance about human physiology, in that any person, independent of culture, social context or lifestyle, has the capacity to acquire a physical and/or cognitive impairment. Impairment, as previously mentioned, is intrinsic to human beings; it is not the preserve of a minority group (Zola, 1989; Bickenbach et al., 1999). In broader terms, some respondents feel that the regulation specifies technical standards to the detriment of relating access issues to moral and ethical questions about 'what is the appropriate and right thing to do?' As one officer suggested, 'builders should be reminded about their moral responsibilities, to provide decent design'. For some officers, the provision of access to the built environment is a matter of responding to human rights or, as an officer commented: 'I would like to see Part M go into the philosophy and rationale behind the actual requirement . . . I feel it would help "sell the ideal".'

Such sentiments underpin officers' views that Part M ought to be changed. Thus, most survey respondents (164 or 70 per cent) would like to see revisions to the regulation or, as a respondent said, 'Part M appears to have been a very rushed regulation poorly thought out . . . a lot more rational guidance should be built into such a haphazard regulation'. For most officers, changes to the regulation should include: the extension of Part M to flats at any level where lift access is provided; greater clarifi-

	Number (%)
Usually	1 (0.43)
Often	2 (0.85)
Sometimes	29 (12.39)
Usually not	128 (55.70)
Never	74 (31.20)

Table 6.2 Do house builders submit proposals that exceed Part M standards?

$n = 234$
Source: Author's survey, 2002.

cation and guidance on how to achieve the regulation; more formal guidance and details about the design and layout of toilets; the inclusion of all physical and mental impairments in Part M; all fixtures and fittings to be at a height suitable for wheelchair users; clarity about the relationships between planning and building control and their respective roles and responsibilities in adjudicating access matters; large extensions and conversions to comply with Part M; access to be provided to amenity areas such as gardens; and, as a minimum, the adoption of lifetime homes standards as the basis for the design of accessible dwellings (see Lifetime Homes Group, 1993).

Interpreting and seeking to achieve Part M

The central stipulation of Part M, as outlined in Chapter 3, is the requirement that 'reasonable provision shall be made for disabled people to gain access to and to use the building' (DETR, 1999a: 5). For one officer: 'we have little idea what the term "reasonable provision" means ... it's confusing'. Others concurred with another officer, noting that the 'reasonableness' clause has led to endless debates with builders about how to apply the regulation: 'this is the game that you play. It is endless debate and negotiation.' Others were aware of contrasting interpretations: 'there are good reasons for the regulation but the interpretation and perceptions are too greatly ranged'. An officer aptly illustrated this point:

> the guidance in NHBC documents is that they don't use the seven fifty millimetre rule for the wash hand-basin, they use the six hundred, which is for ambulant disabled people, not people in wheelchairs. So I'm finding discrepancies there between the two, but to be fair, that's not the only discrepancy you'll find, you'll find discrepancies in our office between building control officer and building control officer, because of the interpretation.

Such interpretative discrepancies work their way into the final design of dwellings, with variable consequences in relation to access (see also Imrie,

6.1 Interpretative discrepancies in relation to access.

2003a). For instance, Figure 6.1 shows how the tightness of fit between house frontage and pavements led to a design solution that some officers might well deem not to be meeting the requirements of Part M. The stepped approach, in the foreground, is to a property in which there is a slight incline between the front door and the pavement; the ramped approach, in the background, is where the incline has disappeared. In both instances the 'solutions' are problematical, in that the former provides a step in a context where the topography is more or less flat, while the latter comprises a ramped access that is steeper than the required minimum of 1:12. However, these outcomes were deemed 'reasonable' by the local authority, and were therefore judged to be in accord with the requirements of Part M. Likewise, Figure 6.2 shows another attempt to achieve ramped solutions in a context of 'tight fit' between dwellings and pavement.

The interpretation and application of Part M is guided and assisted by an 'Approved Document' (AD), although, as one officer said, 'as a guidance document it is very limited and woolly'.[2] Likewise, as another officer suggested: 'the AD is poor: interpretation of the guidance is difficult, it is half-hearted with limited detailing that does not cover all aspects of the built environment'. Others concurred, with one officer noting that the 'guidance is too ambiguous, resulting in the building industry having to battle it out to come up with acceptable solutions'. Another officer was particularly scathing about the guidance in the AD, and recalled a familiar scenario:

6.2 Attempting to achieve ramped solutions in a 'tight fit' situation.

the electrician's been in there, whacked in all the sockets and switches, we go round and say 'Oh, they're at the wrong height, you haven't got them correctly.' And so they've had to alter them. But it's not clear in the Approved Document, or it is clear in the fact that it doesn't say anything.

This is particularly so in relation to the guidance on WC provision. As one officer stated, 'I feel that the recommendations for the WC are very poor and short of the mark.' These require builders to construct outwardly opening doors, which wheelchair users, once inside the WC, are unable to reach in order to close the door. A number of respondents were horrified by the human and practical implications of this guidance. Thus, one officer noted that 'you cannot use the wheelchair to transfer to the toilet and also close the door and this is, therefore, close to performing in public' – a view echoed by another officer, who said that 'the WC provisions are particularly inadequate and undignified for disabled people'. The guidance in the AD, as Figure 6.3 illustrates, also seems to confuse some officers (and builders) about the precise width of the WC. An officer noted that 'most

6.3 Transgressing part of the regulation. A common interpretation of Part M, by builders, is to provide the minimum width for the WC and then to add fixtures and fittings. This has the consequence of reducing the space standards in the WC to less than the legal minimum prescribed by Part M. The width of the WC, according to Part M, should be 950 mm for oblique access, as measured from wall-to-wall. However, by fitting in a radiator on the sidewall of the WC, the width, in this instance, was reduced by 100 mm. The builders said that 'the building control officer has told us not to put radiators here, and we'll have to move this one. But, we've been doing it elsewhere, although, to be fair, this authority has let us off once before so it's not surprising that they're coming down on us now. It's just a mistake putting it there, as it seems the best place for it.'

builders measure up the width before they put on the plaster board, radiators, and other things . . . so if you're not careful in checking, the WC can end up a lot smaller than it should be'.

For most officers, part of the problem is that builders have incomplete knowledge of Part M, and are slow to absorb new standards into their designs (see Table 6.3). As one officer said, 'it takes two or three years before builders get in tune, and they can demonstrate resistance to standards'. Similarly, builders sometimes fail to communicate with project managers and others on site about how to apply Part M. Site or project managers will work from drawings produced by a builder's design team. More often than not, drawings do not provide any sense of topography and they convey site details in no more than one or two dimensions. As an officer noted:

it's transposing that onto the practical building site, because on a lot of plans, well, say on some plans, for instance, they always show a level site. You know, they draw a straight line and you draw the building, it looks fine, doesn't it, but when you get on site you find, yeah, there's a gradient and it falls this way and that's when you get problems.

Others suggested that implementation issues arise because 'designers have failed to give or offer design solutions on site, leaving site managers to build what they consider is required'. One officer recalled the following tale by a builder:

the site manager here never meets the architect and he tends to get on with it . . . that's led to some right cock-ups, the drawings don't show any detail . . . I have to let the site manager get on with it, but it can lead to some strange looking ramps.

Some officers, however, tend to ascribe such implementation problems, in part, to the 'design and build' mentality of builders which, as a respondent said, 'encourages the building trade to cut costs and not consider design too seriously' (see also Imrie and Hall, 2001a; Chapter 7). Typically, design issues are often an afterthought or, for one respondent, 'the lack of design

Table 6.3 How knowledgeable are builders of the provisions of Part M?

	Local house builders Numbers (%)	Regional house builders Numbers (%)	National house builders* Numbers (%)
Knowledgeable of all aspects of Part M	2 (0.85)	34 (14.53)	86 (36.75)
Knowledgeable of most aspects of Part M	49 (20.94)	156 (66.66)	124 (52.99)
Little knowledge of Part M	152 (64.96)	38 (16.24)	24 (10.26)
No knowledge of Part M	31 (13.25)	6 (2.56)	0 (0.00)

*The NHBC, as an approved inspector, tends to deal with the applications of national house builders.

$n = 234$

Source: Author's survey, 2002.

thought in the early stages from builders means Part M is often thought about towards the end of the project and consequently compromised'.

Aspects of building control, such as builders' use of building notices, are also implicated in potentially poor applications of Part M. More often than not, a builder will submit a building notice rather than a full plans application to gain building control consent.[3] While the latter contains constructional drawings and is checked by officers for compliance with building regulations, the former has none of this (see Figure 6.4). Officers check for adherence to the regulations on site. However, as an officer suggested, this can lead to fraught situations:

the difficulty then is on site you're dealing with the developer, not the architect and not the owner. So you turn up on site and you say to the developer, 'What provision have you got here for disabled access?' 'Well, there's nothing on my plans.' 'Well, that's irrelevant, you still need to provide it.' Then you start to get in a conflict situation because he may not be aware of the requirements of the approved document because he's simply a builder.

6.4 House-type approvals.

The Local Authority National Type Approval Confederation (LANTAC) offers builders, developers and construction industry professionals a quick and easy route through building regulation plan approval. LANTAC is a service provided by local authorities across England and Wales. Builders make just one application to a local authority to obtain national type or system approval. This allows the builder to repeat a LANTAC-approved design throughout England and Wales with a minimum of checking for Building Regulation approval. To use the LANTAC system, builders deposit their plans in the normal way, attaching a copy of the type-approval certificate. Building control will not check type-approved plans, and will only look at site-related matters that are not covered under the LANTAC certificate. The system is seen as 'time saving' and 'flexible', although there has been little or no research to see how it operates in practice.

However, for some disabled people the system has capacity to lack sensitivity to local context. As one respondent said: 'They've obviously got their house-type, which they probably used in Newcastle and they're using it here in Wales and whatever, and that's been approved by one authority, and the plan appears down here, and often, you know, there are issues around levels and about, you know, whatever, and it's all detail that in some respects they don't want to get too involved in.' Others concurred, and for another disabled person 'we would like the local building control office to adjudicate all the applications for development here, because they know what we need and we feel that designs that have had approval elsewhere will not necessarily work well for us'.

Officers felt that builders with house-type approvals were reluctant to respond to their observations. For one officer, 'we've had it on a number of things, where the plans come in to us for development within our borough, but it's almost just for information, just for rubber-stamping, because it's all been approved by a different authority, and under this agreement our building control officers are not then meant to get into negotiation around the design, because that's all been approved. And you know, there's been occasions where I've had real issues with what's actually been approved, but it's like you can't do anything about it because it's been approved by another authority and under this agreement that's what then stands. So it's all about consistency as well, of course, across the country.'

However, the majority of building control officers feel that Part M is 'easy to achieve' and, as one respondent said, 'the document isn't asking for a great deal'. Indeed, as an officer noted:

> we haven't had what we'd anticipated, which was a lot of people raising or lowering their sites so that they could get around the idea of putting ramps in and putting staircases in instead, because of the steep site. There was a concern at the time that people were going to do that to get round the regulation. But that doesn't seem to have happened.

However, one officer said that they have constantly to counter builders' feelings that Part M 'is over the top', while another suggested that 'builders feel it is unfairly prescriptive and restricts freedom of design'. Officers are, as a respondent said, 'having to explain why Part M is a good thing', although most concurred with another officer who said that builders are 'indifferent at the moment as with any change to regulations, but they will adapt and accept Part M over a period of time'.

Compliance, enforcement and seeking to extend standards

In relation to compliance with Part M, one officer suggested that 'at one time or another every possible transgression has occurred', an observation echoed by another who said that 'basically all areas of Part M are not complied with on some sites or other'.[4] The most frequent is probably in relation to access into the building with some form of step being maintained. This was a common view, with others suggesting that builders often transgress Part M by providing level thresholds and ramped access to the rear of the dwelling rather than to the principal door. Other transgressions include the provision of principal entrance door widths of less than the 775 mm minimum, the use of ramped access constructed out of moveable timber features, and the tendency for builders to 'forget things like switches and socket heights'. The latter is often the main problem and relates, in part, to builders' limited control over subcontractors. Thus, as an officer noted, 'we have problems with the light and socket heights because most of the electricians that builders use are unaware of the regulation'.

One common transgression relates to builders misjudging pavement and door entrance levels and constructing dwellings in which it is difficult to achieve level or ramped access. One instance is illustrated in Figure 6.5, in which a builder made a genuine mistake with the levels on site, and, according to the access officer for the local authority, 'they saw the provision of temporary metal ramps as an easy way out'. The building control officers adjudicating the development did not deem this as reasonable provision, and asked the developer to provide permanent ramps. This has subsequently been done, although the ramps that have been provided are 1-in-9 in places and, as the access officer stated, the development has 'now been signed off by Building Control, and a completion certificate issued without my agreement'. For the access officer, 'the best solution would have been to raise the courtyard area to the entrance levels, but I suspect that was viewed as the more expensive option and one of the units was already occupied'.

6.5 Failing to achieve the standard. The development comprises six housing units on a level site. Four units were originally built with metal ramps, one had a very steep ramp or a 1-in-4 gradient, and the last unit had a side ramp. The insertion of permanent brick ramps, as a solution, has been less than satisfactory. As the access officer said, 'this was a level site, so there was no excuse really to end up with such a poor result'.

While officers are obliged to enforce the provisions of the building regulations, the reality is one whereby enforcement is usually a last resort. In part, officers' behaviour is influenced by the competitive nature of building control in which builders can use any building control department or, alternatively, private sector inspectors to carry out the control function (see also Figure 6.6).[5] The deregulated nature of the control system appears to be implicated in officers' reluctance to penalize builders or, as one officer said:

> if the measurements are a bit out, do I penalize them and say 'get that door frame off and get back'. I don't, because my competitors might say 'We'd have accepted that.' You've always got that. I'm not going to do that. I'm not going to put men's jobs on the line.

Others concurred: 'if there's something wrong on site, we try to discuss and communicate with builders rather than enforce. A good inspection regime reduces the need to enforce, because as soon as you start enforcing you might lose that business.'

Most officers feel uneasy about enforcing a regulation that seems open-ended: 'it is difficult to enforce a requirement you don't understand yourself, for instance, trying to explain why closed risers are required on ambulant disabled stairs'. Some also feel powerless to stop builders 'retrofitting' or, as an officer said, 'knowing that the builder will alter the work after completion to suit the purchaser makes enforcement useless'. More often than not officers will stop short of enforcement, and instead accept a level of compliance less than the prescribed minimum. Thus, as an officer said: 'we have allowed for some electric sockets to remain at a lower level than the minimum standards require provided a reasonable amount of other sockets comply'. For others, enforcement will only occur after a warning or caution has been issued to the builder: 'we allowed "one free go" to builders and made sure that they were aware that we would be enforcing the regulations in the future – we also produced our own guidance notes'.

6.6 Approved inspectors.

The Building Act 1984 contained important provisions for the private supervision and certification of building work by private approved inspectors as an alternative to control solely exercised by local authorities. These provisions were brought into effect in November 1985. In effect, it introduced the privatization of building control and the opening up of it to market forces. This has led to competition between inspectors for business from developers and applicants seeking building control consent (see also Meijer and Visscher, 1998). Interviews with local authority building control officers and disabled people highlighted their concerns about approved inspectors, and a perception that the approved system was diminishing the quality of control. As one disabled person, in interview, said: 'building control's major problem is that it is now in direct competition with the approved building control inspectors ... the approved inspectors are not maintaining the standards, they are not making the builders build to what Part M says'.

This person amplified the point by saying that 'we went through the list of all the sites being dealt with by approved inspectors, and we went to look at all of the sites and we found mistakes on every one. The problem is that the approved inspectors are not enforcing the regulations, and because local authority building control know that they aren't able to go out into the market place and win the business, they are dropping their standards.' While it is difficult to substantiate such allegations, they appear to have taken root amongst local authority officers' understanding of the approved inspectorate. As an access officer said, 'I am concerned about some of the things that I've seen under approved inspectors ... we had a refurbishment of a hotel. I did a lot of work for planning to make sure that wheelchair-accessible rooms were provided; we sorted out the parking and it's got a gym and a restaurant and things like that. I went to a conference there the other week and found that, you know, silly things, like the door opens inwards on the disabled person's toilet.'

Many officers said that because they have to compete with approved inspectors it meant that they had to be careful about how they treat applicants; they could not afford to upset them unduly or discourage them from using the local authority service. An officer felt that this was leading to a situation of weaker control: 'we are now not enforcing the building regulations like we ought to, and the quality of outcome is a lot worse as a result'. However, others suggested that the system of approved inspections had sharpened practices, and was leading to a better system of control. One local authority officer commented that 'there's no reason for us to go onto sites being controlled by an approved inspector. I've got to guard against paranoia, because I know that local authorities are paranoid about the competition that they're facing from the approved inspectors. Certainly I don't think that you'll find anybody who's got an awful lot of hard evidence to suggest they're doing a bad job.'

Seeking to enforce the provisions of Part M is hampered, so officers claim, by lack of staff and resources to inspect all aspects of building work (see Figure 6.7). As an officer said, 'we enforce compliance with Part M on plans, but we have no information on how this is carried through on site'. In particular, officers rarely if ever monitor material alterations to dwellings once sold by builders to purchasers. Yet, as one officer said, there is evidence that some purchasers alter Part M features once they have occupied the dwelling. As he said: 'I've had reports, I haven't seen it, but I've had reports from my lads that say the builders here are supplying the ramps and everything else per detailed on the plans, but the householders them-

A legal agreement (Section 106 of the Planning and Land Use Act, 1991) was used on the Littleover estate in Derby requiring the developer to construct all dwellings to visitability standards. As the access officer explained: 'I met up with all the relevant parties in advance of construction, including the architect, the developer and site manager. The site manager left a few weeks later without me knowing, and the new site manager obviously wasn't aware of the legal agreement because steps were appearing everywhere and I didn't pick it up until a lot of the dwellings were occupied.' This example illustrates one way in which aspects of the design process can break down. The new site manager was not familiar with visitability criteria (this was before Part M was introduced) and a lack of communication on site, and between the architect and the site office, meant that the new site manager had not been made aware of the legal requirement to construct level and/or ramped access to the dwellings. He continued to do what he was familiar with: to construct stepped entrances.

By the time the access officer was made aware of the transgression, 25 dwellings had been constructed with a stepped entrance. The access officer asked the developer to write to the occupiers to offer to construct level and/or ramped access at no extra charge. Five of these dwellings were subsequently converted. As the access officer said: 'the enforcement of the local plan or any regulation on site requires time, effort and constant monitoring, but we can't pick up everything that goes wrong'. He noted that one of the lessons he learnt is never to assume that access will be implemented, or, as the access officer said: 'it's all right sitting down with developers and agreeing things round a table, it's actually when the site agents just come from somewhere else, building this house-type with a step and then he builds the same house-type here and there's some differences. And if you're not careful the people who are building it, the site workers, won't know any different and will just build whatever.'

Source: Watts, 2002.

6.7 Problems in the implementation of Part M: Littleover estate, Derby.

selves are taking them away.' As he explained, rectifying this situation was only likely if it was reported by a member of the public:

I could serve notice, if I find, if somebody reports it to me, I haven't got enough staff to go policing the area after people buy a property. If people were to report it and say 'Hey, he had a ramp there, threshold and everything and he's taken it away.' I would have to serve a notice on that owner, because it's a material alteration.

Not surprisingly, building control, as an activity, is not characterized by officers seeking to exceed the legal standards, and 173 (74 per cent) survey respondents said that they do not promote standards beyond Part M. One officer provided a typical response: 'it is not the job of building control to promote any aspect of work. The job is to enforce minimum standards.' Others concurred, with an officer suggesting that his department always adopted a cautious approach. As he said:

we may suggest that something might be better than Part M, but the difficulty is that we have to draw the line at what is the standard, what can we actually ask for, and we can't really go beyond that. Yes, we quite often give advice on any of the documents saying, you know, 'If you did this, this might be a better solution.' Or 'Just move that slightly it would work slightly better.'

For another, the need to encourage development was paramount in the application of the regulation: 'we can't go beyond Part M because it will drive investment away.' This respondent did, however, express his frustration:

> Disabled people would love me to go further. I can't. I can only apply the minimum standards and I can market that and say we're only applying the minimum standards. I can't market that we're exceeding the regulation! I'd love to be able to say to a big housing developer, 'Listen, why don't we do something different, why don't we cater for Part M first and then design the rest of the house around it?' That would be nice, wouldn't it?

However, a minority of officers (61, or 26 per cent of the survey respondents) encourage builders *to consider* standards in excess of Part M.[6] According to one officer, 'we always emphasize to developers that the regulations relate to minimum standards and that people with certain impairments may need a higher standard of provision'. Others related their approach to personal circumstances: 'as a carer for my mother I can see the shortfalls and I try to promote improvements and give reasons for it'. For another, 'higher standards are enforced (albeit illegally) through the authority's planning policies and guidance and conditions'. As this person admitted, this approach 'creates a "double standards" approach and results in a lot of bad feelings and criticism from house builders and developers'. For others, additional modest design features were sometimes requested. Thus an officer said that 'where it is reasonable, we ask builders to provide a sloping grab rail on the back of the toilet door'.

More often than not such exhortations fall on deaf ears and end in frustration and failure. As an officer suggested, 'we try to promote the lifetime homes concept, but this doesn't work very often'. Others concurred, with another officer noting that 'we try to cajole and persuade builders to do a bit more and we give them copies of design guides on access . . . but they rarely look at them'. Some officers felt that their own limited knowledge of disability and design issues inhibited proactive advice or guidance being offered to builders. As a respondent said: 'we know what Part M is and what is required to achieve it, and it is difficult to know what else to advise builders to do'. Thus, while a majority of respondents claim (180 or 77 per cent) to have heard of 'lifetime' home standards, few (58 or 24.7 per cent) have knowledge of, or use, related publications such as *Meeting Part M and Designing Lifetime Homes* as a specification guide. As an officer said, 'it's in the nature of the profession to follow the rule book'.

6.4 Conclusions

Part M of the building regulations is one of a broader series of initiatives by government to improve the quality of urban design in England and Wales, and to encourage builders to construct dwellings to higher standards than has hitherto been the case. Such initiatives include the production of good practice guides on housing and urban design (National Housing Federation, 1998; DETR and CABE, 2003), the promotion by government of a

Clients' Charter (ODPM, 2000a, 2000b) to encourage an improvement in building practices and, more recently, the publication of a manifesto by house builders pledging themselves to commit to high-quality housing schemes (see www.buildingforlife.org). These initiatives are based on providing no more than encouragement and advice to builders, and they do not guarantee that building practices will change or that the quality of dwellings will be enhanced. In this context, Part M, and the building regulations more generally, assume a critical legal role in seeking to ensure the development and delivery of design quality in the built environment.

However, the evidence from this chapter indicates that there are reservations, by building control officers, about how far Part M is able to enhance significantly the design of dwellings in relation to the access needs of disabled people. In particular, officers were concerned about the limited scope and objectives of the regulation. Most feel that Part M is half-hearted and tokenistic, and that it does not address the real housing needs of disabled people; that is, for livable rather than visitable housing. These feelings were conveyed powerfully by a respondent:

> there is a danger that people look at Part M now as the standard, and there's an awful lot of things required for disabled people that aren't covered in Part M, and they're being led to think that Part M is the document to use . . . and it's not really, it doesn't go far enough.

In this respect officers noted the absence of inclusiveness in the regulation, with most suggesting that it should take into account, explicitly, the design needs of people with vision impairments, impaired hearing and cognitive disorders.

While the prime purpose of the building regulations is, as Baer (1997:46) suggests, ensuring the standardization of activities and products, the evidence in this chapter shows that the interpretation and application of Part M is a messy and indeterminate affair. This is partly due to its discretionary element – that is, the 'reasonable provision' clause – that permits diverse interpretations to be made by officers of how to achieve the standard. Such interpretations are characterized by a complexity of applications of the regulation, with the effect of different types of design outcomes. Transgressions of the regulation are common, and there is evidence that building control officers are often unaware of poor applications of Part M by builders, and/or will choose to overlook them. The implication is that the design of dwellings, since 25 October 1999, will exhibit varying levels of access that both correspond to and diverge from the design guidance and advice as laid down in the approved document.

The data also demonstrate that officers will usually adopt a risk-averse approach to the interpretation and application of Part M that rarely involves them asking builders to exceed the legal minimum. This confirms the observations of other commentators, who note that building regulations or codes encourage design practitioners not to exceed the minimum standards and, as Goodchild and Furbey (1986: 96) point out, 'the controls do not and cannot encourage private developers to build better quality dwellings . . .' (see also Wylde et al., 1994; Goodchild, 1997; Carmona, 2001; Franklin, 2001). Officers' risk-averse behaviour is also characterized by their reluctance to upset builders by what might be seen as over-zealous interpretation of Part M, and most regard the regulation as 'over the top' in that they see it as responding to a minority concern. Given this, it is difficult to envision how the building control system, in its present form, will significantly enhance the quality of dwellings for disabled people.

One way of enhancing design is, of course, to raise the minimum standards, although this does not solve the problem of builders refusing to build beyond them, or some of the other problems associated with the building regulations more generally. In some countries, fiscal and other incentives are used to encourage builders to enhance quality in the design of dwellings. In the State of Illinois in the USA, for example, a State ordinance permits officers to relax density standards if builders are willing to provide access features that exceed the legal minimum (City of Naperville, 2001). This initiative, the planned unit development, involves a simple trade-off; more dwellings per plot in return for an enhancement of design. Likewise, English Partnerships (EP) is experimenting with a scheme called Part M+ in housing schemes in Thames Gateway, London. The trade-off is one whereby EP will provide developers with access to subsidized sites in return for design that exceeds the minimum standards of Part M.

However, fiscal incentives and other trade-offs ought to be complemented by changes to the practices, culture and discourses of building control in ways that seek to transcend the strictures of 'standards' (see Baer, 1997; Franklin, 2001). In particular, officers ought to be encouraged to be proactive in promoting inclusive and sustainable design to builders, and to adopt the idea, after Goodchild (1997), that the design process ought to be concerned with (as suggested in Chapter 1) the 'house as a home'; that is, as a place of social and emotional significance and attachment. In addition, officers ought to use their discretionary powers (of interpretation) much more creatively than is apparent from this study (and it is an interesting empirical issue as to why they rarely do so). More often than not, officers will ensure that there is a close 'fit' between the standard (as a written and codified rule) and the design outcome rather than seek to push the boundaries of interpretation of what 'reasonable provision' is or might be.

Further reading

Surprisingly little has been written about building control and regulation. Two of the more important pieces are by Dobson (1968) and Meijer and Visscher (1998). Much has been written about building standards, and the best readings are by Bentley (1999) and Rowe (1993). The article by Franklin (2001) is particularly good and thought-provoking, and is highly recommended. *Prospecta 35* (2004), an architectural journal published by Yale University, is a special issue about building codes, and contains some of the best articles to have been published on the subject of building codes and standards.

Case study
Securing accessible housing in two
English towns*

The building regulations provide scope for interpretation, and this is a basis for variations from one place to another in terms of how Part M is achieved. In Forest Town, the approach to the regulation of Part M is pragmatic in that officers regard it as their job to follow 'the rule book', and do no more than enforce the minimum standard. The Principal Building Control Surveyor (PBCS) suggested that while the building regulations are part of a 'grey system', his job is to try and make it clear and obvious to applicants for building control consent about 'what will be required from us'. As the PBCS said:

> it's a minimum standard, that's the trouble with building regulations, they're a minimum standard, and if you can achieve something better without causing grief and probably with a little bit of thought touched on it, then that's the way we'll go, but most of the time we can do no more than insist to builders on the minimum level of compliance.

The PBCS tries to encourage builders to adopt Part M as good practice that will benefit their business. As he commented:

> I try to point builders in the direction of the fact that they should use it as a sales advantage, rather than jumping up and down about how bad it is. I mean, promote your house, that it's accessible in all situations, get it to make that difference.

To this end, the PBCS felt that the message of inclusive design, that the regulation has applicability beyond disabled people, ought to be conveyed to builders. In this respect, the approach of the building control officers in the borough is to stress that Part M is related

> to lifetime health as much as anything else … there's a whole gamut of people, even when I've broken a leg or you know, there's all sorts of

things, and you're talking in terms of a lifetime home. I mean, I've got elderly parents and that sort of thing and they've got a staircase in their house, and you're sitting there thinking 'Well, that's a situation where they're going to have trouble later on.'

However, this statement was sometimes contradicted in interviews with other officers, one of whom suggested that the regulation was 'over the top' and asked too much from builders. As this officer said: 'it's aimed at what everyone would class as a minority, but that minority is very vociferous in certain areas and has achieved it because of it. I mean, that sounds terrible but it is a fact, isn't it?' In contrast, the access officer in Forest Town felt that the major issue with Part M is its inflexibility, despite the degrees of interpretation that officers were able to apply to it. As she suggested, Part M tends to foreclose debate about what can be achieved in relation to access:

> as soon as you get to the Part M stage builders are asking me, 'What do we have to do?' and there's no room for negotiation, you know, it's sort of difficult because you get builders saying 'Well, why are you asking for a bigger toilet and that?', and I have to say to them 'because Part M clearly states this'.

The access officer described her legacy in the borough as one of trying to persuade colleagues that access issues are important:

> what they had done as a planning and building control division has been absolutely minimal, you know, really bottom-line stuff, and I think in a lot of cases access wasn't considered. And to be honest, you know, I mean it's awful to say, because I've been here six years, but I'm not totally sure how much more we've achieved.

For this person, her role permits officers to pigeonhole access issues, and to defer them all to her. She finds this problematical because:

in terms of negotiating with planning applications and checking plans and working with building control, our surveyors and the planners have, in some respects, taken a back seat. And I think, you know, the planners tend to think, 'Oh well, you know, she hasn't made any comments on that application therefore everything should be okay.' And I think there's a real lack of understanding within the professions.

This is compounded by the weak support from members for access issues. As the access officer said, 'my position was described to me by one of our leading councillors as "One of those fashionable, politically correct posts that are not needed." But I managed to prove my worth and sort of secure my position.' However, while the access officer feels that 'we should challenge councillors more than we do, as officers, but obviously that has to be led from the top, or driven from the top', this is not likely given that, as she said, 'the officers, because they're used to this environment, don't push forward on certain issues'. The access officer noted further that planning and building control officers' behaviour in the borough was inherently conservative and reactive. As she said: 'within this authority, you know, you do tend to be talking about "Well, what can we do? You know, what's the absolute maximum we can ask for?" They're often not prepared to negotiate and go for best practice.'

In relation to Part M, some officers in the borough felt that it was not achieving much. As one officer noted: 'I think it's very interesting that the feeling that you're getting back from builders is either to strengthen it or abandon it. And I think a lot of disabled people would agree with that actually. It doesn't really do anything at the moment.' The access officer concurred in highlighting 'the downstairs WC

issue' which, as she said, was one whereby 'you only have to talk to our building control officers, and they just don't know what they're meant to do, and there's so many issues around it'. However, for the access officer the main problem remains one of officers' attitudes. She described the attitudes of building control officers as reluctant to enforce Part M and, as she noted, 'they will say to me, "Oh, you know, we should be adapting homes, we should be providing grants for people to adapt their homes, we shouldn't be requiring it as a new build issue on all houses." '

Achieving the standard is usually straightforward and, as the PBCS said:

where it's been built into a scheme from the outset it's never normally a problem, where it's the afterthought of the architect, builder, whatever, after the scheme's already gone through that initial phase it tends to then look like an add on. I mean, a lot of the level pathways and such like and gentle slopes to pathways, obviously you've got level access and such like, but it's obviously just not part of the whole landscape scheme.

The access officer recalled some examples:

a single house in Cotby, they ran the drive, curved it in, settled it back down again, and the whole thing flowed, so basically when the person came in s/he had a completely level access, it was beautiful, really looked nice, and yet I've got a small site of houses just down the road there, where literally it's just a straight slope up. I mean, you see the ramp like a, well, like a disabled person's ramp basically, it just sits there in splendid isolation [see Figure 6.8].

One of the problems for building control officers in the borough is that builders with type-approval will often want to modify aspects of the design to suit local conditions, but, as the PBCS said, 'the drawings they present to us

6.8 'In splendid isolation.'

don't necessarily end up being what's constructed on site'. As the PBCS said:

> we check drainage, we check Part M access, we'll check all that sort of thing, as a separate entity on the site itself, so although you might get a picture of a house, that bears no resemblance to what eventually is built, ground wise and such like, because of the way they've done it.

Likewise, the access officer noted some problems in achieving satisfactory outcomes because of type-approvals missing access features. As she said:

> if we confront builders, they will say, 'Oh, well. It's been approved under that authority. They never picked it up, they were happy with it, why are you, why are you raising it as an issue?' It's like 'Well, I'm not interested what they approved, this is how it is here.'

In contrast to the reactive nature of the political and officer systems in Forest Town, Green Town Council's approach to issues of accessible dwellings is derived out of a political commitment to disabled people's rights that has its roots in the late 1980s. By 1988 the access officer for the town, who is still in post (at the time of writing), noted that:

> it was clear to me then that we were not going to be able to have a significant influence on the built environment, and housing in this particular context, unless we had something in the local plan, because developers were all going to point to 'Where is it in your local plan about a housing policy? How can you condition, what are these negotiations? It doesn't say anything in your local plan about accessible housing.' So unless you'd got the background of what, as a local authority, we were trying to achieve, unless you'd got that and that had been through the local plan process and had been agreed and got written into the local plan, then it was going to be difficult really to make a significant difference.

This reasoning led the access officer to suggest to councillors that the use of the local planning system to secure accessible dwellings was possible. However, as the access officer said, 'the first thing we did was get members onboard'. A supportive socio-political environment helped him to achieve this. The access officer noted that:

> a lot of it is because of disabled people themselves, disabled people in this area and their organizations have always been fairly proactive, and I know that some disabled people were politicians, and one or two of them who worked for the Coalition for Independent Living at the time were councillors on the county council ... there were discussions amongst members at the county council and the town council, and issues about accessibility were being brought forward, were being put on the agenda by disabled people.

As a result, the access officer suggested that 'I've never had nothing but total support. I think members can take a great deal of credit that access issues were on the agenda at an early stage, when perhaps they weren't so nationally.'

The approach taken by Green Town Council was to try and secure visitable dwellings through the local planning system although, as a building control officer stated: 'it had to be on a voluntary basis'. He explained further by noting that

we had difficulty persuading the government to let us set targets for what to achieve. They didn't like us putting the words 100 per cent, or 10 per cent or whatever; we could negotiate, we could have that figure in our mind but we couldn't write it down in the local plan. So members instructed officers to go away and negotiate a 100 per cent visitability and 10 per cent mobility. This was a bold approach because, legally, developers were not bound by the council's objective to secure accessible dwellings.

However, the access officer said that the approach was 'to try and persuade them, hopefully by the positive benefits there will be for the whole community. Builders were told, "You're going to have difficulty getting your planning application approved unless you comply." '

This approach had some dangers and, as the access officer highlighted:

our legal people were very apprehensive about all this policy, because they were concerned about appeals. So what members decided to do, very craftily, and they must have had some advice, they were advised legally that they would be on dodgy ground refusing a planning application purely on the grounds that the developer wouldn't play ball, but members just deferred them, and asked officers to go away and keep negotiating. So a developer saw his application deferred for further negotiation, and deferred again for further negotiation. The way that it worked was that when it came to determining a planning application, the planning officer would say, in planning committee, that 'we haven't been able to negotiate any visitability or mobility units with the builder; members said 'We're not happy about it', and 'We'd like you to go away and continue your negotiation and come back to us at the next meeting.'

The result was, as the access officer commented, 'that members only had to ever defer applications once, because I think it demonstrated to the applicants that the council was committed . . . that signal got around the house builders' network' (see Figure 6.9). The situation was helped by the town council's ownership of large segments of land in the town which, when selling on to builders, provided them with the opportunity to set conditions on the terms of sale. A building control officer outlined the context:

6.9 Houses constructed in Green Town, pre-Part M.

6.10 A patchwork quilt.

the local press'. The Regional Director of Wimpey did not like ramps and told the project manager on site to stop constructing them. The access officer gave Wimpey 'ample time' to comply with the legal agreement: 'they tried to get out of it by saying that they would fully comply in the next phase'. The council turned down this offer, and the publicity to the press meant that the company decided to do the 'decent thing'. By then steps had been constructed in some of the occupied dwellings, and it was impossible to go back to these to construct level and/or ramped access. The phase is a patchwork quilt; some dwellings have stepped entrances, others have ramped and/or level access.

The advent of Part M has potentially provided the town council with additional means to secure accessible dwellings. The approach to Part M by officers reflects the broader ethos of the town council in seeking to gain the maximum from builders. An officer explained the situation:

perhaps it's difficult for the developers to get their heads around the actual site that they're building on, particularly if it is a steeply sloping site. But there are solutions and I remember going to a presentation by the government's head of building regulations, Paul Everall, and one comment that still sticks in my mind is that he said, 'With some imagination and with good design there should be very few dwellings where ramped or level access cannot be achieved.'

The officer noted that this had become their 'bottom line', and, as he suggested, it was working because 'I'm not aware of any developments in the last twelve months here in the town where we've agreed to steps.'

members felt that there was a lot of development going off in the town, and that this was an opportunity to create a more accessible environment for everyone. I remember, at that time, the council was selling lots of land, we had lots of land, and in the terms of sale of that land, if I want to sell you a piece of land we can negotiate whatever we want to negotiate between us, we'll sell you the land if you'll do this, and you do that or whatever . . . that's the way we made it stick . . .

The council took a hard-line approach with builders not complying with the visitability criteria. In the early 1990s, Wimpey plc had a legal agreement with the town council to construct dwellings to include ramped and/or level access. However, as Figure 6.10 shows, some of the dwellings were constructed with stepped entrances so, as the access officer said, 'we let the members know about this through a committee report, and we reported it to

*   To preserve the anonymity of particular individuals who were interviewed for this part of the research, names have been changed.

7 Experiential knowledge as a component of housing quality

7.1 Introduction

> There can be no dichotomy between good design and usable design or between beauty and function in architecture.
>
> (Sommer, 1972: 4)

As previous chapters have intimated, the conventional understanding of housing quality, which conceives of housing as a physical structure and system, ought to be extended to incorporate an understanding of housing as a multidimensional and complex process – what Habraken (1972) and Rapoport (1977) refer to as 'dwelling' (see also Norberg-Schulz, 1985; King, 1996). An important dimension of the processes that underpin the constitution of dwelling relates to the users and/or occupiers. As Goodchild (1997: 60) comments, 'good practice in housing design may be understood as a process of empathy with the users' (see also Luck *et al.*, 2001). Likewise, Callado (1995: 1666) notes that the crux of housing quality is the issue of usability of dwellings or, as he suggests, whatever the physical or technical standards of dwellings 'they may all come to nothing should there be any limitation on the usability of space'.

The conception of the user, in whatever guise, is, however, alien to the contemporary house-building industry in which the social relations underpinning the design and construction of dwellings are characterized, for the most part, by little or no interaction between producers and users. This is particularly so in relation to the design of dwellings, which is preset and standardized and rarely altered in any significant sense from one construction site to the next (see Chapter 2). The process prompts actions and behaviour by builders and other building professionals which does not value, or seek to respond to or incorporate, consumers' practical knowledge or experience. Rather, users are labelled as 'consumers' to denote that the relationship is, first and foremost, a market transaction. Builders claim that they know what consumers want, and that there is no need for much market testing or interaction with their customers prior to the point of sale.

This chapter describes and evaluates disabled people's interactions with builders and building professionals. I begin by outlining the broader debates about the role and significance of users' involvement in and control over aspects of the design and construction process. I develop the proposition, after Brattgard (1972), that the success of a building depends in part on its acceptance by those who use it. In a second part, referring to interviews that I did with builders, building professionals and disabled people, I document their contrasting feelings and experiences about the role and importance of users' interactions with and involvement in the design and building process (see Appendix 1 for more details about the interviews). The material shows that disabled people rarely meet builders or related professionals, and that builders have little or no knowledge of disabled people and their needs. I conclude by describing the possible ways in which the design and construction of dwellings can be related more closely to the experiential knowledge of disabled people.

7.2 The relevance of experiential knowledge in the design process

A perennial debate in environmental design relates to the interrelationships between the aesthetic and the functional characteristics of the built environment. Since the earliest writings on design, and evident in Vitruvius's (1960) *The Ten Books of Architecture*, there have been endless disputes and debates about the appropriate role and *raison d'être* of architecture, architects and design professionals more generally (see Venturi, 1966; Bentley, 1999; R. Hill, 1999; Forty, 2000; J. Hill, 2003). These debates range widely, including the views of those (such as Le Corbusier, 1923: 35) who sought to propagate architecture as an artistic endeavour: 'architecture is a thing of art, a phenomenon of the emotions, lying outside questions of construction and beyond them ... architecture is a matter of harmonics, it is a pure creation of spirit'. For Le Corbusier (1923) the architect was conceived of as a supreme individual or, as Bentley (1999: 28) notes, 'a "heroic form giver", in which the built form is the product of creative and talented individuals'.

Such conceptions tended to elevate the architect or designer to a preeminent social position, in which the aesthetic style or form of buildings was privileged over its use (or usefulness). Here, the occupant or user was to be provided with and be given the benefits of architects' expert knowledge of spatial form and process. For Bentley (1999), such discourses, still propagated by elements of the architectural profession, are problematical because they tend to exclude certain subject matter from consideration by emphasizing the artistic, technical or investment attributes of buildings and the design process. The consequence is that the social, institutional and cultural context of design, relating to the social and political conditions that underpin and give shape to the production of buildings, is rarely considered. However, as Frampton (1989: 19) suggests, the social and political contexts that condition the building process are neither ephemeral nor insignificant and, as he says, 'society tends to transform the subjective originality of the work through the process of appropriation'.

One element of this relates to the fragmentation of the design and building professions into different 'expert systems', in which what is designed is dependent in part on the ways in which the views and practices of different professionals are combined (see Knesl, 1984; Jackson, 1996; Rabinowitz, 1996; Imrie and Hall, 2001a). The architect is one amongst many 'experts' that condition and influence the design process; this is indicative of, as Bentley (1999) suggests, the rise of modernist design (values) in which the application of science, technology and management, through the context of a multiplicity of experts, became paramount in the post-war period (Haviland, 1996; Ward, 2004). Thus, from the expertise of the interior designer to the application of the expert knowledge of building control and planning officers, design and construction processes post-war were characterized by the rise of a professional cadre, and what Bentley (1999: 250) refers to as 'design culture's systematic devaluation of lay knowledge'.

The devaluation of lay or experiential knowledge was characterized by the propagation of functionalist values and practices that were in turn creating environments that, in Illich's (1992) terms, were characterized by 'a world that has been made' (see also Rowe, 1993; King, 1996; Hill, 2003). For Illich (1992), and others, the functionalist paradigm of planning and design differentiated between 'those who know and those who don't' and, as Gloag (1945, quoted in Oliver *et al.*, 1981) suggested, architects, planners and others 'have become social reformers intent upon telling the contemporaries how to live, instead of providing them with the best background for living in their own way' (see also Hertzberger, 1991; Bentley, 1999; Hill, 1999). Others concurred, with Sommer (1972: 5) suggesting that the 'inescapable nature of architecture' is that people usually have no choice about occupying buildings, but do so with few opportunities to influence their design.

This view was one of a number that sought to (re)centre the user in the design process. For instance, Louis Mumford (1928: 298) wanted a reorientation in architectural ideas towards a broader, holistic understanding of people and nature, or, as he suggested, 'we must look for a finer relationship between imaginative design and a whole range of biological, psychological, and sociological knowledge' (see Hatch, 1984). For Mumford (1928), the 'good city' could only come about through a revived democratic society, and the 'recovery of civic participation' in design and planning processes (Luccarelli, 1995: 20). Others, such as Le Corbusier (1925: 52), were critical of design that did not respond to the human scale, or, as he suggested, the objective of design was 'to tie buildings back to the scale of the human being'. Likewise, for Alvar Aalto (1940: 16) buildings, to be worthy, had to be sensitive to human needs: 'to provide natural or an artificial light which destroys the human eye or is unsuitable for its use means reactionary architecture'.

These broader critiques have been mirrored by various commentators in relation to the design of mass or speculative housing, in which the theme of people's estrangement from the act of dwelling is evoked (see also Chapters 1 and 2). Thus, in commenting about mass housing, Le Corbusier and de Pierrefeu (1948: 23) presented a familiar refrain: 'men are ill lodged . . . nothing in nature is mass-produced, nor are ways of life and reason'. Habraken's (1972: 92) observations about the delivery of housing unaffected by user or experiential knowledge are not dissimilar in noting that 'we have the need to concern ourselves with that which touches us daily . . .' (see also Rowe, 1993). For Habraken (1972: 13), the problem was that the design and provision of mass housing, public or private, 'cannot be called a process of man housing himself. Man no longer houses himself, he is housed!'

The emergence of building professionals' focus on the user or consumer of the built environment, in the 1950s, did little to redress (lay) individuals' estrangement from the (modernist) systems of building design and production. As Forty (2000: 313) suggests, the term 'user' became part of 'the canon of modernist discourse', or a shorthand expression for those regarded as 'a source of information from which design could proceed'. Here, the user was conceived of in narrow, passive terms, as providing the material through which architecture, as Swain (1961: 508) suggests, might realize its potential by evolving 'techniques to help us to analyse the needs of the users of buildings . . .'. The user was, therefore, the object of social surveys and questionnaires, part of a process akin to forms of market testing. For Forty (2000: 314), the term 'user' also helped to describe the functional relationships between constructed (designed) space and social (or user) behaviour, in which the former, it was assumed, determined the latter.

Not surprisingly, far from challenging traditional functional discourses of architecture and design, the 'user' was, according to Forty (2000), a construct of advocates of functionalist design and process to legitimize their ideas and practices. In the post-war period, the need for mass housing and large-scale urban renewal elevated the spatial disciplines – architecture and planning – to a pre-eminent position in facilitating the reconstruction of society. As Forty (2000: 314) suggests, architects and planners were entrusted with the development and delivery of major public sector infrastructure programmes, based on the premise that the creation of the built environment 'would induce – in the face of persisting social differences – a sense of belonging to a society of equals'. Thus, throughout the 1950s to the late 1970s, consultation with and analysis of users was a feature of planning and architectural practices, although, as Forty (2000) implies, it was often half-hearted and never challenged the underlying socio-political structures of the building professions.

For instance, government reports and recommendations about housing quality were rarely based on experiential data or surveys of consumer tastes or desires, let alone proactive involvement from users in the construction and implementation of such survey work. From the Tudor Walters report of 1918 to the Parker Morris standards of 1961, government officials produced domestic design standards that were devised by and for professionals. Others concur, and Carmona (2001: 119) notes that probably the best-known housing design guide of all produced in the UK, the Essex design guide of 1973, 'was never based on any survey of residents' opinions' (see also Booth, 1982). When user involvement did occur, it tended, as it still does, to be as part of a post-occupancy survey, at the end rather than the beginning of the process, and so foreclosing opportunities for users to influence much of the content of the design and construction of the dwellings that they were to inhabit (see Hooper, 1999; Luck et al., 2001).

The marginalization of the user was compounded by the ill-defined nature of who or what the user was and, for Forty (2000), the user was 'a person unknown . . . an abstraction without phenomenal identity', that is, without sex, gender, impairment, ethnicity or any social ascription or sense of individuality. Lefebvre (1991: 362) was also guarded about the term 'user' and, as he suggested, it 'has something vague – and vaguely suspect – about it. User of what one tends to wonder.' For Lefebvre (1996), the (Cartesian) rationality of architects' and planners' practices, which conceived of space as 'represented' and pre-designed according to expert principles, reduced the user to a 'type', or an inhabitant of abstract rather than lived space. The everyday activities of users, as Lefebvre (1996) suggests, are not abstract or singular in type, but are part of a social morphology – that is, lived experiences analogous in complexity to a living organism.

Since the early 1960s, and especially in the 1990s, the term 'user' has been the subject of critique and reformulation to mean something more proactive than a 'provider of information'. One definition is of people or persons involved actively in the design process in which, in Hertzberger's (1991: 103) terms, they have 'the freedom to decide for themselves how they want to use each part, each space'. Others have sought to take this further. Instructive here are Lefebvre's (1996) writings on cities, in which he notes that the right to the city must involve active participation of people in its political life, management and administration, on terms which recognize the right to be different (see also Young, 1990; Isin, 2000). By this, Lefebvre (1976: 35) suggests that core to social justice is the 'right not to be classified forcibly into categories'. Such categories, for Lefebvre (1976), essentialize human behaviour and interaction, and in doing so deny, even suppress, the multiplicity of possible social encounters and experiences in cities.

Here, Lefebvre (1976, 1991) highlights the importance of local or vernacular knowledge in creating vitality in cities. Others concur, and, in the housing context, King (1996: 101) notes that the process of dwelling is a vernacular one which 'arises out of practice and voluntary discussion'. For King (1996: 101), it has to be a non-imposed process that evolves 'out of the practice of individuals relating together'. Dwelling cannot be planned nor manufactured; it is a reaction to 'the centralization and standardization of daily life' (King, 1996: 165). He notes that the role of government, housing professionals and others, such as builders, ought to be 'strictly prescribed' to ensure that dwellers are able 'to control their own dwelling environment'. Likewise, Brattgard (1972: 31) notes that accessibility can be compromised if the dwelling is regarded as a single solution 'that can be proceeded with in a mechanical way as a matter of arranging . . . physical materials'. Rather, a dwelling that functions well will best be achieved through a participatory design process.

The expectation that house builders will be receptive to the views of those such as Lefebvre, King and Brattgard does not seem tenable, because there is no culture of interaction between builders and customers in the building industry, other than through superficial forms of market testing. As Belser and Weber (1995: 125) note, 'although most builders seem to understand that the environment has an effect on the user, few give this much consideration when designing'. Indeed, most builders treat the customer or user as a 'generalized category', not differentiated by individual traits or characteristics. Such perceptual schema of customers does not provide for ease of identification of specific customer needs or demands, although certain categories of consumers, such as disabled people, tend to be seen by builders as requiring 'special provision' which, they argue, is not their concern (see also Chapter 5). A consequence is that disabled people, for the most part, are invisible within the context of the house design, construction, sales and purchasing process (Burns, 2004; P. Thomas, 2004).

The relative absence of a customer or user focus in house building more generally can be understood, in part, by some of the organizational and social relations of the building industry and, in particular, its commitment to design which is 'tried and tested', standardized and pre-set prior to the construction of dwellings (see Chapter 2). Naim and Barlow (2003) note that there are inbuilt inflexibilities in the house-building design and construction process that reduce the potential for builders and their design teams to be responsive to customers or users, or to even contemplate the use of experiential knowledge (Hooper, 1999; Carmona, 2001). Foremost is that, as Naim and Barlow (2003: 92) say, even if house builders wanted to introduce a greater range of house-types and designs, it is doubtful this could occur easily because 'the typical house building supply chain is simply not robust enough to cope with variabilities in customer demands'.

The demand for dwellings outstripping their supply also means that (at the time of writing) builders can choose to be indifferent to customers beyond a range of minimum design specifications. Naim and Barlow (2003) suggest that even if builders wanted to tap into experiential knowledge as a means of product development, it is difficult to do so because such knowledges are multiple and differentiated, and there are no clear techniques or methods to translate them into realizable products. They also highlight the role of building regulations and the regulatory contexts in prescribing design guidelines that reduce, so they allege, the scope for introducing greater diversity to house types. In this respect, while a customer focus in the design of dwellings ought to address how far customers or users are able to influence builders, it also needs to consider the mechanisms for user interaction with systems of building regulation. As section 7.3 outlines, the scope for disabled people to interact with and influence either builders or building control officers is limited, with builders and other building professionals placing little value on the use of (disabled people's) experiential knowledge.

7.3 Interactions between disabled people, builders and building professionals

Since the early 1990s, builders in the UK have been encouraged by successive governments to improve all aspects of their performance, including the development of sustainable construction techniques and practices, the adoption and use of new technologies, and the closer integration of market knowledge with systems of design and product development (see Egan, 1998; Naim and Barlow, 2003). Part of the changing context relates to governments' desire to enhance the quality of the design of the built environment by the encouragement of a paradigm shift in which construction, in the terms of the Commission for Architecture and the Built Environment (CABE, 2003: 12), 'should be about building places rather than just predicting need and promoting the basic accommodation to fulfil that need'. As part of the change, the government's sustainable communities plan (ODPM, 2003: 11) suggests that a prerequisite of attaining livable places, and the 'good city', is 'effective engagement and participation by local people ... in the planning, design, and long term stewardship of their community'.

This provides some encouragement to house builders to tap into, and use, lay or experiential knowledge, although government advice about how to achieve this is short on details. For instance, PPG3 (DETR, 1999a, paragraph 55) encourages local planning authorities to 'develop a shared vision with their local communities of the types of residential environments they wish to see in their area', but does not say how this should be done. More fundamentally, CABE's (2003) report on the value of housing design and layout says nothing in its 51 pages about the value of lay or experiential perspectives on housing quality. Likewise, the influential document *By Design* (DETR and CABE, 2000: 3), while encouraging designers to listen to lay persons' viewpoints, does so in such a way as to reinforce rather than challenge expert-based perspectives. Thus, the document says that good design will depend 'on the skills of designers and the vision and commitment of those who employ them'.

In some respects this may be sound advice, given the pre-existing social relations of design and construction, and the not unimportant roles of expert knowledge in the design process (Bentley, 1999). However, it ought not to preclude other possibilities, and it does make one wonder how far and in what ways the views of particular users, such as disabled people, fit into the processes that underpin the design of the built environment. The rest of the chapter turns to this theme, and, referring to testimonials based on interviews with building professionals and disabled people, seeks to describe and evaluate the different ways in which disabled people interact with builders and other professionals in the context of the design and construction of dwellings. I divide the discussion into two. First, I provide insights into builders' attitudes and practices in relation to responding to the needs of potential consumers or users, such as disabled people. Second, I describe disabled people's interactions with builders and other building professionals, and the effects on the quality of domestic design.

Professionals' approaches to the dwelling needs of disabled people

Welsh (1994: 5) notes that builders' interactions with customers are characterized by a marketing-led approach, in which volume house builders 'have no need to ask or build the public what they really want'. Aside from meeting estate agents, prospective purchasers of dwellings find it difficult, if not impossible, to meet or interact with builders, architects or others involved in the design and construction of dwellings. The main point of interaction of customers with builders and their agents is at the point of purchasing a dwelling, but even here the quality of interactions is such that the user or customer input is usually reactive. As already intimated, builders tend to regard the sales and marketing of dwellings as a non-problematical process that does not require much interaction with customers. As one builder, interviewed by me, said: 'we are supplying as much as we want to, and we have never have a problem selling'. Another builder suggested that 'we don't get that involved in consulting with customers on the design of our houses, we get on and design them and they sell easily enough'.

While builders say that they are prepared to respond to customers' requests to customize aspects of design and/or the layout of dwellings, this occurs within strictly defined parameters and rarely translates into substantial changes (Barlow, 1999; Carmona, 2001; Imrie, 2003a; Naim and Barlow, 2003). For instance, one builder noted that he was likely to have difficulties in responding to what he regarded as the specific, or specialized, requirements of disabled people because 'everything we use is pre-designed, packaged and already assembled, and it isn't easy to change any of this'. Others concurred, and for another builder, 'unless I get asked early on in the process, I can't change much, and, even if I do get asked early on I still can't do a lot'. Another builder felt likewise in noting that 'why should we do anything differently for disabled people, we've got a large customer base and can't customize everything'.

Builders rarely consider the provision of specific design features in dwellings unless prompted by a customer drawing attention to their 'special needs' (Heywood et al., 2001). As one builder recounted:

> Sensory perception is, it's never considered, never. We would never think of putting a hearing loop in a house, unless we had a customer who had a particular problem and came to us at the earliest point and said 'I'm different, can you do something for me?' We'll say, 'Well, yeah. Course we will, if we can accommodate it we'll do it for you, what do you want?'

Other builders said that they would rarely refuse to listen to a request for the provision of design features that departed from their standard designs and, as one builder suggested: 'I've had requests to lower the level of windows, and provide slip-proof paving, larger WC, corridors, the lot, and we can do it as long as whoever wants it gets to us before we start building, and is willing to pay a bit extra.'

The responsiveness of builders to disabled people's needs depends in part on the market segment that their companies are operating in, and the willingness of the design teams to incorporate into the process what are seen as additional design elements (see also Imrie and Hall, 2001a). For instance, the Chief Executive of a company that specializes in the construction of prestige dwellings for sale to wealthy consumers, suggested, in interview, that responsiveness to clients' demands is part of their approach to the process. As he explained: 'the nature of our clients dictates our approach. Most people get in quite early on ... they get in and specify some of the design elements to suit their own requirements inside.' This company was very happy to respond to anyone and, as the Chief Executive said: 'we've adapted a few properties in the past, not many, I must say, we haven't sold many properties to disabled people, but we have done them for wheelchair users, and they've had an input into various elements of the design process'.

Small building companies provide evidence of responding to the specific, customized design needs of disabled people. In one example the builder was approached by a couple, one of who was dependent on the use of a wheelchair. As the builder recounted to me in interview, 'they came to me with a clear understanding of what they wanted, they owned the land that the house was to be built on, and they approached us with a proposition and we did the rest'. The end result, depicted in Figure 7.1, is a dwelling made to the customers' specifications, including ramped access and level entry through all entrances, an accessible garden, all rooms at ground floor level, the provision of grab rails, reinforced walls, non-slip footpaths, and a WC facility large enough to permit ease of closure of the door. As the builder commented: 'we provided them with a one-stop job, and a local architect we use was more than happy to draw up the spec, and we've done a lot more than Part M'.

Such examples are, however, a rarity, and more likely than not disabled people have to take what is available or keep looking until they find something suitable. However, research by Burns (2002, 2004) suggests that disabled people believe builders to be reluctant to engage with the idea of property suitable for disabled people (see also P. Thomas, 2004). As one of Burns' (2002: 183–184) respondents said: 'Well, as far as the house builders are concerned they're not really interested in adapting or making new houses in the first instance to suit disabled people.' Other respondents were put off searching because past experience had led them to expect that nothing suitable was available: 'I think we just thought all the houses were the same. Laura's been in lots of shared houses and things and they're just silly sizes' (quoted in Burns, 2002: 185).

These observations support the feeling, highlighted in earlier chapters, that builders have little or no perception or understanding of disability, and

7.1 A customised house.

very few could recall selling dwellings to people that they regard as a 'disabled person' (see also Imrie, 2003a; Burns, 2004; P. Thomas, 2004). As one builder, in interview with me, recalled: 'I've never sold a house to a disabled person, and I've never ever heard of my sales staff talking to them about buying from us' (see also Chapters 2 and 5). Rather, builders tend to regard disabled people as 'disadvantaged consumers' who ought to be catered for by specialist housing providers, or, as a builder said: 'they've got their own providers to take care of them, it's not our job to do this' (see also Imrie and Hall, 2001b; Burns, 2004). Most builders said that they rarely get requests from disabled people to provide bespoke accommodation, and most conclude, therefore, that disabled people do not constitute an 'effective' demand.

However, as suggested in Chapter 5, the pre-conditions for disabled people to choose are not always present (e.g. the lack of income, the absence of accessible dwellings, etc.), and more often than not their housing needs are unheard or not articulated. As a disabled person, interviewed by me, said: 'how can we influence them, they don't see us as legitimate customers and until you change that attitude then they won't do anything'. Others expressed similar sentiments, with one person highlighting that they had given up searching for a home because they knew that there wasn't anything suitable to purchase: 'I've searched and searched, and I'm fed up looking for something that isn't there.' Another disabled person said, in interview, that 'I don't bother looking for places anymore, because there's nothing there and builders don't seem to listen or understand . . . I only hope that Part M and the DDA make builders react and listen to what we want and what we need.'

The prospects for this seem doubtful given that, as already intimated, the majority of builders rarely interact with disabled people and their organizations, either directly or through intermediaries, such as their architects or project managers (see also the next section). A typical exchange with a builder in interview was as follows:

Rob: On this site, have any disability groups, such as access groups, been involved in providing you with advice, or have you consulted with disabled people?
House builder: No, no, we haven't, no. I've never seen an access group. I've never witnessed them or seen them in action. They've never, they've never been to see us or make contact.
Rob: Has the local authority made any representations about disability issues?
House builder: No, no, and we wouldn't want to get involved in talking with them about these things.

This attitude appears to be framed by the broader logic, or rationality, of the building industry that regards (some forms of) consultation as a potential waste of time and detraction from their main business. Very few builders could provide examples or instances where they had interacted with disabled people in relation to issues relating to the design of dwellings. In one instance, a national builder recalled that their 'sales offices had stepped entrances:

so whilst we were providing level thresholds into the houses we weren't providing level thresholds into sales offices. We now ensure that we have got a level threshold, but only because this was picked up by the local access group who put us to rights.

For most builders, however, the approach to achieving accessible dwellings is one whereby they follow the legal rulebook, or Part M of the building regulations, and they do not want to enter into much dialogue about aspects of the design that departs from it. As one builder said:

The book is there, that's it. That's what we're going to deal with. And building control officers don't say 'we'll try and explore a mediation on your behalf through a consultative body'. They'll say, 'You tell us how you're going to do it, and apply by the approved document.' So it's then up to us to go through any consultative bodies to achieve something, and that's the way it works. Now, with all due respect to these bodies, we don't have time to attempt to get in touch with them . . .

The rationale for minimizing involvement with disabled people's organizations, or any organization for that matter, tends to be related to the possibility of time delays and the potential for loss of profit. One company explained this in the following terms:

we are in the commercial world, it would be wrong for me to say that we would be readily available to change anything, depending on the lobby of the disabled person. What we do, as I'm sure it's the case with many other developers, is the minimum. Because it costs money. Not a lot of money, but every bit counts.

Others felt that access groups and/or other disability organizations have their own agendas and fail to take into consideration wider issues and implications of the design and building process. In particular, builders referred to the narrow-minded nature of disabled people's groups as being caught up in their very specific concerns, often to the detriment of other building users. Thus, as one respondent commented, 'most of these organizations are unlikely to accept that their own interests are only one part of designing a building. There are many other considerations.'

For most builders there was the assumption that the regulatory or statutory parameters, such as the Building Regulations and the Disability Discrimination Act (DDA), are the legitimate results of consultations with the relevant groups and that no more is required in taking disabled people's views into account. For instance, as a builder's architect commented: 'I believe that mandatory requirements incorporated into legislation are the result of extensive consultation and that they are constantly evolving. I do not, therefore, see the need for such additional consultation.' Another voiced similar sentiments, and added that consultations are counterproductive in that 'if builders tried to satisfy all parties at all times then nothing would be built'. In this sense, even if builders wish to consult with disabled people and/or their organizations, they may very well be constrained by wider imperatives and pressures within the house construction process (see also Imrie and Hall, 2001a).

Interactions between disabled people and builders

In interview, disabled people were critical of builders' ignorance of their housing circumstances and needs, and felt that the content of Part M, and builders' approaches to design more generally, betrayed an absence of use of experiential knowledge (see also Burns, 2004; P. Thomas, 2004). Some questioned how far one could refer to Part M dwellings as comprising 'quality design', in a context whereby experiential knowledge was missing from the process: 'builders never talk to us, the regulation is weak, and we have no input into influencing what is built . . . it's not surprising that what we end up with isn't much good'. Others were scathing about general societal attitudes towards disability that they felt underpinned builders' approaches to the design of dwellings. As one person said:

> There are built in assumptions that carry on. Built in assumptions that it's okay to go to the back of the building, built in assumptions that we're not going to use some services, that we don't require some services, or that it's all right for other people to access those services for us, like posting a letter.

Some respondents, who were living in private dwellings that required adaptations, were particularly frustrated by the lack of consultation between themselves and the builders contracted to carry out the changes to their homes. One individual recalled the construction of a downstairs WC that did not accommodate their wheelchair:

> if my loo had been built eighteen inches longer it would have meant I could have got my whole wheelchair in, but I wasn't consulted about this. I thought that they would do a proper job . . . I was made to feel by the builder that I should be extremely grateful for what was provided.

Others were critical of architects and other professionals, such as building control officers, ignoring their expertise, and also felt that it was difficult to convey their points of view: 'it's our experience, we know what we need but we don't know quite how to get that over to them . . . they can easily ignore us and they haven't got into the habit of asking you'.

In particular, respondents were perplexed by differences between architects' drawings that had been presented to them for comment, and the final outcomes that did not always follow the original plans. For one respondent it was a matter of trust to let builders get on with it, but, as he said, that had been a mistake in relation to the conversion of an under-the-stairs cupboard into a WC:

> on the plans there was going to be a small corner sink where I could have a little bit more access, but no, to cut the costs down, I've got a damn great big washbasin, which is lovely, but it's something else I have to manoeuvre around. I wasn't told about it, I didn't have a say, it's just there and a nuisance.

Another person recalled the (re)adaptation of his bathroom, an episode that left him worse off:

I have a bathroom that had to be converted so I could use it. After it was done I said to the builder that it was wrong; I just wasn't actually consulted, and I had to move out of my house four times to keep having it altered. In the end, I told them that they were complete crap ... the whole thing had to be knocked down, and rebuilt for nine grand. To actually get somebody to do what was supposed to be done in the first place was nigh impossible, because the builder was so bloody-minded, saying, 'I'm right, I'm the builder, I know what to do.'

Others told similar stories, with George highlighting his frustration at not being able to influence a builder that he was negotiating with to change some of the basic features of a new build property. As he said:

the assumption is that you wouldn't know what your patio door should look like. A simple question from the builder like, 'Would you like a threshold?' might have avoided the threshold that's there now, and other mistakes being made too. But the assumption, I presume, is that you've got no skill or knowledge that would actually have been of value to the person putting in your door.

Likewise, Anne was less than pleased with her builder's approach to the recent conversion of her kitchen, which she described as one of indifference to and disinterest in her needs. As she said: 'he was hostile to suggestions that I made and that's the interesting assumption about disabled people, isn't it, we obviously have got nothing to contribute back ... he never paid any attention to me'.

There were, however, some exceptions, where builders were prepared to work closely with prospective purchasers in customizing aspects of the design of the dwelling. For instance, Sheila had heard that a new development was likely near where she lived and approached the builder at the pre-planning application stage. She wanted to purchase a bungalow built to her specifications, although, as she said, 'I had very limited knowledge of what they do or anything.' The builder introduced her to his architect and, as Sheila recalled, 'he did spend an awful lot of time then just popping in and talking to me and finding out what my needs were ... it was pretty good. I was glad I was able to say "Actually, I don't think that would work." ' As Sheila admitted:

I was very lucky, like I say, with my own housing here, because they literally did everything virtually that I asked them to do at not much extra cost. I just think I made a bit of a pain of myself in the end so they just thought, oh, you know, but I did have a very good working relationship with them.

Seeking to influence builders at a strategic, non-individual level is more problematical, and respondents, as members either of access groups or other disability organizations, said that there are few formal mechanisms for them to meet builders or their architects or agents. A member of an access group said:

> time and again planning applications seem to get through the system even though we don't like a lot of the design details. We never meet the builders or architects or anyone for that matter who might be important. The chair of the access group says there's no need because it will all be handled by the planners and the system ... well, it isn't from what we can see.

Other groups and/or individuals expressed similar experiences, noting that builders do little to facilitate access and usually ignore disabled people's views. As the chair of an access group said, with regard to a recently completed development: 'I spoke to building control and said that the scheme wasn't conforming to Part M ... I've written to the builder and they've ignored me and I've been on site to talk with them there but I was escorted off.'

Members of access groups recalled similar events whereby their presence on site was either not welcomed by the project manager and his team, or received with what one respondent called 'polite indifference'. For instance, members from one access group, based in a southern English coastal town regularly visit building sites, sometimes unannounced, and in recalling a recent visit one of its members said:

> I see the builders on site sometimes, and just have a chat with them. They'll listen to you, but then at the end of the day they'll ignore what you're asking. You know, some will take it into account, they'll say 'Oh well, I'll speak to our architect about that, see what he knows about it.' But that's only word of mouth, you know.

For others, the difficulty is trying to set up visits to building sites. A familiar experience was recalled by John: 'we did try to arrange a meeting with builders on-site, and we did try to arrange to meet some architects and have an afternoon with them telling them about our concerns ... but it never came off, there isn't the interest there'.

Off site, the main institutional route for disabled people to influence access issues is through the context of access groups. These are voluntary organizations that may receive funding by local authorities, and their remit is to comment on the impact of proposed (local) development on access. However, while access groups regularly comment on planning applications relating to non-residential development, there is no evidence, from this research, that disabled people are consulted about applications relating to dwellings, either prior to the submission of a planning application or building notice or at any stage in the process. Some do not see this as a problem, because they feel that the design of dwellings is not their business. As a disabled person said: 'in all the years the access group has been meeting up with architects, we've never met a house builder or commented on a housing development ... I've never thought that we should get involved in this'. Others concurred and, as another respondent remarked: 'there is an assumption that housing is a private matter and no concern of ours...'.

While others did not really disagree with this sentiment, it was felt that Part M now provides disabled people, through the context of access groups, with good reason to comment on applications for housing development. As a respondent from an access group said: 'we've chatted with one or two builders about housing but that's unusual, but we've never had the reason to do it ... Part M might now change all of this'. Others expressed stronger feelings than this and, as a member of another access group noted, 'we're here to push for accessible design, and we'd like to comment on everything, but officials here won't let us do this ... they don't think that housing is any of our business' (see also Imrie, 1996, 1999). This was a common observation, and reinforced by the chairperson (a local councillor) of one access group who, in justifying his stance that the inspection of planning applications in relation to dwellings was beyond the remit of the group, suggested that 'the members don't have any expertise to comment on such planning applications'.

The consultative process is therefore 'hit and miss', and influenced by variations in the nature of access groups and builders' receptiveness to disabled people's comments (if they are received at all). Most respondents said that big companies were the least likely to listen to them:

> The big building companies, they'll ignore us, they've got their own architects, they've got their own designers, but the small people, they tell us, 'Yeah, we can do that. We can adapt to that.' And you see the next time they put the next set of drawings in or plans, I said, 'Hey, look. They're listening.'

In one example, the access officer invites builders to present their proposals to the access group. As he said: 'I get the planning officer and developer to give a presentation on the detail, so that disabled people can feed in. Sometimes it takes a bit of persuasion to get them in but they usually come in if they think it might assist the planning process.' However, as he admitted, 'we rarely know how the views of the access group are absorbed into the final details, and we can't easily monitor this ... there's never much follow-up'.

This is a recurrent issue for disabled people, in that they do not often know what happens to the results of their consultations with builders. For some, there is the feeling that planning and building control officers do not follow up their suggestions with builders. As a respondent said: 'maybe it's passed on by officers and ignored. But in that case then building control could say "Well, stop work." You know, "Until you put that right you're not doing anything else." But I don't know if they do that.' Others related similar experiences of not knowing the results of consultations until too late in the process: 'we never see anything come back on them. The only time we've actually come across where we know they've ignored us, is where we've done our own walk round.' Likewise, another respondent noted that 'we know that our comments go to planning and building control, but whatever happens after that we don't know. The only way we find out is by turning up at some of the sites, and then you can see they haven't taken any notice.'

7.4 Conclusions

The testimonials in this chapter paint a picture of the building industry that is wedded to a hierarchy of social relations, in which the role of the customer or user is reactive and passive, and usually confined to interactions with builders at the point of market exchange. Beyond the sale and exchange of dwellings, builders' interaction with customers involves no more than market testing or research to gauge consumers' views about the product. Even here, builders do not 'market test' accessible design features (see Chapter 5; also Burns, 2004; P. Thomas, 2004). For most builders, the consumer is conceived of as a general category that is rarely provided with human characteristics or differentiated by social type or identity (Imrie and Hall, 2001b). Categories such as 'disability' or 'disabled people' are not likely to feature in builders' understanding of who a house is to be provided for, nor in the subsequent design, construction, marketing or sales of housing.

The relative absence of user input in to the design and production of housing, by disabled people and others, seems to revolve around the problematical assumption held by some that housing is a private good which is privately produced and consumed, and is not therefore an object of public scrutiny. Such views were articulated by most disabled people that I interviewed, and this was reinforced by their experiences, in access groups, of rarely being asked by officers to comment on the design elements of planning or building control proposals in relation to proposed residential developments. As members of some groups suggested, the practices of planning and building control officers appear to reinforce the view that residential developments are 'off limits' to scrutiny by access groups. However, the design and construction of housing is patently part of a process of public regulation and comment, from the specification of planning standards on densities to the application of building regulations in relation to matters such as lighting and drainage.

In particular, the contention of this chapter is that housing quality, and the construction of accessible housing, is dependent in part on user input and forms of user control over the design and construction process. The opening up of such processes to user scrutiny and control will depend on a shift in values about what is regarded by builders and other professionals as legitimate forms of user involvement in design and construction processes. Does this mean or entail backward integration of users into the formative stages of the design process, and user involvement in project formulation and development? How might this practicably occur? Likewise, if users are to be more than just the appendage of the professional, that is, an abstract tool and component, or self-serving part of a process, then they have to be given some substance and content (which may provide some clues as to users' uses of and interactions with the built environment), and means to exercise control over professional and expert opinion and action.

However, while this observation points to problems with 'expert culture', that is not to say that all forms of design expertise and practice are problematical or ought to be changed substantially. As Bentley (1999: 239) says, 'the problem . . . lies not so much in the fact that designers feel they are experts, as in the kinds of experts they feel themselves to be'. Far from denigrating the knowledge or expertise vested in architects or other design professionals, commentators such as Bentley (1999) and Brattgard (1972) note that there needs to be a rethink about the conception of expertise, and the development of structures and practices which draw on experiential knowledge, rather than deny or sideline it. As they suggest, the use of lay and or experiential knowledge in and of itself does not guarantee any improvement in the outcome of the design process. The essential task is to combine and conjoin different forms of expertise (lay and otherwise), in such a way that housing is designed and constructed as habitable dwelling space.

Further reading

One of the best pieces of writing about users and architecture published in recent years is Jonathan Hill's (2003) book, *Architecture and Users*. Readers are also advised to consult his edited text 'Occupying architecture: between the architect and the user' (Hill, 1998). Ian Bentley's (1999) book on 'Urban Transformations' is insightful and thought provoking, and one of the best about the interrelationships between users and experts in the design process; so too is the text by Richard Hill (1999), entitled *Designs and their Consequences*. In relation to disabled people's interrelationships with building professionals, it is worthwhile looking at Imrie (1996) and Imrie and Hall (2001b).

Case study
Cultivating influence through disabled people's organizations

This case study compares and contrasts the activities of two disabled people's groups, one in Wales and the other in the USA, that in their different ways have campaigned for accessible housing (and accessible environments more generally). The first example is the Welsh access group*. This was formed in 1988 after encouragement by Disability Wales, a national campaigning organization. Its first project was the pedestrianization of the town centre, and by the mid-1990s a full-time access officer's post had been created, although this was later disbanded. In its formative years the group received some nominal funding from the council or, as the present chair said: 'they said to us, "we'll give you fifty pounds a year to run the group", and now that's stopped and they're paying other people to get rid of us, I think [laughs]'. This comment is revealing of the poor relationships between the access group, council members and officers, in a context whereby disabled people feel excluded from the main decision-making procedures and processes in the town. As the chairperson of the group said: 'with what we're doing at the moment and asking for, I think they're probably going to hope that we vanish'.

The access group has become frustrated with what they regard as poor planning and lack of officials' attentiveness to access issues in the town centre. The chairperson pointed out, as depicted in Figure 7.2, a range of design deficiencies around the town that detract from the overall quality of the environment. As he said: 'look at the way the clutter gets in the way of my wheelchair, it's a mess, and the tactile walkways take you nowhere, or more likely make it dangerous for vision-impaired people'. In relation to housing, the group has met with 'nothing but official indifference, and just rudeness by some of the people we deal with'. In trying to push for more than Part M, the chairperson, John,

7.2 The route way for wheelchair users has to be shared with lampposts and other pieces of street furniture, while the tactile paving directs people with vision impairments straight into the main road!

wrote to the chair of the housing committee and, as he said: 'I asked her to consider lifetime homes and she never even bothered to reply to me. I spoke to the people at the council later on and she said "Yes, I've read your letter." And that was the end of it. That was their attitude, not bothered.'

The chairperson explained that the strategy of the access group is 'to try and persuade certain large house builders in our area to do what they should be doing, and also to change what's going to be built'. However, as he noted, they were getting little help from officers in planning and, in particular, building control: 'what is happening in building control at the moment, is that there's a lot of things that aren't happening . . .

* To preserve the anonymity of particular individuals who were interviewed for this part of the research, names have been changed.

and it is the same with transport and highways'. As John suggested;

the way that I'm trying to attack it is that I'm trying to change the fundamental way of thinking of the council, by persuading them that it's not our job to go and tell them that each dropped kerb that they put in is wrong, I'm trying to get them to understand that they need to understand what is needed to be done for disabled people ... they have to take the issue of empowerment right across the board, and to take it more seriously.

John described the relationship with the council as one whereby disabled people are trusting in authority, but are frustrated by the unresponsiveness of officials. As he noted:

You were told what was going to happen and you tried to influence but you didn't have a lot of influence, you didn't have the knowledge either to say what you really wanted, you relied on building control officers and planning officers saying 'This is what so and so's done, and do you like that?' Or this is what, you know, we've done, and you thought they were right. Now it turns out that a lot of things here aren't totally right, but that was all we knew at the time.

Another member of the access group recounted the resignation of the access officer:

I met him some time afterwards, and he said that he left because everything he tried to do, he just ran into a brick wall, and he said he got fed up of hitting his nose into brick walls ... he actually walked away because he was so despondent, dispirited, broken.

The lack of an access officer is a problem, because it means that the access group has no one inside the council to supply them with information. As a member of the group explained:

We still have a meeting with the council once a fortnight and we do try and ensure that all the houses are to Part M standards and the council were saying 'Yes, we would do it.' And unfortunately they weren't, which is where John got wound up about it and started going to town on it, now whether or not they are now, because being a small access group, you know, in all fairness most building sites are not accessible, when they start building a house you look at plans and you say 'Well, there's a step there.' Or whatever or that toilet you can't get a wheelchair into it or whatever, and they say 'Oh, we're sorting it out, we're talking to the builders, we're talking to the designers.' And again, you're at their mercy, they know better. And you think they're doing it, but whether they are, you wouldn't find out until the house was built.

A particular difficulty for the group is that the house plans they see do not convey much detail. As the chairperson said: 'one set of plans came in last month with, say, thumbnail sketches, thumbnail drawings of houses in the bottom right-hand corner, a drawing at the side and small house footprints on the corner. Now you couldn't do anything with them. I said, "Where are the drawings?"' To compound this situation, the group was told that the scheme in question was not being adjudicated by the council's officials, but by approved inspectors (see Chapter 6), and that they had no (legal) right to see detailed drawings. As a member of the access group said:

That's a real problem, now, that is a real problem, because it's going to go through the privatized approved inspectorate and then ... we have no rights whatsoever to go onto the land and look at the physical state of how a building is built on any location, unless it is open to the public, to the general public.

In seeking to circumvent officials, the group has taken matters into their own hands by making direct representations to builders. One of the struggles the access group referred to was trying to persuade builders to provide ease of access to their sales offices (as depicted in Figure 7.3). In making a representation to one builder, about removing steps into a sales office, a member of the access group was told by the site manager: 'there's no need to move them, we never get any wheelchair users here and if we did we'd come outside to talk to them'. This comment is not without irony as it was made to a wheelchair user who was visiting the site but, as this person said: 'legally we can't seem to do anything about this, and no one in the council is willing to support us'. He pointed out that the housing on site had been constructed with level access and thresholds, 'so why can't they do the same for the sales office?'

On another construction site, the group had more luck. They observed that a sales office had a stepped entrance, and that some of the (under construction) housing did not conform to Part M. The builder was operating with a type-approval from another local authority, and the group felt that their only recourse to get things changed was to approach the builder. The chairperson said that 'we proved to the builder that the approval that they had was wrong'. The builder conceded that both the sales centre and some of the dwellings were below the standard required. In a letter to the access group, a director of the company said:

> we will carry out a number of amendments to the sale centre … with regard to accessing ground floor toilets, a review of our complete range was carried out and the inadequacies pointed out by yourself were also evident in other house types, in the interests of clarity I have attached a compilation sheet in a before and after format, detailing improvements to all house types which have now been adopted by the company.

This 'little victory' was the exception rather than the rule, and, in contrast,

7.3 A sales office.

there is much more positive interaction between disabled people, officials and house builders in the village of Bolingbrook, a municipality of 67,000 residents located 35 miles southwest of Chicago, USA. Until early 2002, the preponderance of single-family homes being built in the area, which are excluded from the accessibility provisions of the FHAA, meant that very little of the new housing stock was being constructed to accessibility standards (see also Chapter 3). However, in February 2002 the Village Board developed a set of advisory or voluntary guidelines for the construction of accessible housing (including single-family dwellings). These guidelines required wider doorways, reinforced bathroom walls, a ground-floor bathroom that allows a wheelchair user to shut the door, accessible outlets and switches and, most crucially, at least one entrance without a step. Since the guidelines were developed, more than 1,500 accessible homes have been constructed in Bolingbrook. These guidelines were given legal status in November 2003.

The possibility for developing guidelines for builders, relating to the design and provision of visitable dwellings, was first raised by an organization called the Coalition for Citizens with Disabilities in Illinois in 1997. The Coalition was founded out of a context in which rules and regulations in relation to dwellings were nonsensical. For instance, the law relating to public access to goods and services, derived from the ADA, is such that a sales office on a housing development has to have level or ramped access to permit wheelchair users to enter. However, the homes that builders were constructing in Bolingbrook did not necessarily have to be built to visitability or any standards of access. As Edward Bannister, former chairperson of the Coalition, noted, 'All the sales offices have a ramp to go in, and that's what I told the Mayor. I said, "they have ramps to allow you to get in and look at the blueprints but when you leave that office you can't go and look at the houses ... it didn't make sense" [see Figure 7.4].'

Bannister contacted one of the key officials in the municipality, the Community Development Director (CDD), and suggested to him that a policy initiative to develop accessibility standards ought to be instigated. As Ed Bannister said:

I met with the CDD and I explained what was going on here, the fact that we didn't have any accessible homes, and he thought that a policy initiative on this made sense. So he started moving the ball forward and three months, four months, five months, eventually he got to a point when he said, 'Ed, I don't believe I can take it any further, you'll have to take it from here.' So I said fine and I set up a meeting with the Mayor.

Thus, the Coalition approached the Mayor to highlight the problem of the lack of accessible dwellings. As Bannister said:

I explained to him that people, good people, were moving out of Bolingbrook because they had nowhere else to go if they became disabled or elderly. There just weren't any appropriate dwellings. The Mayor's reaction was to survey all builders, asking them what they were going to do to rectify the situation.

The Mayor's reaction highlights the importance of the local political environment in influencing the attitudes and actions of builders. In Bolingbrook, the local political environment consists of a strong Mayor who is supportive of access issues, staff with good knowledge of the needs of disabled people, and the Coalition that draws elected officials' attention to access and related issues. As Ed Bannister stated, 'We are respected here. Disabled people are respected and we are listened to.' Bannister further explained, 'it is what I like to call inclusion, the people of Bolingbrook have accepted, and understand, that there are disabled and elderly people here and they have enough vision to know that people are living longer and therefore requiring more assistance in living, and accessible housing is one of them'. Given this, Bannister was not surprised by the Mayor's reaction because, as he commented, 'he is a no-nonsense, let's get this thing done, person, and his attitude is appreciated'.

This was demonstrated by subsequent events that made it clear to builders that they would not be doing any construction in Bolingbrook unless they conformed to advisory guidelines being drawn up on visitability. The

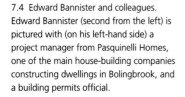

7.4 Edward Bannister and colleagues. Edward Bannister (second from the left) is pictured with (on his left-hand side) a project manager from Pasquinelli Homes, one of the main house-building companies constructing dwellings in Bolingbrook, and a building permits official.

Building Commissioner outlined the position that emerged:

> If you want to build in Bolingbrook, you need to apply for a permit from the Building Commissioner. The Building Commissioner will explain the advisory guidelines on visitability. You could then speak to the CDD or even the Mayor. They would all ask the same thing to any developers and that is to follow the visitability guidelines.

However, at the outset of the policy initiative to develop accessibility standards, Ed Bannister agreed to proceed incrementally. As the Building Commissioner commented:

> Ed [Bannister] asked if we could mandate just at least one model home to have visitability ... the mandate I got from the Mayor was every one of them should conform to visitability standards, why should it just be confined to one model or just the models themselves, why can't we do it all. And that's how it mushroomed into where we are at today.

An important part of the success in gaining builders' acceptance of visitability standards in Bolingbrook was the willingness of one building company,

Pasquinelli Homes, to take the lead (see Figure 7.5). Bannister recalled that when the Chief Executive of Pasquinelli was presented with the proposed standards, he said, 'Oh, we think that's fair and we can do this.' As Bannister said:

> they were the only builder not to give us any static. They were the first builders to build accessible homes and they are the ones that we go to whenever we want to show people what can be done. They welcomed us with open arms, not only do they make the first floor visitable, but they made the

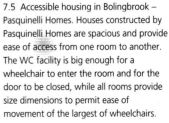

7.5 Accessible housing in Bolingbrook – Pasquinelli Homes. Houses constructed by Pasquinelli Homes are spacious and provide ease of access from one room to another. The WC facility is big enough for a wheelchair to enter the room and for the door to be closed, while all rooms provide size dimensions to permit ease of movement of the largest of wheelchairs.

second floor visitable too. So if a disabled person moves into one of those units and they needed access to the second floor they can put in a rail-ride to ride up to the second floor, and when they got there the doors are wide enough, and the bathrooms are large and everything.

Staff in Bolingbrook suggested that Pasquinelli's attitude and actions were vital to the success of the visitability codes because, as one inspector said, 'now we have other builders coming here and seeing what has been done and saying, well, I'm sure we can do that'. The inspector continued by saying that

the fact that Pasquinelli took a strong position in support of visitability allowed other builders to see for themselves how easily visitability standards could be implemented. Once you have the houses in place it's easy to just go see, to take other builders out to show them, and it's easy to look at the plan, you know, pull it out of the file, say here's what they're doing with their homes you can do with yours.

The Building Commissioner concurred, and commented:

after Pasquinelli, we had a meeting with another house builder, I forget who it was, and they said, 'Well, we can't do the no-step entrance.' I said, 'Who said that?' They said, 'Well, our architect.' I said, 'Well, Pasquinelli's architect figured it out, your architect must not be as smart as theirs' [laughter].

Despite the strong political support for the development and enforcement of the visitability codes, some builders try to side-step them. However, as Bannister said, a national builder, Pulte, is constructing (at the time of writing) 1,200 new dwellings to visitability standards. However, this builder was not initially enthused by the idea of building all

dwellings to the visitability code, and Bannister recalls that they 'suggested an alternative to the no-step entrance'. Bannister amplified by recalling that:

They had a portable ramp that they were going to install in the garage and hang on the wall to use when needed. The Mayor said 'no', he said, 'I'm not going to make that call, you need to talk to Edward Bannister.' So they got to me and they said 'We want to do this.' I said, 'we cannot sanction that'. The end result was Pulte's compliance with the access codes.

In seeking to ensure compliance with the access codes, the approach of building inspectors is proactive and is characterized by a positive attitude towards disabled people. As the CDD said:

in the building division we have six building inspectors, and they are knowledgeable about access issues and determined to make sure dwellings comply fully with the standards. The process here is that builders have to submit their building plans, and the elements of visitability have to be contained in those plans, and then they're required to call us at certain stages of construction to go and inspect it. So there will be a rough framing inspection, there will be a rough plumbing, rough electrical, prior to that we'll just check the footing and foundations and make sure that they're adequate and deep enough and so forth, and then they have to call us up again. They have to do that because if they cover something up, if they put sheet rock on a wall and we haven't checked the plumbing or electric, they will need to remove the sheet rock. You cannot by-pass an inspection.

In contrast to the attitudes of building control inspectors in England and Wales, who felt that Part M was adding to their workload, inspectors in Bolingbrook said that the codes relating to visitability did not generate any additional work, and that they were a welcome addition to the range of codes that they have responsibility for. As an inspector explained:

in a single-family home we'll do twenty inspections by the time construction has ended, including the driveway and the front sidewalk and stoop, and, regardless of visitability, it has no impact on the amount of inspections we do because we're either inspecting a concrete porch and sidewalk or a concrete ramp and stoop, it makes no difference. It doesn't have any impact on our department what so ever, other than producing the code text for visitability standards,

The inspector concluded by noting that, 'it's a pleasure to enforce a code that will improve the lives of people here in Bolingbrook'.

PART III
PROMOTING ACCESSIBLE HOUSING

8 Inclusive domestic environments

8.1 Introduction

We shall only solve our problems if we see them as human problems arising out of a special situation; and we shall not solve them if we see them as . . . generated by our being somehow unlike others.

(Kwame Anthony Appiah)

It seems an irony that at a time when television programmes and other media outlets in the UK are presenting housing as the ultimate consumer good, many disabled people can barely afford to rent or purchase a property that is responsive to their access, and other, requirements.[1] The apparent rise of the nation's obsession with property values, and the encouragement of consumers to search for the idyllic house in the appropriate setting, contrasts with the realities for many, in which a decent property is either unaffordable or inappropriate in meeting particular needs. For many disabled people, particularly those who use a wheelchair, most houses are impossible to get into without assistance and, even if an accessible threshold is provided, they do not provide wholly livable spaces or design features that facilitate ease of use. Rather, as previous chapters have conveyed, the design of much housing is poor by its failure to accommodate bodily impairment and the multiple, often unpredictable, ways in which people seek to use dwelling spaces.

There is no single reason for the inaccessible nature of much of the housing stock, but rather a multiplicity of factors that conjoin in different ways to produce houses that are rarely designed in ways that are sensitive to the needs of disabled people. In particular, the attitudes and practices of builders and other building professionals should not be held to blame for deficient design of housing; rather, builders' understanding of and reactions to the needs of disabled people cannot be separated from broader societal definitions of and practices related to disability, or from the rationalities of real estate that underpin the speculative building process (see also Imrie and Hall, 2001a). This is not to absolve individuals from particular actions and the consequences of them, but to situate such actions in the broadcloth of social, political and institutional relations that enframe and give content to the different ways in which professionals in the building industry respond to disabled people's needs for physical access into, and movement and mobility around, housing.

In this respect, one of the arguments in the book is that the design of housing in the UK, and most other Western countries, revolves around prescribed standards (of physical dimensions and performance) which, allied to the industrialized processes of mass production, provide limited scope for flexibility in/of use. This observation forms the cornerstone of arguments of those who, like Papanek (2000: 220), regard contemporary design and its objects as (re)producing no more than 'a utilitarian and aesthetic standard often completely unrelated to the consumer's need' (see also Habraken, 1972; Turner, 1976; Bloomer and Moore, 1977; Rowe, 1993; Bentley, 1999; R. Hill, 1999; J. Hill, 2003). Rather, consumers' needs have tended to be defined by builders and designers in relation to the provision of specific building 'types', or pre-set design packages that, as previous chapters have suggested, are based on what Rowe (1993: 62) terms 'a generic characterization of occupant populations and their spatial requirements'.

This generic characterization, as Bloomer and Moore (1977) note, is usually deployed by architects, builders and others in ways which leave it devoid of references to sex, gender, ethnicity, disability or other social categories such as children. As material in Chapter 1 suggested, government reports on housing standards in England and Wales, from Tudor Waters to Parker Morris, have said little about how changes in internal layouts and the deployment of specific physical standards might benefit or be sensitized to disabled people. In part this is because of discourses (of disablement) that are underpinned by a medical conception of disability, which conceives of the defective (impaired) body as a deviation from the normal physiological or organic state and, as such, an aberration confined to a small part of the population. Disability in this view is a minority concern, and ought to be responded to either by providing medical cure and rehabilitation, or alternatively by recourse to special measures or programmes, such as mobility housing, to accommodate those that cannot be 'cured'.

Either way, disabled people are conceived of as separate from the mainstream and, as a consequence, not an object or subject of the design and building professions. For instance, the testimonies of some builders and building control officers, in Chapters 5 and 6 respectively, suggest that they have limited knowledge about disabled people and their needs, and regard them as a minor consideration in building projects. Disabled people are seen as insufficient in numbers to constitute an effective demand, and as a consequence Part M is seen as being 'over the top' and excessive. Builders in particular have argued for a 'proportionate' response to the housing needs of disabled people, in which the requirement should be for no more than a quota of housing to be constructed to accessibility standards. For most builders, access regulation, so they allege, increases costs of construction, reduces scope for innovation in design, and will reduce the overall quality of housing. However, the evidence to back up such claims is, at best, equivocal.

This final chapter considers the main messages from the substantive parts of the book and, in particular, addresses three issues. First, I develop the argument, after Illich (1992), King (1996) and Habraken (1972), that one potential way to develop accessible housing for disabled people is by a vernacular housing process. I describe the elements of this process, and evaluate how far it is able to provide quality of habitation for disabled people. Second, I consider what the components of a policy 'agenda for change' ought to be, with respect to the provision of accessible housing, and what they realistically can be, given the pre-existing social, institutional and political contexts of housing provision and consumption. Finally, I conclude by providing some thoughts on future research directions and priorities in relation to issues of accessible housing, disability and the built environment.

8.2 The inclusive dwelling

Part M, and regulations like it, are part of a broader system of values and attitudes that seek to minimize the scope of policy intervention in builders' practices and, in doing so, to rely on their goodwill and voluntary conduct to achieve high standards of building quality. However, builders tend to construct to the minimum standards, and observations about Part M, by builders, building control officers and disabled people, often pointed to the regulation's palpable lack of quality in requiring not much more than modest adjustments to the design of housing (Imrie, 2003a). For instance, the experiences of builders since the inception of Part M have led most to say that the regulation is easy to achieve. As material in Chapters 5 and 6 suggest, builders and building control officers tend to think that the regulation is half-hearted because it does not respond to the needs of those who are not wheelchair users and/or individuals without mobility impairment, nor does it provide ease of use of spaces within the home environment.

Thus, as evidence in Chapter 5 indicated, some builders were sceptical about a regulation that did not permit people to live with ease of independence in the house, and were puzzled as to why certain requirements (such as provision of lifts in flats), were excluded. Likewise, building control officers, like builders, were sometimes perplexed by aspects of the regulation (such as the dimensions of the WC) which they felt were not well suited to the objective of Part M – that is, to create a context for disabled people, particularly wheelchair users, to visit a dwelling (and have access to a downstairs WC). For most builders and building control officers, then, Part M appears to be contradictory, and lacks clarity in relation to its technical guidance. However, despite the fuss that builders made about the introduction of the regulation, there is little evidence, as suggested by material in Chapter 5, that it has had detrimental effects on any aspects of the construction process.

The extension of Part M of the building regulations to incorporate the access needs of disabled people might, at face value, seem to signify a qualitative shift in attitudes and practices by builders and others towards the provision of accessible housing. However, while I do not doubt that the regulation has some positive aspects, it is problematical because of its encouragement of a physical or technical approach to housing quality. As outlined in Chapter 1, a technical approach to housing quality is concerned primarily with the house as a functional system that performs according to prescribed physical standards. It is an approach to housing that, for Habraken (1972), King (1996), Rowe (1993) and others, encourages builders to focus on and seek to attain often preset, usually standardized, aggregate physical structures, within the context of rule and regulation characterized by 'authoritarian direction and centralism' (King, 1996: 158).

Such authoritarianism underpins the broader rationale of regulation, post-1997, in which successive Labour governments in the UK have developed policies that promote the 'rights and responsibilities' of citizens. Within this framework, as suggested in Chapter 3, disabled people's rights to social support, and other forms of state welfare, are conditional on their discharge of responsibilities to develop their capacities and capabilities to lead independent, self-directed lives in which a reduction of (their) dependence on the state is a key objective (of government). The state's regulation of access to housing is, arguably, part of the deal in which a disabled person's rights to access, as guaranteed by law, provides in turn a context (i.e. an accessible house) in which independent living, free from social support, might take place. Seen in this way, access legislation and regulation may have little to do with housing quality *per se* as the paramount objective, and more to do with the restructuring of particular aspects of state–citizen relations.

That access regulations, in the UK, the USA and elsewhere, appear to fall short of helping to create houses with potential 'to activate' disabled people, or provide them with living spaces that facilitate ease of use and, potentially, greater independence, is in part a reflection of the political struggles between builders, disabled people and others in seeking to determine the scope of legislation. Such struggles tend to occur within a political and policy context or culture that is characterized by terms of engagement dominated by professional or expert opinion about what housing policy ought to be. As King (1996) suggests, policy and practice in relation to housing revolves around provision and utilization, and physical structures and their material values. The focus here of policy-makers and builders is primarily output of units, and the control of costs and maximization of (developers') profits, in which the role of regulation is to prescribe and control for the material substance and layout of housing.

In turn, construction and building practices are directed, potentially, towards 'fixed' or prescriptive design solutions that demonstrate ignorance of physiological differences and do not, in Wylde *et al.*'s (1994: 1) terms, 'support the variations in human abilities'. This observation helpfully draws attention to the reductive mentality of 'standards' which, as Franklin (2001: 86) suggests, have intuitive and practical appeal for both builders and regulators because they facilitate the ease of understanding and operationalization of regulations. However, such understanding is, problematically, couched in terms whereby the FHAA, Part M and other regulations are seen as 'additive' – that is, comprising a set of special features, rather than essential or intrinsic to good design. The emphasis on 'standards' is also likely to encourage builders and regulators to regard them as 'ideals', as the best possible solution, 'rather than the minimum that they are' (Wylde *et al.*, 1994: 248).

In seeking to understand what housing quality is or ought to be as the basis for influencing the content of accessible design for housing, one of the arguments of the book, following authors such as Turner (1976), Habraken and Illich (1992), is that a house is much more than a physical structure or its valuation as a commodity for exchange. Far from being just a 'thing', an object or material artefact, a house is, for Humman (1989: 272), 'the place of manifesting and creating identity of self, and between self and community'. Testimonials from disabled people in Chapter 4 confirm the potency of place of habitation in influencing (self) identity and, as Turner's (1976) study of housing suggests, the important thing about a dwelling is not what it is but what it does in people's lives. In this respect, 'dwelling' ought to be, as suggested in Chapter 1, a context that facilitates the capabilities of citizens to perform what Nussbaum (1999: 39) refers to as 'central human functioning' or activities 'that are definitive of a life that is truly human'.

These observations form part of a tradition of thinking that rejects the values and policy content of modernist housing production and consumption, and instead seeks to offer alternative ways of habitation which are centred on and derived from the dwellers' affective and material needs and feelings (see also Chapter 1; Bloomer and Moore, 1977; Wright, 1980; Rowe, 1993). In particular, King (1996: 169) suggests that the discourses of modernism perpetuate a situation in which 'housing is provided for people rather than by them – it is made and equipped by others according to standards made by others'. The result, as Habraken (1972: 16) suggests, is the estrangement of the dweller from the dwelling, characterized by the determination of what the dwelling is 'before the occupier is in any way concerned'. For Habraken (1972: 13), the inhabitant (of mass housing) remains 'lodged in an environment which is no part of themselves'.

Habraken's (1972) point is part of a broader series of ideas espoused by those who regard speculative housing processes as having failed to produce and deliver quality housing to citizens (see Noberg-Schulz, 1985). Turner (1976) calls for changes in the social relations of housing production, not dissimilar to King's (1996) observation that what is required is a vernacular housing process. Building on the work of Illich (1992), King (1996: 161) notes that a vernacular process is based on the provision of housing 'that is not planned, manufactured and imposed on communities and households'. Rather, housing as a process, as a dwelling, is more than just the provision of a material structure but is, for King (1996: 162), 'a layered process in which our private refuge is linked to public institutions, urban space, and human settlement'. What is required, so King (1996: 164) suggests, is to return to the pre-modernist traditions of housing production and consumption, based on (alleged) processes of housing design that are sensitized to context and 'localized through referencing to historical links'.

An important part of this vernacular housing process, as intimated earlier, is control by individuals over their dwelling circumstances or, as Turner (1976: 162) notes, 'only when housing is determined by households and local institutions and the enterprises that they control, can the requisite variety in dwelling environments be achieved'. The vernacular approach to housing emphasizes the importance of the 'self-made' place, or what King (1996: 166) notes is 'the habitual, the traditional, the familiar', and not that which is imposed. For King (1996), the vernacular process provides the basis for creating the 'inclusive nature of dwelling', or that which is, so Norberg-Schulz (1985) suggests, the means to enhance and maintain our familiarity with the environment (see also Rowe, 1993). Inclusive dwelling is characterized by autonomy or self-control over housing circumstances (see also Somerville and Chan, 2001). It is where one acquires what Spinelli (1989: 109) refers to as an authentic mode of living, that is, 'independence of thought and action, and subsequently feel in charge of the way our life is experienced'.

Most disabled people seeking to find accessible housing will empathize with such sentiments. However, given the present social and institutional relations of housing provision and consumption, it is difficult to imagine how far, and in what ways, a vernacular housing process can be encouraged. The pursuit of a vernacular process ought to be cautious about rejecting, in total, 'modernist' housing and the processes underpinning their production and consumption. It is problematical to characterize all housing designed and constructed in the period since the late nineteenth century as failing to respond to particular human needs. The rise of mass housing was, for Giedion (1929: 9), a response to the shortage of housing and the need for 'dwelling for the common man'. Likewise, Norberg-Schulz (1985: 108) notes that mass housing 'undoubtedly represented a significant contribution to the improvement of man's living conditions'.

The idea of vernacular housing also appears to refer to an age in which, so it is claimed, the provision and consumption of housing was closer to the ideal of 'inclusive dwelling'; this viewpoint harks back to some sort of 'authentic existence' (King, 1996). However, this is an overly romantic and probably erroneous understanding of previous periods of housing consumption. Even if it contains some degree of accuracy, it is unclear how housing contexts, in different periods of history, might be (re)created as part of a process to provide accessible housing. The emphasis of the vernacular housing process on 'self help', and autonomy or self-control, raises issues about whether society comprises a range of competing cultural and social groups and/or individuals with separate, distinctive needs and interests, or, alternatively, whether it is a collective whose needs can be expressed and understood through universal needs and discourses.

The distinction between the particular and the universal here is important, if only for disabled people and others to articulate their housing needs in ways that, while recognizing specific contextual features (e.g. impairment), does not diminish the importance of their shared human characteristics with others. The dangers of an emphasis on 'the vernacular' is that, in identifying the needs of specific cultural and diverse social groupings, a politics of housing might result that plays one group off against another, opening up new political conflicts and forms of oppression (see Fainstein, 1995). Thus, in Fainstein's (1995: 34) terms, there is the danger that a vernacular process, by opening up a multiplicity of individual and/or group identities, may well lead to a 'cycle of hostile action'. In this respect, the pursuit of 'inclusive dwelling' ought to have regard to specific needs and demands, but within the overarching context of what Fainstein (1995: 34) calls 'a consistent generalisable ethic, regardless of the specific circum-stances'.

In relation to disabled people and housing, this ethic ought to relate to the inability to inhabit or to be a full person, in a context where the processes of construction and design of housing prohibits their entry into and ease of use of habitable spaces. As Thomas Hobbes (1996) noted, mobility is fundamental to the liberty of the human body, a point that is relevant to dwelling or access to a place where basic forms of (bodily) reproduction can be carried out (with dignity) (see also Blomley, 1994; Law, 1999; Imrie, 2000b; Imrie and Hall, 2001a). That most of the housing stock does not provide disabled people, especially wheelchair users, with the means for dignified bodily reproduction ought to be an observation that is the starting point of an agenda for change which at its core should be underpinned by the premise that, given the intrinsic nature of impair-ment in society, it is an issue of concern to every person.

8.3 An agenda for change

The emergence of non-disabling home environments, or places that facili-tate the movement, mobility and access of disabled people, is far from being realized. While a practical politics of disability can address imme-diate, tangible, concerns about the inappropriate design of housing and home environments, it needs to be aligned to a broader agenda of change (see, for example, UPIAS, 1976). This agenda, at its root, ought to consist of a programme of transformations in attitudinal and value systems towards disability, housing quality and design (see Oliver, 1990; Barnes *et al.*, 1999). As Dikec (2001: 1793) notes, this ought to comprise nothing less than the development of 'new sensibilities that would animate actions towards injustice embedded in space and spatial dynamics'. This, for Dikec (2001) and others, should engender a political process and programme to challenge the conceptual and moral terms of reference, as well as the practical activities, of those individuals and their organizations involved in the (re)production of the built environment.

At its broadest level, the challenge should not underemphasize the possibilities of the perpetration of unjust process and outcome in and through the institutional processes of real estate. As suggested in Chapter 1, injustice can be related, after Young (1990), to systematic exclusion, domination and oppression, in which domination (in spatial terms) is exemplified by the (re)production of unequal spaces, such as inaccessible houses, that permit some people to enter housing and others not. Such inequalities play a significant role in the reproduction of the conditions of domination, and have the potential to create oppression or situations in which individuals, unable to gain access to a house, are prevented from developing and exercising their capacities and capabilities (as human beings). While the absence of control and/or choice associated with oppressive social actions cannot be disassociated from the social relations of real estate, it is improbable that much will change. However, a number of politically pragmatic and practical options ought to be considered.

An important part of the process ought to be the (re)education of pro-fessionals working in real estate, including the teaching of access issues on appropriate degree and continuing professional development courses. Such teaching ought to raise issues relating to the morality of spatial form and process, and to issues about just process and outcome in relation to the design and construction of housing. There are, however, limits to what education can achieve, and some commentators are cautious about its role and potency in reducing acts of unfair treatment against disabled people (MacDonald, 1991). Tisdale (1999: 13), writing about racial discrimination, notes that 'the push to make education a remedy for racial discrimination is predicated on the assumption that discriminatory acts are perpetrated by well meaning but slightly biased or uninformed persons'. For Tisdale (1999), education is a necessary yet insufficient means of changing prejudices and practices, and it ought not to be the dominant means of seeking to change unfair treatment.

In this respect, a legislative route or response to guarantee accessible housing appears to be inevitable, although, without changes to some of the underlying assumptions in legal discourse about disability, it will be limited. Indeed, as suggested in Chapter 3, law and legal process may be part of the problem and not the solution (see also Blomley, 1994). This is because legal regulation, such as Part M, perpetuates a discourse of design that does little to acknowledge the complex ways in which people's identities and emotions are entwined with domestic settings or environments. Rather, the legal regulation of access to housing is, problematically, underpinned by values and practices that seek to evoke prescriptive 'physical standards and rules'. These are premised on a reductive, medical conception of disability as a phenomenon that is derived from and determined by impairment. This combination, as argued in previous chapters, is a recipe for a static approach to building design that has potential to 'blame the victim' for (his or her) lack of access to and usability of housing.

In seeking to overcome some of the problems of Part M, builders' attitudes and practices in relation to disabled people, and the failures of the speculative building industry in providing accessible and livable dwellings, a practical politics of access needs to be developed (see Imrie and Hall, 2001a). This politics ought to work within the existing structural constraints of the speculative house-building process, while seeking to push its main actors and agents towards practices that have, at their core, a commitment to disabled people's housing needs. A broad range of interrelated issues needs to be addressed:

- The main approach by government to housing in the UK is based on the method of 'predict and provide'. This method is one whereby government is concerned, as King (1996: 33) notes, 'for the numbers of dwellings of a particular type' and with creating the conditions for new construction. Arguably, it is a necessary part of the process of housing quality (i.e. the supply of housing) but, in and of itself, it is a singular approach to what are broader complexities relating to the provision and consumption of housing. 'Predict and provide', in relation to housing, is apparent with the government's estimation that 4 million new households will be formed by 2020, and that they will have to be catered for by providing new housing (ODPM, 2000a). The method is one of extrapolating existing demand to some point in the future, and then seeking to match the projected demand with the supply of the relevant good (i.e. housing). The problems of the method are well known, and include the generation of latent demand by virtue of increasing supply (see Vigar, 2002). The approach is more concerned with quantitative than qualitative aspects of housing, and is not likely to focus policy attention on those aspects of housing quality that relate to dwellings as integral to supporting 'ways of living'. 'Predict and provide', as core to government's housing strategies, ought to be modified in ways that permit alternate measures of housing quality to come to the fore.

- In this respect, a more sensitized direction, in seeking to achieve housing quality for disabled people in relation to the design of housing, is for academics and policy-makers alike to recognize the importance of an understanding of the interrelationships between corporeality, design and dwellings: that is, with the embodied nature of dwelling. Such understanding ought to contribute to the interlinking of housing studies to studies of disability by recourse to, I would suggest, theories that acknowledge the complexities of the body and corporeal processes (see Shilling, 1993). An objective ought to be the recognition of and responses to the diversity of bodily needs in the built environment, by (re)producing flexible forms that affirm (bodily) ambivalence and irony (rather than seeking to reproduce a static, singular conception of the body) (see Bloomer and Moore, 1977; Grosz, 1994). Reflexive building practices are required: these ought to be 'open-minded', without boundaries or borders, and sensitized to the corporealities of the body. To translate such observations into practical plans and designs for housing may seem difficult, but it is not impossible. As a first stage, designers, project managers and others ought to be provided with guidance, through appropriate design manuals, about the multiplicity of human (bodily and sensory) needs in relation to habitation.

- An example relates to making simple, yet important, differentiations between different 'types of bodies' and/or users of domestic spaces. For instance, inclusive housing design is often inattentive to particular people, especially children, and is, in Allen's (2004b) terms, 'adultified'.[2] In research conducted for the JRF, Allen et al. (2002) note that barrier-free homes often have small gardens because it is assumed that only single adults will live in them. The assumption is that disabled adults tend to be single and do not need the garden space. However, it is not uncommon for disabled adults to live with other people and to have children who may well want garden space for play purposes. Allen et al.'s (2002) research highlights a situation where a small family (e.g. two adults with a disabled child) was allocated to a house that was basically designed for a single-person wheelchair user. While the width of the living room door was wide enough to allow a wheelchair to pass through, the living room space appeared to be calculated according to the assumption that one wheelchair user would use it. As Allen (2004b) suggests, 'so what if there is a family living there? They could not all use the living room at the same time.'

- A range of commentators note that accessible design in housing depends in part on the use of experiential knowledge in the design process (Bentley, 1999; R. Hill, 1999; J. Hill, 2003). However, there is social, cultural and political resistance to changing user involvement and/or participation in housing and construction processes. In part this is because housing is seen as a private good and not of concern to the wider public. As material in Chapter 7 indicates, while access groups regularly comment on planning applications relating to non-residential development, there is no evidence that disabled people talk with builders (or their representatives) either prior to the submission of a planning application or building notice, or at any stage in the process. Disabled people themselves do not regard their lack of involvement with builders as an issue. Builders assume that the regulatory or statutory parameters, such as the Building Regulations and the Disability Discrimination Act (1995), are the legitimate results of consultations with the relevant groups. As such, builders feel that no more is required in taking disabled people's views into account. Such attitudes, and related practices, reinforce a system of 'expertism' that is unlikely to draw on much experiential knowledge – a situation that ought to be remedied.

- Seeking to achieve accessible housing will not be easy, given the complexity of building contexts that underpin the provision of accessible dwellings (see Imrie, 2003a). The research in this book demonstrates that achieving the minimum design standards is often beyond some builders. A complex combination of site-specific or locational conditions, the process of project management, the difficulties of interpreting an ambiguous regulation and the inconsistencies of building control practice can all combine to produce a variety of design outcomes. In this sense, a contribution of the research is to highlight 'interpretative and implementation' gaps that prevent builders achieving Part M, by seeking to understand shortfalls in design in relation to aspects of the social relations of the building process. Such gaps could be specified in detail and (re)presented to builders and other building professionals in the form of a 'good practice' guide or manual, with training provided by relevant organizations (e.g. the NHBC). An example relates to achieving access on sloping sites. Most builders will say it is difficult, when, as the examples in the Case study in Chapter 5 show, a range of easy-to-achieve design solutions is available to consider and replicate.

- Likewise, the implementation of legislation on access depends on clear design guidance being issued and made available to builders in easy to digest formats for project managers and others on site. At present, the approved document Part M, which provides technical advice on how to achieve the requirements of the regulation, is not liked by most builders and building control officers. It should be re-drafted by the ODPM in order to provide clearer advice about how the regulation can be achieved (and indeed this appears to be happening at the time of writing). In particular, diagrams in the approved document are confusing and difficult to interpret, especially in relation to the WC requirement. The reference to 'reasonable provision' in the requirement is difficult for builders and officers to interpret, and most would like more advice about what the term means. It is the source of variable and inconsistent practice and application of the regulation (see Chapter 6). Comments from builders and building control officers suggest that the

ODPM should provide a menu of fully worked through examples of what reasonable provision is deemed to be.

- A significant gap in builders' understanding of what accessible housing is relates to the lack of promotion, by government, of the broader merits of legislation and policy in relation to the provision of accessible housing. Government departments, such as the ODPM, ought to 'sell the concept' of accessible housing to builders, and explore the real costs of seeking to achieve quality standards in excess of Part M. Such costs ought to include some estimation of the cost involved (to disabled people, the care industry, etc.) of not achieving minimum standards of access to dwellings. The concept of visitability is not well understood by professionals in the building and design trades or by most building control officers; less so ideas about LTH and accessible housing more generally. The ODPM should spread the message that visitability is not an 'add-on', but is integral to the design of good-quality housing. At a practical level, advice should be provided to all builders and building control officers about the philosophy and moral rationale behind vis-itability (through the auspices of various channels such as the RICS, the NHBC and the HBF; also, see Imrie, 2003a). Most training provides pro-fessionals with advice on how the regulation can be achieved. However, little is said about how and why the regulation is important.

- The requirement that Part M seeks to provide for visitability and a *measure of use of dwellings* for individuals who are not just wheelchair users should be clarified (see also Truesdale and Steinfeld, 2002). This broader remit is the intent of Part M, but most builders and officers see the regulation as relating solely to the needs of wheelchair users. Part of the problem is misinterpretation and/or lack of understanding of the regulation, and the often-limited interpretation, by builders and build-ing control officers, of its scope. In this respect, design guidance in the approved document should be extended to include advice about how the needs of individuals with impaired hearing or sight can be accom-modated in order to discharge the requirements of the regulation; that is, for disabled people 'to gain access to and use the building' (DETR, 1999a: 5). Practical examples, with appropriate diagrams and illustra-tions, ought to be provided as the basis of guidance. At the time of writing, such matters are likely to be addressed by a committee set up by the ODPM to consider the introduction of LTH standards as the basis of a revised Part M.

- Any attempt to develop a coherent response to the access needs of dis-abled people will require changes to conflicting policies. The most significant is the UK government's urban renaissance agenda, in particular its strategies for the densification of cities (ODPM, 2000a, 2000b). The core of the densification agenda is PPG3 and, as discussed in Chapter 5, it does not address the housing needs of disabled people.[3] It is premised on achieving the maximum numbers of units on each developable site, with the consequence that the size of units is small and they are not particularly accessible to wheelchair users. Most builders and officers feel that PPG3 makes Part M difficult (if not impossible) to achieve, and often the regulation is overlooked where builders are adhering to PPG3 directives. Given this, there ought to be much more dialogue between planning and building control officials in government departments to ensure that policies are not conflicting, or likely to have effects or outcomes that are contrary to what is intended. The difficulty here is that PPG3 is framed within the mentalities of the 'predict and provide' approach to housing policy. It propagates a conception of housing quality that will serve to maximize developers' profits at the expense of providing living spaces that can accommodate the needs of particular people, such as wheelchair users.

- The research of P. Thomas (2004) and Burns (2004) shows that a deterrent to disabled people finding housing with access features is the frustration of the search process, in which the lack of information about access features leads to wasted time and effort viewing inappropriate properties. In a context of shortage of accessible housing, property agents ought to be required to list an inventory of access design features in houses in order to provide disabled people with information about how accessible available properties are. Few estate agents either document, or draw attention to access features in housing, because agents do not see such features as providing a 'sales advantage'. However, there are some exceptions. For instance, 'Mobility Friendly Homes' is operated by Reid & Dean, an estate agency and lettings service based in Eastbourne, southern England, that specializes in marketing accessible and adapted property around the UK.[4] On their website they state that:

  if you are looking for a home for life, or if easy access is important to you, then one of our 'Mobility Friendly Homes' may meet your requirements. Accessibility features are clearly listed and described, and some property may also contain adaptations designed to meet the needs of someone with a physical impairment

  (www.mobilityfriendlyhomes.co.uk)

- The development of accessible property registers has also occurred in recent times. One example was the Cardiff Accessible Housing Register, an initiative in the late 1990s between the Voluntary Action Cardiff Housing Access Project and some estate agents in Cardiff. Estate agents, using an access guide, inspect each others' property to identify barrier-free elements. Properties were categorized into one of four types to indicate levels of accessibility: negotiable, visitable, livable and universal. This information was included as an integral part of the property details made available to the general public. More recently, an Accessible Property Register (www.accessible-property.org.uk), which aims to provide coverage of property throughout the UK, has been set up by a group of disabled people in Sheffield. Their objective is to work closely with estate agents so that they become more aware of the physical barriers facing older and disabled people in relation to housing.[5] While such initiatives are likely to provide a helpful contribution to the search process, their existence is symptomatic of the problem, in which much of the housing stock remains largely inaccessible to and unusable by a large proportion of disabled people.

8.4 Conclusions

In setting out part of the Labour government's policy agenda for disabled people, Tony McNulty (2003: 2), Parliamentary Under Secretary of State at the ODPM, said that:

the Government is fully committed to an inclusive society in which nobody is disadvantaged. An important part of delivering this commitment is breaking down unnecessary physical barriers and exclusions imposed on disabled people by poor design of buildings and places.

McNulty's statement provides an insight into a changing policy agenda in relation to responding to the access needs of disabled people, in which there is implicit challenge to the notion that any one (or limited group of) lived identities should have privileged status within a polity. Central to social justice, from this perspective, is the recognition and respect given to diverse perspectives and ways of life. In turn, terms such as 'diversity', 'difference' and 'inclusion' have come to the fore in requiring policy-makers, including building control officers, to be increasingly aware of and responsive to the multiple needs of a diverse population (see Booth et al., 2003).

The 'diversity agenda' is one that is encouraging, so government statements allege, the development of policies to enhance sustainable and socially inclusive neighbourhoods and patterns of living. Part of this, as previously mentioned, is the likelihood that Part M will be changed to incorporate LTH standards and, in doing so, to try and ensure that new housing provides livable and/or usable spaces. This is a welcome, even unexpected, development, and one that could not have been envisaged ten years ago. However, LTH standards are, in reality, modest in scope, and are no more than the extension of a building regulations route in seeking to provide accessible housing. The standards can do little to change the social relations of the building industry;[6] nor can they do much about the negative ways in which some builders regard disabled people. Rather, they are derived out of the discourse of 'housing as a system' that, first and foremost, has recourse to technical and physical 'fixes' to overcome problems which are deeply embedded in social, attitudinal and political relations.

There are dangers here that the agenda relating to inclusion and diversity may turn into not much more than empty rhetoric and small-scale, incremental technical changes that leave intact the social relations and practices of real estate. As suggested above, the Labour government's record to date, in relation to accessible housing, reinforces the (medical) view that small-scale adaptations to the design of dwellings, such as the removal of doorsteps, will facilitate inclusion. While it may encourage particular patterns of social interaction previously denied to some individuals, Gleeson (1998) notes that the focus first and foremost on technical adaptation and change is part of a political culture that sees impairment as the problem. Here, (bodily) deficits are to be compensated by the provision of technical adaptations, and provided with the means to be 'fitted' to the contours of domestic design. This reflects the mentalities of Part M, LTH standards and the FHHA, which seek in large part to fit 'people to design' rather than 'design to people'.

In addition, one of government's preferred routes to tackle attitudes and practices in relation to the provision of housing is to encourage consumer pressure on builders. The extent to which a shift in building culture and practices will take place by virtue of this is doubtful, and more so for disabled people, who, as the book has recounted, are prevented from ease of access to or dialogue with builders and other building professionals. In the absence of effective consumer pressure, the present government, like previous ones, continues to place its faith in the goodwill of developers to 'do the right thing'. For instance, on 8 July 2003 the Deputy Prime Minister John Prescott launched *The Building for Life Standard*, a three-year initiative that, in the words of its chairperson, Terry Farrell (2002: 2), will 'try and up the sights of the UK's large-volume house builders and persuade them that good design is achievable and brings social, economic and environmental benefits'. As the Deputy Prime Minister, John Prescott (ODPM, 2003: 2), said: 'the launch of this Standard will help house buyers identify new housing that lives up to the Government's vision of good place making, high design principles and creating a sense of community'.

While encouragement of this type has a role to play in guiding the design and construction of accessible housing, it is likely to propagate 'more of the same' – that is, the supply of standardized house-types in which the design of housing is not attentive to the needs of specific consumers, such as disabled people. House builders show little understanding of the differentiated needs of their customers and, as RADAR (1995: 1) has noted, 'developers in the private sector have resisted, and continue to resist, any change to tried and tested practice'. Without changes to the social and institutional relations and practices of house building, and to the broader discourses of disablism in society, many disabled people's choices of where to live and who to visit will be difficult to facilitate.

Further reading

The writings of Peter King are interesting in respect of issues relating to conceptions of dwelling. They are derived, in part, from the works of Habraken, Illich and Norberg-Schulz, and interested readers ought to read these original writings. John Turner's book *Housing by People* is excellent, and it provides good guidance about broader principles and specific practices in seeking to develop the context for the production and consumption of dwellings sensitized to individual needs.

Endnotes

Introduction

1 Karn and Sheridan's (1994) research also shows that only a few properties with ground-floor entrances (5 per cent of private properties and 3 per cent of housing association properties) were internally negotiable and had a WC, and none of these had visitable entrances.

2 Part M was originally introduced in 1987 to cover disabled people's access needs in newly constructed and/or substantially renovated public buildings; private dwellings were not considered, at that time, as a legitimate focus for regulation (see Chapter 3 for a fuller discussion of Part M; also Imrie, 1996, 1997). A similar regulation exists in Northern Ireland (Part R) which, in relation to dwellings, came into effect on 1 April 2001. In Scotland there is no separate regulation relating to disability and access, although there are substantial references to access issues in Parts M, Q and S of the Scottish building regulations. Access to housing is primarily covered in Part Q.

Chapter 1

1 Age Concern is a charity that, as it claims on its website (www.ageconcern.org.uk), 'supports all people over 50 in the UK, ensuring that they get the most from life. We provide essential services such as day care and information. We campaign on issues like age discrimination and pensions, and work to influence public opinion and government policy about older people.'

2 On a study visit to the USA in February/March 2003 I met Ed Bannister, who for many years has championed the rights of disabled people in the village of Bolingbrook, near Chicago. Along with colleagues, he has campaigned for a building code to ensure access to dwellings in all new private (for sale) dwellings. See also the Case study, Chapter 7.

3 Most physically impaired people live in mainstream dwellings and, where necessary, are cared for by parents or a dependant. Few live in care or residential homes or settings, although Parker and Mirrlees (1988) estimate that 25,000 physically impaired people under the age of 65 years were living in residential homes in 1950 – a figure that had declined to 11,000 by 1968.

4 As Bull and Watts (1998: 21) note, the Housing Act 1974 (Section 56) provided 'discretionary improvement grants for works required for making a dwelling suitable for the accommodation, welfare or employment of a disabled occupant'. Mandatory intermediate grants were also available, 'for installing standard amenities (e.g. toilets) which were lacking or for installing suitable alternative facilities where existing amenities were inaccessible to a disabled person' (Bull and Watts, 1998: 21).

5 In particular, the CSDP Act stipulated that developers should provide access to new buildings where practical and reasonable, and only to existing buildings where 'substantial improvements' were being undertaken. The CSDP Act is still a significant piece of legislation regarding statutory provisions on access in the built environment. However, this is

problematical because it is underpinned by the idea that minimum control over private investment decisions in the built environment should occur.

6 The Department of Environment (1974, 1975) issued guidelines that distinguished between wheelchair and mobility units. The former was intended for people who were 'totally dependent on wheelchairs'; steps were to be avoided throughout the dwelling and fitments were fixed for the convenience of the user. Space standards were in excess of the recommended standards for mainstream housing. In contrast, design standards were less stringent in mobility housing; there was no additional space beyond the minimum requirement for mainstream housing. The approach to the dwelling had to be ramped, and doors to main living areas and bedrooms had to be a minimum width of 900 mm.

7 Margaret Thatcher's Conservative government introduced 'right to buy' policies in 1980. It permitted tenants living in council or state-owned homes to purchase them at a discount. Since then, more than 1.5 million homes have been sold. The policy has helped to boost the level of home ownership in Britain from around 55 per cent in 1979 to around 70 per cent today. However, there is increasing concern that the policy is adding to the growing housing crisis, insofar as at least half of the homes sold have not been replaced.

8 The situation was not dissimilar in England and, as the DoE (1991: 44) data indicate, just over a quarter of the housing stock in England in 1991 had level access and facilities. These were primarily bungalows and flats with lifts, and were most likely to be local authority and housing association dwellings. The low numbers of accessible dwellings are revealed by other data, too. For instance, a housing needs survey prepared by the Joint Client Services Group in Hammersmith and Fulham Council (2002) identified 128 people with a physical impairment who needed rehousing. Need is broken down into wheelchair housing, sheltered and wheelchair housing, sheltered mobility housing, mobility housing and people who require housing on a level access. The report showed that demand for accessible housing had been double the available supply in the three years prior to 2002, and projections indicated a widening gap.

9 The NHBC was set up in 1937 as a not-for-profit company with the purpose of raising standards in the new-house building industry and providing consumer protection, through warranty and insurance schemes, for new homeowners. It is independent of the house-building industry and has a governing council of 73 people, including representatives from the Local Government Association, the Royal Institution of Chartered Surveyors and the Consumers Association. Of builders in the UK, 18,000 are registered with the NHBC and agree to comply with its rules and standards. The NHBC is the largest provider of building control services, and inspects half of the new homes built in England and Wales.

10 In a similar survey of disabled people about their housing circumstances, conducted by the Michigan Statewide Council for Independent Living (2001) in the USA, familiar themes about independent living, affordable and accessible housing were voiced. For one respondent to the survey, 'accessible housing is not as bad as it used to be, but still there are slim pickings'. There was also a perception that disabled people have little choice and are usually consigned to the 'wrong side' of town. As a respondent said, 'more housing is needed in safer areas'.

11 The EHCS is run by the Research Analysis and Evaluation Division of the ODPM to provide information on the changing condition and composition of the housing stock, and the characteristics of the households living in different types of housing. The survey is a key tool used to measure the effectiveness of current policies and to underpin the monitoring of ODPM's Public Service Agreement measure of decent housing. Up to and including 2001, the survey has been conducted every five years. However, the EHCS moved to a continuous format from April 2002 to enable, so the ODPM (2002a) claims, progress towards the government's target relating to decent social housing to be monitored annually.

12 Karn and Sheridan's research also shows that only a few properties with ground-floor entrances (5 per cent of private properties and 3 per cent of housing association properties) were internally negotiable and had a WC and none of these had visitable entrances. Evidence from the USA is not dissimilar. For instance, of the 10,460 public housing apartments managed by Washington, DC housing authority in 2001, only 191 (or 1.7 per cent) were classified as accessible to disabled people (Leonnig, 2001).

13 The Scottish House Condition Survey (Scottish Office, 1996) noted further that 144,000 households had someone with a mobility impairment, of which 20,000 were wheelchair users. Of these households, 110,000 included a disabled person requiring adaptations to the property to make it suitable for their housing needs.

14 Even where purpose-built accommodation is provided, it has not always catered for all needs. A survey by the OPCS (Buckle, 1971) of impaired people's working and housing circumstances indicated that only 1 in 20 impaired persons was living in purpose-built accommodation, provided by either a local authority or a voluntary agency. Ten per cent were unable to use some of the rooms in their accommodation, with the inability to climb stairs being the main factor in preventing use of some rooms. Others mentioned doors and corridors being too narrow for wheelchairs as a constraint on the use of some rooms

15 A range of disabled people and organizations have made similar observations to those of Nussbaum. For instance, in 1976 the Union of Physically Impaired Against Segregation (UPIAS, 1976) noted that a fundamental right of disabled people was their access to and habitation of conveniently sited and accessible housing. Likewise, in 1981 the Derbyshire Coalition of Disabled People (1981) noted that of the seven needs that were paramount in the lives of disabled people, access to livable dwellings was a priority.

16 The inability for many disabled people to gain access to good-quality housing is related in part to their incomes relative to housing costs. For instance, Bournemouth's survey of housing need shows that the incomes of households with a disabled person were, in 1998, far lower than those for households as a whole. This confirms other research that shows a persistent pattern of inequality of incomes between disabled and non-disabled people. Thus, in the USA, Weeks (2000) notes that most people with a developmental impairment rely on social security payments of between $6,000 and $9,000 per year. As Weeks (2000: 1) comments, 'any housing developer or provider will assure you, an income like that doesn't open many doors'.

17 In contrast, in the USA the Fair Housing Amendment Act (1988), while not requiring owners to make a dwelling accessible, provides tenants of rented property with the legal right (albeit at their own expense) to make appropriate changes to facilitate access.

18 There had been little improvement on this definition by the time of the 2001 EHCS. In the surveyor's manual (ODPM, 2001b: 2), level access was defined as where 'there are no more than 1 or 2 steps up or down to the entrance to the dwelling from the street (this need not necessarily be the front door), and there is space to install a ramp'.

19 Housing Associations are required, as a condition of their receipt of government grant through the Housing Corporation, to design dwellings in accordance with the Scheme Development Standards. These require new dwellings to adhere to mobility standards, and these include a plethora of provisions such as: the construction of staircases suitable for a future British Standards-specified lift; passageway widths of 900 mm generally; the provision of slip-resistant and smooth pathways on the approach to the dwelling; extra space for wheelchair users to circulate, transfer, use furniture and fittings; and so on. These standards are in excess of the provisions laid down in Part M, and full details are available in the document by the Housing Corporation, 2003, Scheme Development Standards, HC, London.

20 However, a statement by the Building Regulations Advisory Committee, a committee set up to provide advice to government on revisions to Part M in relation to dwellings, has said that government ministers have agreed that 'new housing should be built to LTH standards, and be delivered through a revision to Part M of the building regulations' (see ODPM, 2004).

21 For instance, in 1921 the German State Efficiency Board (entitled Reichskuratorium fur Wirtschaft-lichkeit, or RKW) identified and 'publicised efficient means of production and procedure, including applications to domestic circumstances' (Rowe, 1993: 64). Rowe (1993: 64) cites the case of the RKW-employed architect, Alexander Klein, 'who applied graph theory to determine the most efficient domestic layouts'.

22 Such needs and lifestyles rarely related to disabled people, and Ravatz (1995: 80) suggests that 'the design and policy of twentieth century housing ... were devised in the interests of the nuclear family', or what was referred to as 'the nursery of society'. This policy focus was not new, but reflected early Victorian conceptions of the 'good home', and the significance of physical space, such as the design of the dwelling, in determining forms of habitation and social behaviour.

23 An important moment in the development of housing design standards was the recommendation of the Dudley Committee in 1944 to move the bathroom and water closet from the ground to the first floor of housing. As the report suggested, 'if, as we recommend, the living space on the ground floor is enlarged, the bathroom cannot remain there without producing a larger area on the ground floor than is required on the first floor for the bedrooms. Therefore, both the bathroom and water closet should be upstairs. This arrangement, as our evidence has made abundantly clear, will also be far more convenient to the

occupier, particularly in cases of illness' (Ministry of Health, 1944: 15). This was perhaps one of the more problematical changes in the layout and design of dwellings for disabled people, especially wheelchair users, because potentially it cut them off from ease of access to the most important part of the dwelling. The change appeared to have been made not for practical reasons relating to bodily care and maintenance, but to ensure that the overall footprint of dwellings did not exceed specified dimensions.

24 The Joseph Rowntree Foundation first mooted the concept of LTH in 1993 (Lifetime Homes Group, 1993). It suggests that the design of dwellings ought to be 'inter generational' in the sense that they should contain design features that will accommodate any person at any stage of the life course, from the very young to the frail and elderly. Dwellings ought to contain design features that do not require expensive adaptations to be made at a later stage. Part M contains some of the design elements of lifetime homes; lifetime homes also feature stairs that are designed to take a stair lift and ceilings suitable for fitting a through-floor lift.

25 Further details about the Housing Quality Indicator system can be accessed by visiting www.housing.odpm.gov.uk/information/hqi.

Chapter 2

1 Since 2001, Zurich Insurance has commissioned an annual survey of customers' attitudes towards new housing in the UK. Their most recent survey, in 2004, suggests that builders are making little progress in keeping customers happy. As the report says, the common refrain of most buyers is that 'once they had my money, they just don't care'.

2 Such housing was commonly referred to as 'Jerry-built', a term that refers to something that is built of bad materials, to sell but not last. Israel (1997) notes that the origins of the term are not clear, although he speculates that it may well be connected to the term 'jury-rigged' which comes from 'jury mast', a seventeenth-century nautical term to describe a temporary mast made from any available material. Alternatively, Israel suggests that 'jerry-built' is more likely to be derived from the pejorative use of the term 'jerry' in eighteenth- and nineteenth-century Britain (e.g. 'jerry mumble', to knock about; 'jerry sneak', a hen-pecked husband; 'jerry', a cheap beer house).

3 These are a few examples of what were many scathing comments and observations about speculative builders in the nineteenth century. Dyos (1961: 122) notes that the term 'specu-lative builder' 'was used to name not only a particular economic function but a meretricious scale of values and a dubious social status'. Such views have been repeated time and again, and reached their apogee in the mid to late 1990s. The Council for the Preservation of Rural England (1995: 3–4) observed that 'in place of distinctiveness we have ubiquity – row upon row of near identical brick built family units – it is the victory of uniformity over distinctive-ness'. Likewise, John Gummer (1995: 1), Secretary of State for the Environment in the last Conservative administration, expressed his disquiet with the uniform design of speculative housing and declared it to be 'an insult to our sense of place to offer precisely the same house in Warrington as in Wallingford, Woodbridge or Wolverhampton'.

4 Other comments, elsewhere, were not dissimilar and a feature in *Building News* recalled the delights of the modern, speculative-built home: 'we could hear the merry laughter of the next door inhabitant . . . into the partition of the modern house no reasonable person expects to drive a nail to hold a picture of more than half a pound in weight' (Anon, 1866: 755–756).

5 By the 1920s, commentators were raising concerns about the emergence of suburbia and the standardization of dwellings and domestic environments. For instance, Le Corbusier (1967: 42) referred to the modern dwelling as a monstrous lie, suggesting that 'if the social relations between men were as false as taste (or more likely the ethics) which govern the construction of our houses, we should all be in prison'.

6 Thus, the least cost nature of the procurement process tends to marginalize design to a peripheral activity and, as Carmona (2001: 119) notes, 'design costs are usually less than 1 per cent of total unit costs', or less than a third of that spent on marketing.

7 Builders attempted to defend the integrity of the door step on the basis of practical and cul-tural grounds. As the HBF (1995: 3), and others pointed out, in modern domestic dwellings it is standard practice for builders to raise the ground floor at least 12 inches (305 mm) above the surrounds (see also Finn, 1995). This necessitates the construction of steps to

facilitate ease of access to the dwelling. While builders justified a stepped entrance as a practical means of damp proofing, Pugh Associates (1969: 3) and others note that the stepped entrance has an important psychological function in helping 'to delineate the boundary between public and semi-public and private territory within the house' (see also Milner and Madigan, 2001).

8   There is, however, nothing new about this and the editorial of an American trades journal, *House and Home* (1952: 108), recounted a familiar tale told by builders in the early 1950s: 'the most expensive thing about today's house is the local building code . . . with its countless unpredictable and often senseless variances from sound national standards. The variances cost the home buyer (and the house builder) a lot more than it would cost to make all the living rooms and all the bedrooms 20 per cent larger – more than wall-to-wall carpeting, more than complete insulation and double glazing, more than an extra bathroom.'

9   Different builders reacted in contrasting ways to the DoE's consultative paper. Some were vitriolic and dismissive about disabled people and their dwelling needs. An example is provided by Clancy (1995: 1), who stated that 'I fear that this is a letter written to the truly disabled in government – those who will not see that the solution is not as that proposed, those who are deaf to commonsense arguments and those who use lame intellects to push through politically correct ideas which do not address the real issues . . .'. Others, while not necessarily well disposed towards Part M, were more temperate, if still sweeping, in their judgements. For instance, Rivermedd Homes Ltd reacted angrily, and its managing director, Smith (1995: 1), stated: 'in order to comply with these requirements, there will be many disadvantages to able-bodied customers, resulting in less sales, less houses being built and less developers surviving the economic climate' (see also Chapters 3 and 5).

Such views did not go unchallenged, and disabled people and their organizations felt that the draft proposals were a weak response by government that did not address the issue of creating livable and usable space in dwellings for disabled people (see also Milner and Madigan, 2001). As a respondent to the consultative document noted: 'the proposals have adopted a minimalist approach to the issue. The tone of the proposals is grudging . . .' (Bristol Churches Housing Association Ltd, 1995: 1). Likewise, a spokesperson for the Derbyshire Coalition of Disabled People commented that 'we are not hopeful that the points we are putting forward will receive much support . . . due to the limited horizon of the DoE's consultation which is based on the patronizing idea of visitability standards' (Hemm, 1995: 1). RADAR's (1995) representation argued that the limited appeal of Part M to builders was due to the document referring primarily to wheelchair users as beneficiaries of the regulation, with little reference to the fact that accessible design has the potential to benefit everyone. As they concluded, the draft proposals 'are excessively cautious'.

10 Many other representations were made to the DoE about the cost implications of Part M, including by Barratts Development plc, whose representative noted that 'the additional cost for constructing the ramps as drawn is £3342', while other 'adaptations could total £2000 to £3000 extra in pure construction costs' (Finn, 1995: 2; see also arguments and information in Chapter 2).

11 For instance, in 1990 the Department of Housing and Urban Development (1990) in the USA estimated that the provision of adaptable housing would add no more than 1 per cent to construction costs. On a unit costing $75,000 to build, the average marginal cost per unit was calculated to be between $287 to $389.

12 For instance, it has been argued that in the UK context, the provision of accessible dwellings provides the opportunity, at least in the longer term, for reduced welfare spending on adaptations or adjustments that, in the financial year 2002–03, cost the exchequer £700 million (see Heywood *et al.*, 2002).

13 Anecdotal evidence also suggests that there is plenty of demand for accessible dwellings. In a letter to the Department of the Environment about the draft proposals for Part M, Age Concern (1995: 1) said that 'we receive many enquiries from older and disabled people seeking a new home that is suitable for increasing frailty . . . we are therefore not convinced by the argument that there is little demand for accessible housing as argued by house builders and developers motivated to keep their costs as low as possible, at the expense of space standards and accessibility'.

14 A survey of 250 disabled people by Fanning *et al.* (1991) confirms this observation, in that 67 per cent of the sample said that they had difficulty in acquiring information about the availability of affordable barrier-free housing, with 36 per cent reporting this as a severe problem for them.

15 The AIA Center for Livable Communities and the AIA Housing Professional Interest Area, in partnership with the US Department of Housing and Urban Development, sponsor an annual award related to exemplary models of residential, community and accessible housing design.

Chapter 3

1 In 1974, a United Nations resolution suggested that governments ought to encourage the construction of accessible dwellings. The resolution stated that 'in order to permit free choice, the construction of adaptable dwellings is recommended. A dwelling is adaptable if it is accessible and if it permits modifications at low cost for the benefit of disabled people in wheelchairs. Such adapted housing will accordingly be very suitable for persons with other disabilities and for older persons' (United Nations, 1974: 4).

2 The voluntaristic nature of governments' approaches to issues of housing quality and livability is evident in Japan, where in 1999 the Housing Quality Assurance Law (HQL) came into force. One of its performance requirements is 'designing for ageing' in dwellings, although, as Kose (2000) says, it is not obligatory for house builders to respond to the directives. Kose (2000) speculates that high-quality house builders are likely to apply for the performance rationale available to those that implement the directives of the HQL, although to date there is no evidence to indicate how far this has occurred.

3 In the UK this switch in emphasis has led to the emergence of a plethora of home improvement agencies, such as 'Care and Repair' and 'Staying Put'. Care and Repair was set up in 1986, and its objective is, as its mission statement states, 'to innovate, develop, promote and support housing policies and initiatives which enable older and disabled people to live independently in their own homes for as long as they wish'. They are in competition with many organizations, such as 'Anchor Staying Put', a Home Improvement service that, as they state on their website, 'provide a service to older and disabled homeowners across England, helping them with repairs, adaptations and improvements so that they can remain in safety, security and warmth'.

4 'Supporting People' is, so government allege, a new integrated policy and funding framework for housing support services introduced from April 2003. The aim is to provide good-quality services, focused on the needs of users, to enable vulnerable people to live independently in the community in all types of accommodation and tenure.

5 The American National Standards Institute (ANSI) standards were substantially revised at the end of the 1970s (ANSI A117.1 1980) and have undergone periodic revisions since then. As Toran (1999) notes, it is generally accepted by the private sector, and it is the basis for most state and local building codes. The 1980 version marked a significant change in the contents of the ANSI by providing information about design and access to dwellings.

6 These requirements are stated in the Fair Housing Act, as amended, 42 U.S.C. 3604 (f) (c). The requirements are described in detail in HUD's (1991) publication, *Fair Housing Accessibility Guidelines*. These are supplemented with a *Supplementary Notice: Questions and Answers About the Guidelines*, published 28 June 1994. In particular, multifamily housing is defined under the FHAA to include owner-occupied housing with five or more units and renter (i.e. privately rented) housing with four or more units.

7 Robertson (2001) amplified by saying that at this first meeting 'there was a lunch, you see, and I was talking to these house builders, and they were passing comments about the Prince saying that "Well, he's out of his mind." You know, it's sort of like how they rubbished him on talking to plants, "Of course you couldn't do this." I mean, "people would never buy houses that were suitable for people in wheelchairs", and you know, their minds were totally blank to the fact that they might be using a wheelchair or their son or daughter might have an accident. And that was the initial reaction.'

8 In responding to the inadequacies of the FHAA, the Inclusive Home Design Act was reintroduced on 5 June 2003, a bill that requires all newly built single-family homes receiving federal funds to provide an accessible route or 'zero-step' into the dwelling, 32-inch clearance doorways on the ground floor, and a wheelchair-accessible WC. The Act seeks to close a loophole in which 95 per cent of federally supported dwellings do not have to meet any accessibility standards. For US Representative Jan Schakowsky, sponsor of the bill, 'it defies logic to build new homes that block people out when it's so easy and cheap to build new homes that let people in' (House of Representatives, 2003: 1).

9 DETR (1998) was required to produce an impact assessment of Part M which noted that the regulation had the potential to cater for a wide range of people, including wheelchair users, people with temporary mobility impairments and pregnant women. This message, however, is missing in the final approved document, and references are made only to wheelchair users and ambulant impaired people.

10 One such exemption is that Part M does not require lifts to be installed in apartments or flats. As Approved Document M (DETR, 1999a: 28) states: 'for buildings containing flats, the objective should be to make reasonable provision for disabled people to visit occupants who live on any storey. The most suitable means of access for disabled people . . . is a passenger lift. However, a lift may not always be provided.'

11 The lack of accessible dwellings has had, so Leonnig (2001) argues, severe repercussions for some disabled people (see also Gold, 2000; Stephen-Kaye, 2003). In one case, a young adult of 18 who has cerebral palsy has to wear diapers (nappies) because he cannot get access to the first-floor bathroom. In another case, a 20-year-old person with multiple impairments is unable to get into the narrow toilet. Instead, he relies on a catheter and bed liners. Likewise, a 10-year-old has to drag herself on her knees and elbows up the stairs to the toilet in the family's town house. The family has been on the waiting list for seven years for a public housing unit (Leonnig, 2001).

12 That is not to say that legal action against builders does not occur or, when it does, is unsuccessful. There are examples where builders in the USA have been taken to court for transgressions of the FHAA, and have been required to retrofit accessible features (at their own expense). For instance, John Buck Co., a Chicago-based developer, lost a federal lawsuit brought by the Justice Department alleging that a five-year-old apartment block, Park Evanston, was inaccessible to disabled people (see O'Connor, 2002). The developer was required to refit all of the 283 units in the block at an estimated cost of $1 million and to pay $50,000 into a fund for persons who were unable to rent at Park Evanston. The major problem at the apartment block was that doors were three to four inches too narrow to accommodate wheelchairs. The refit will include the widening of doors, and the alteration of kitchens and bathrooms to allow manoeuvring space for wheelchair users.

   In August of 1997, Baltimore Neighborhoods, Inc. (BNI), a non-profit Fair Housing organization located in Baltimore, Maryland, settled a lawsuit against The Falls Gable Condominium Residents' Association, Falls Gables Limited Partnership and Gables Development Company. BNI's lawsuit alleged that the condominium units and several of the common areas were inaccessible to people who used wheelchairs. BNI said that Falls Gable had insufficiently and incorrectly designed kerb cuts and handicapped parking places; inaccessible common-use areas and facilities; and inaccessible decks, patio areas and bathrooms in individual units. Without admitting liability, Falls Gable agreed to pay BNI $75,000, of which $7,500. went to the owners of ground-floor units who wished to make them accessible. The remaining funds would be used to make common areas accessible and to pay damages, legal fees and costs.

13 Most municipalities are cautious in their approach, and either stop short of requiring no-step entrances or provide 'get out' clauses for builders. For instance, in Arizona the Pima County Board of Supervisors approved a no-step entry requirement on 5 February 2002, along with other requirements for wider doors, lever hardware, reinforced bathroom walls and accessible electrical outlets. However, builders in Pima are able to opt out of the no-step entry if it costs more than $200 (per entrance) due to the topography of the site. The problem with this clause is that it is relatively easy for builders 'to prove' that a no-step entrance will exceed the cost of $200.

14 However, there are some initiatives that seek to provide disabled people with help to find accessible property. In the USA, for instance, the Rehabilitation Research and Training Center on Independent Living and Disability Policy has produced an Accessible Housing Database package that provides a tool with which users can identify accessible rental housing in their communities. It permits users to evaluate the levels of affordability and accessibility of different properties. Kate Toran developed the AHD in 1999; she is contactable at ktoran@uclink4.berkeley.edu).

Chapter 4

1 In a communication with Chris Allen (2004b), he helpfully pointed out that post-modern literature emphasizes the increasing and universal importance of self-identity in contemporary societies, and that this analysis has been taken up in the meaning of home literature which examines the issue of self-identity, etc., in relation to home. But, as he said, 'surely the identification that disabled people have with home is more crucial than for other people? Given the higher likelihood of disabled people's exclusion from the labour market, they may well spend more time at home.'

2 Sending transcripts back to respondents is important in order to clarify points of detail or to give respondents the opportunity to change their story or qualify points that they have made. Some respondents did not reply, and others were concerned about how they would 'come across' or 'sound'. They either deleted certain expressions or changed the wording of parts of the transcript. Respondents were sent a draft copy of this chapter for comment, but no one has asked for any details to be taken out or rewritten; all respondents have been presented anonymously, and revealing details about them have not been included.

Chapter 6

1 The lack of time and resources to enforce building and other regulations is a recurrent observation of the planning and building control systems. For instance, Burdett's (1883: 238) comments about building inspection in the late nineteenth century have a familiar tone to them. As he said, there was 'no one to look after their construction except the surveyor to the Local Board. He, poor man, often without an apology for assistance, cannot be in every part of his scattered district at the same time, even if we wished to supervise all of his class of work efficiently. Besides, it too frequently happens that the jerry builder is a member of the Local Board himself, or has powerful friends there, and in such cases the surveyor finds it inexpedient to interfere . . .'

2 The building regulations in their present format consist of a small number of functional requirements that are supported by 'Approved Documents'. These documents give guidance on how the requirements of the regulations can be met. There is, however, no obligation to adopt particular solutions set out in the document if the builder wishes to satisfy a requirement in any other way.

3 Builders can choose to submit either a detailed application showing all design details, or a building notice. The building notice method is most suitable where small works are to be done. No formal approval is given, so good liaison between the builder and building control officer is essential to ensure that the work does not have to be re-done.

4 Officers suggested that compliance is less likely in small housing units and where driveways are split-level and constructed with gravel paths. They also reported compliance problems with specific house-types, such as town houses with ground or basement garages, and housing opening directly onto public footpaths or highways. In relation to minor transgressions of Part M, authorities are often lenient.

5 The Building Act 1984 contained important new provisions for the private supervision and certification of building work by approved inspectors as an alternative to control solely by local authorities. These provisions were brought into effect in November 1985. In effect, it is the privatization of building control and the opening up of it to market forces (see Meijer and Visscher, 1998)

6 There is much confusion and misunderstanding by builders, architects and other professionals in the construction industry regarding the differences between Part M and other accessibility standards, such as LTH. More often than not, professionals will conflate the different standards or fail to recognize that there are any significant differences between them. For instance, the City of Derby's Local Plan Review (2000) contained a policy requiring developers to construct dwellings to lifetime home standards that were objected to by a range of organizations. The HBF (2001: 1) said that 'it is not clear what this policy is seeking to achieve that is not covered in Part M', while the local NHS Trust (2001) suggested that 'the policy duplicates the requirements of the building regulations without justification'. Likewise, builders, including Westbury Homes and William Davis Ltd, considered the policy to be 'superfluous in the light of Part M of the building regulations' (William Davis Ltd, 2001). However, as Mick Watts (2002: 2), Derby's access officer, pointed out, 'the building regulations do not however adequately address the concept of lifetime homes'.

Chapter 8

1 In a single week of viewing on British television in November 2004, it was possible to watch the following 'lifestyle' programmes about housing: on Monday 15 November, the schedules included *I want that house* (ITV1), *House doctor* (Channel 5), *Escape to the country* (BBC2), *Houses behaving badly* (BBC1). These programmes featured every day that week. In addition, on Tuesday other programmes included *Selling houses* (Channel 4) and *Time to get your house in order* (Channel 4). On Wednesday, *Property ladder returns* (Channel 4) was one of the feature programmes, and on Thursday programmes included *No going back* (Channel 4) and *Smart living@home with technology* (Channel 4). Finally, on Friday Channel 5 had a string of programmes in its evening schedule, from 1930 to 2200, including *House doctor*, *Hot property*, *Housebusters* and *House doctor: designs for living*.

   The sheer number of programmes about housing and the propagation of them has been referred to by some as the rise of 'property porn'.

2 Another example of 'adultification' provided by Chris Allen (2004b) was in situations where local authorities could not deal with dual impairment households. As Allen (2004b) said, 'so we saw examples where households with a wheelchair using adult *and* a visual impaired child were allocated to an adapted house with a chair lift (in response to adult need) even though the narrowness of the chair lift presented a danger for the visual impaired child'.

3 In a personal communication with Chris Allen (2004b), he mentioned some of his recent research studying city-centre living in Manchester in which he found a number of pressures compromising housing quality in the city centre. As Chris Allen suggested, 'an extremely large proportion of *new build* (as opposed to converted) apartments are purchased (sometimes *en bloc*) by investors. There is also a high level of competition in the rental market that has a downward pressure on rents. This combination of factors has resulted in a significant reduction in space standards as investors seek to minimize purchase costs so as to be able to offer competitive rents whilst developers spot an opportunity to put more units on each site. The result is lots of studio apartments that you can't swing a cat in! So, who is the urban renaissance for?'

4 On their website, Mobility Friendly Homes note that to qualify as an accessible property a house must fall into one of the following categories:

   It can be: **Accessible** with:

   - Off-street or unrestricted on-street parking within 25 metres.
   - No steps between the point where a car could be parked the entrance to the property, although there may be a slope.
   - Level access to at least one entrance to the property. The entrance may incorporate an access ramp or a small threshold.
   - Level access to all main living floor rooms.
   - A WC on the same level as the entrance to the property (or lift access to a WC on another floor).

   or **Adapted**, meaning:

   - The property contains fixed equipment or adaptations designed to meet the needs of someone with a physical or other impairment.

   or it can be both **Accessible** and **Adapted**:

   - The property meets the access criteria and, in addition, has one or more adaptations or items of equipment designed to meet the needs of someone with a physical or other impairment.

5 Conrad Hodgkinson, Christine Barton and Lindsay Yarrow set up The Accessible Property Register (APR) in 2002. It has developed a nationwide list of approved agencies and, if requested by potential purchasers of property, will recommend approved agencies. APR delivers training sessions to housing associations' staff on issues relating to access and disability, and on improving capacity to identify, record and promote access features and adaptations in residential properties for sale or rent. On the website, it is stated that:

   The Accessible Property Register is a property website with a difference – we only accept adverts for property that is accessible or adapted.

   On this site you can:

   - Advertise accessible and adapted property for sale
   - Advertise accessible and adapted property for rent

- Advertise projects and developments promoting accessible and adapted property
- Search for accessible and adapted property
- Look for property with specific adaptations
- Contact property advertisers
- Register your details and describe the kind of accessible or adapted property that you are searching for
- Find a list of estate agents, housing associations and other housing providers who work with the Accessible Property Register
- Find links to other providers of accessible property
- Find links to organisations and businesses that sponsor or support us
- Read our latest news and find links to useful information and to other websites
- Advertise goods and services.'

6 This is not, however, to deny the significance of building standards and/or regulations. In the course of writing this book, it became evident that there is urgent need for scholars of urban design to consider the building regulations and processes of building control as integral to the understanding of changes in the built environment. Unlike architecture and planning, the building control system has rarely been the subject of academic enquiry and debate. There are few, if any, scholarly writings about the subject and its substance, or comments about its regulatory functions other than in the most descriptive of senses (for an exception, see Baer, 1997). The dominant texts on building control are characterized by useful accounts of its historical origins, and details of the key rules and regulatory functions and procedures (Wright, 1983). While important as teaching tools and aids for trainee building control officers, the content of such texts is indicative of what Dobson (1968: v) suggests is 'the shortage of serious works setting out the general position in a country or on the philosophy or theory of building regulations'.

APPENDICES

1 Research design and methods

Most of the research in the book was generated from a project funded by the Economic and Social Research Council (grant number R000239210) and carried out in the period from July 2001 to June 2003. The research objectives were threefold:

1 What are the attitudes, values and practices of house builders and other real estate professionals towards the access needs of disabled people? How do such attitudes vary, if at all, between builders, and how do they influence house-building practices and processes in relation to the needs of disabled people?
2 How important are regulatory mechanisms such as planning and access directives and/or legislation, Part M of the building regulations, the Housing Corporation's Scheme Development Standards and Lifetime Homes standards in influencing house builders' attitudes and practices towards the provision of accessible housing?
3 How far, and in what ways, are disabled people and their organizations able to influence the attitudes and building practices of house builders (and related professionals)? What forms of experiential knowledge (of disabled people and their needs) do builders bring to bear on the construction of dwellings?

The focus was maintained throughout the duration of the project, with three caveats. First, the project's steering group advised, at the first meeting, that the project should concentrate on new-build dwellings (for sale) in the private sector, particularly in the light of the new requirement (through Part M of the building regulations) for builders to incorporate accessible design features into the construction of new dwellings. The group advised that the original scope of the project, to consider aspects of social (or public) housing in addition to new-build dwellings (for sale) in the private sector, was too ambitious an undertaking. Accordingly, the research was (re)focused to explore the attitudes and evolving practices of builders, with regard to disability and access, through the context of the provision of new dwellings for private sale since the inception of Part M (25 October 1999) of the building regulations.

Second, given that builders' reactions and responses to the housing needs of disabled people are influenced, first and foremost, by Part M of the building regulations, it was decided, on the advice of the steering group, to provide a much more thorough evaluation than was originally envisaged of the impact of this regulation on the design of new dwellings. Thus, much of the project revolved around the evaluation of Part M and its diverse interpretation and application by builders, site managers, building control officers and others (refocusing objective (b) above). Third, during the course of the project it became clear that builders had little knowledge about disabled people and their needs; builders' practices and the content of Part M, so it seemed, were bereft of experiential knowledge or understanding of how interactions between impairment and domestic design could potentially create conditions of disablement. It was therefore decided to extend objective (c) to generate data of disabled people's feelings about and bodily interactions with domestic design

The research design comprised a number of methods:

1 *Key actor interviews and the evaluation of documentary materials.* The research commenced with fifteen face-to-face interviews with a range of key actors in the house-building industry and related professional and other organizations (such as, for example, the Disability Rights Commission, the House Builders Federation, Habinteg Housing Association, various disability charities, etc.). The intention was to generate industry-wide opinion and views about the key issues and concerns relating to the provision of accessible dwellings for disabled people. In addition, archival and desk-based work formed part of the context for later stages of the research. The most significant aspect of this was the inspection and assessment of comments about the Department of Environment's (1995) draft consultation document relating to the extension of Part M to incorporate new dwellings. The draft document was circulated to builders, architects, building control officers, other building professionals and disabled people and their organizations in 1995, and it generated over 1,000 detailed responses. All responses were read and notes were taken. It is a unique data set of opinion and viewpoint about disability, access and housing.

2 *Attitudes and practices of professionals: an aggregate picture.* The second part of the research comprised three postal surveys seeking to gain broad-based information about the attitudes and practices of key professionals in responding to the housing needs of disabled people. House builders, local authority building control officers and private sector approved building inspectors were the target populations. The first survey, of a 5 per cent sample of house builders operating in England and Wales, was undertaken between November 2001 and February 2002. A six-page questionnaire, comprising a series of both open-ended and closed questions, was sent to 721 builders registered with the NHBC. After two postal reminders, a response rate of 29.1 per cent (210 usable returns) was attained. The sample was derived from a NHBC database of registered house builders, with questionnaires sent to named individuals. The sample was random, although proportionally weighted to reflect the size (by volume of build) and geographical distribution of builders.

The second survey was sent to chief building control officers in all local authorities in England and Wales in the period from December 2001 to April 2002, with 382 questionnaires being sent out. After two reminders, a total of 234 (61.2 per cent) usable questionnaires were returned (see Imrie, 2003b). The final survey, sent to the 250 NHBC-registered private sector approved building inspectors, proved more problematical in gaining an acceptable response rate. After two reminders, 53 (21.2 per cent) usable questionnaires were returned (by April 2002). To encourage a high response rate, all postal surveys followed the same procedure: the initial letter and questionnaire were sent out; a follow-up reminder letter and questionnaire were sent out four weeks later to non-respondents; a telephone reminder to non-respondents then occurred two weeks after the initial follow-up.

3 *Interviews and site visits with builders and building control officers.* To develop and extend insight gained from the extensive postal questionnaires, in-depth interviews were conducted with both builders and building control officers. In total, 34 house-building companies and 20 building-control departments, chosen to reflect a mixture of types, were visited throughout England and Wales. The visits comprised an interview with a key contact (that lasted between one and three hours) and the collection of documents (such as architectural drawings, site plans, photographs and other graphics). In addition, visits to building sites were usually arranged in order to meet site managers and see, at first hand, some of the technical and practical issues in achieving accessible design on site. Two firms (one volume builder, one regional/local builder) were visited on three separate occasions during the course of the project, in order to document the ways in which design directives (such as Part M) were being incorporated into the various stages of the building process.

4 *Housing and the structures of building provision – detailed case studies.* The research proposal suggested that builders' responses to the housing needs of disabled people were likely to be influenced by the 'structures of building provision', or what Ball (1998: 1514) refers to as 'the network of relationships associated with the provision of particular types of buildings at specific points in time'. Each network is organization- and market-specific and, as Ball (1998: 1514) suggests, 'associated with historically specific institutional and other social relations'. Thus how builders respond to disabled people, and Part M, will depend in part on contingent, geographically variant relationships. Three local authorities were investigated; Bracknell, Carlisle and Bournemouth – places with contrasting political complexions, social structures and varying levels of disabled people's politicization and types of involvement in seeking to influence access policies.

The case research was based on a mixture of in-depth interviews, attendance at local authority meetings, and inspection of council files and records. The data generated were primarily of a qualitative nature. In total, 40 interviews were conducted with key actors and agents in the case study areas in the period from April 2002 to April 2003. Interviews were conducted with builders, planning officials and officers from social services, building control and architects' departments. Access groups and other disabled people's organizations were contacted, and interviews conducted with a range of disabled people.

5   *Reconstructing the housing histories of disabled people.* in the course of talking with builders and other building professionals, it became clear that they have little or no knowledge about disabled people and their access needs. Not surprisingly, experiential information or data derived from disabled people rarely feature in the design and implementation of building projects or in legal codes, such as Part M of the building regulations. This part of the research comprised two focus groups (eight people per group) and in-depth interviews with twenty individuals living in the case study towns.

In addition, the receipt of funding from the JRF permitted me to develop the scope of the research. A three-stage research design was constructed:

1   *Telephone interviews with builders.* The first part of the research sought to estimate the proportions of housing, constructed since October 1999, that have incorporated Part M standards. This had not been part of the remit of the ESRC research. Two groups were targeted for information: builders and local authority building control officers. Given the large size of both populations, a sample of respondents was derived for each group and a telephone interview was decided as the best method to gather information. A list of the top 73 house builders in the UK, as compiled by the HBF, was used as a basis for deriving a sample of builders to interview. On contact, a number of companies were discounted from the sample because they were constructing solely in Scotland, had ceased to build private housing, or had been involved in mergers with other companies. Fifty house-building firms, of various sizes, were finally interviewed by telephone; 50 per cent of this sample (25 builders) had not been approached in the ESRC-phases of the research.

2   *Telephone interviews with building control officers.* A similar exercise was carried out with a sample of building control departments based in a range of local authorities in England and Wales. Of 382 local authority building control departments, 42 (located in a variety of places) were interviewed. Officers were asked to provide figures for the number of housing units built in their area from October 1999 to December 2002. They were asked to state the proportion of units that they have adjudicated in their area, as opposed to NHBC-approved inspectors, and to predict the number of units likely to come under their jurisdiction in the next three years. In particular, officers were asked to estimate the proportion of housing that had been built to Part M standards, in total and broken down by year on year, since the inception of the regulation. In addition, they were asked to consider each of the Part M standards in turn, pinpointing any difficulties or problems with interpretation and builders' compliance. All bar four of the sample had not featured in the ESRC phases of the research.

3   *Interviews and site visits.* On completion of the telephone interviews, both builders and officers (who had not been previously approached in the ESRC phases of the research) were asked if they would be pre-

pared, if invited, to participate in an in-depth interview at a future date. The purpose of such interviews was to enable the documentation of diverse experiences in seeking to interpret and implement the regulation. This permitted me to enhance the depth of material generated on earlier ESRC phases of the research. From the pool of those agreeing to be interviewed, fifteen builders and fifteen local authority building control departments were selected. They were selected in part on the basis of having knowledge of and being involved in building contexts exhibiting both high and low levels of compliance with Part M, including problems with its application. The interviews generated a range of data, including documentary materials (such as floor plans, site layouts, architectural drawings, etc.), photographs of Part M design features, and oral testimonies from interviewees.

Limitations with the JRF data. Prior to the commencement of the JRF research, four house builders, five building control departments, the NHBC and the HBF were approached by telephone to ask about whether or not they keep reliable data about the proportions of new housing that have been constructed to Part M standards since October 1999. Builders said that they do not keep easily retrievable data, but that they would be able to give what they regarded as 'accurate estimates'. One builder said that they would be reluctant to spend much time on this task because they could not see the benefits to them. Some building control officers said that case control notes would indicate whether or not particular schemes conformed to Part M. Other officers were not sure about whether or not case notes would say anything about the status of applications (in relation to Part M). NHBC and HBF said that they do not hold such data, and both felt that it would be difficult to generate reliable aggregate figures for England and Wales.

In order to gauge the reliability of figures given in response to the questionnaire, each answer was coded as to whether it had been drawn from records, was a reasoned estimate, or was a guess (see Figure A.1). While most builders have accurate data on their annual build and numbers of currently active sites, they tend to be reliant on estimates and guesses about the proportions of housing constructed annually to Part M of the building regulations. In contrast, the initial response of most building control officers, about the proportion of units built to Part M standards since October 1999, was of utmost faith in their procedures. As one respondent said, 'if Part M was introduced into the regulations in October 1999, then the regulation will have been applied'. However, when officers were reminded that proportions of new-build housing may have been built without the need to comply with Part M, they conceded that this may indeed be so, but that there were no figures or records from which to draw this information.

Thus 12 (or 29 per cent) of the 42 local authorities were unable to give any figures for the number of housing units built in their area between October 1999 and December 2002, year on year, that are fully compliant with Part M standards. The reasons given by officers for their inability to produce either recorded or estimated figures were many and varied. For instance, one officer said that 'the information is not available and it is too

A.1 Sources of data.
Source: Author's telephone survey, 2003.

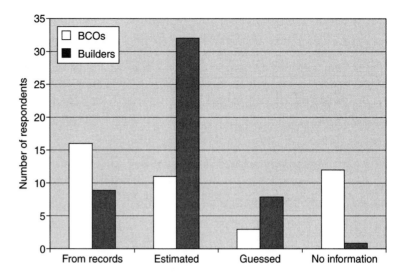

difficult to access', while, for another, 'we don't store this information and we would have to write a software program to access it'. Another officer suggested that 'Part M data are not available and we are not prepared to find time to access the statistics, nor are we prepared to give inaccurate figures'. Others concurred in noting that 'we have no records of Part M compliance', 'we don't maintain these figures as we send them off to the Deputy Prime Minister's Office', and 'we don't keep those figures any more'.

Building up a comparative picture of housing units built in a local authority area since October 1999, and Part M compliance, was further complicated by the variation in individual year-ends. The questions were structured to obtain figures for October to December 1999; January to December 2000; January to December 2001; and January 2002 to December 2002. This does not, however, necessarily reflect individual officers' year-ends; there does not appear to be a consistent pattern throughout local authorities. There is great variation in year-on-year calculations that may run, for example, from May to April, April to March, or October to September. In addition, the research, for reasons of time and cost, chose only to sample officers working for local authorities, although approved inspectors handle much of the building control function. The breakdown of the data, from the telephone survey to builders and building control officers, is presented in Appendix 3.

2 Disability and patterns of housing disadvantage

The discussion in Chapter 1 outlines, in brief, different patterns of disadvantage for disabled people in relation to housing. Such patterns are evident in EHCS data, including the information reproduced below:

Access by dwelling type, by thousands (% dwellings).

Dwelling type	Level access and facilities	Level access only	Level facilities only	None on level	All dwellings
Small terraced house	392 (14.9) (7.2)	2,062 (78.2) (18.2)	25 (0.9) (2.4)	157 (6.0) (8.2)	2,636 (100) (13.4)
Medium/large terraced house	352 (12.1) (6.5)	2,318 (79.7) (20.4)	32 (1.1) (3.1)	206 (7.1) (10.8)	2,909 (100) (14.7)
Semi-detached house	701 (13.3) (12.9)	4,266 (80.9) (37.6)	62 (1.2) (5.9)	243 (4.6) (12.7)	5,271 (100) (26.7)
Detached house	626 (21.5) (11.6)	2,131 (73.3) (18.8)	52 (1.8) (5.0)	100 (3.4) (5.2)	2,909 (100) (14.7)
Bungalow	1,582 (91.2) (29.3)	65 (3.8) (0.6)	39 (2.2) (3.7)	48 (2.8) (2.5)	1,734 (100) (8.8)
Converted flat	479 (35.0) (8.8)	167 (12.2) (1.4)	276 (20.2) (26.4)	446 (32.6) (23.4)	1,368 (100) (6.9)
Low-rise purpose-built flat	1,043 (41.5) (19.2)	289 (11.5) (2.6)	527 (21.0) (50.4)	652 (26.0) (34.2)	2,511 (100) (12.7)
High-rise purpose-built flat	246 (63.8) (4.5)	50 (12.9) (0.4)	32 (8.3) (3.1)	58 (15.0) (3.0)	387 (100) (2.0)
All types	5,421 (27.5) (100)	11,349 (57.5) (100)	1,045 (5.3) (100)	1,910 (9.7) (100)	19,725 (100) (100)

Source: English House Condition Survey, 1991.

3 Telephone survey data

The tables in this appendix provide a breakdown of the data that were gathered as part of the telephone survey conducted with builders and building control officers.

Table A Proportions of housing units constructed by builders to Part M of the building regulations, October 1999 to December 1999.

Units	None	<25%	25–50%	51–75%	76–99%	100%	DK/NA	Total
<50	12	1	–	–	1	3	1	18
51–100	3	–	1	1	1	–	2	8
101–200	6	1	2	–	–	–	–	9
201–1,000	2	–	1	–	–	–	–	3
1,001+	1	–	–	–	–	–	–	1
DK/NA	–	1	1	–	–	2	7	11
Total	24	3	5	1	2	5	10	50

Source: Author's survey.

Table B Proportions of housing units constructed by builders to Part M of the building regulations, January 2000 to December 2000.

Units	None	<25%	25–50%	51–75%	76–99%	100%	DK/NA	Total
<150	2	–	3	2	3	2	1	13
151–300	–	4	–	3	2	2	–	11
301–500	1	3	1	1	2	1	–	9
501–1,000	1	1	3	2	1	–	–	8
1,001+	–	–	7	–	–	–	1	8
DK/NA	–	–	–	–	–	–	1	1
Total	4	8	14	8	8	5	3	50

Source: Author's survey.

Table C Proportions of housing units constructed by builders to Part M of the building regulations, January 2001 to December 2001.

Units	None	<25%	25–50%	51–75%	76–99%	100%	DK/NA	Total
<150	–	2	–	3	1	6	1	13
151–300	–	–	–	2	1	6	–	9
301–500	1	1	–	3	–	5	–	10
501–1,000	–	2	–	3	1	3	–	9
1,001+	–	–	–	1	3	3	1	8
DK/NA	–	–	–	–	–	–	1	1
Total	1	5	–	12	6	23	3	50

Source: Author's survey.

Table D Proportions of housing units constructed to Part M of the building regulations, January 2002 to December 2002.

Units	None	<25%	25–50%	51–75%	76–99%	100%	DK/NA	Total
<150	–	1	1	–	2	7	–	11
151–300	–	–	–	–	1	10	–	11
301–500	–	1	–	–	–	9	–	10
501–1,000	–	–	–	–	2	6	–	8
1,001+	–	–	–	–	2	5	1	8
DK/NA	1	–	–	–	–	–	1	2
Total	1	2	1	–	7	37	2	50

Source: Author's survey.

Table E Proportions (%) of housing units constructed to Part M of the building regulations, October 1999 to December 1999, as estimated by BCOs.

Units	None	<25%	25–50%	51–75%	76–99%	100%	DK/NA	Total
<50	2	1	–	–	–	–	4	7
51–100	1	1	–	–	–	–	–	2
101–200	1	–	–	2	–	–	–	3
201–1,000	1	1	–	–	–	–	–	2
1,001+	–	–	–	–	–	–	–	–
DK/NA	2	–	–	–	1	–	25	28
Total	7	3	0	2	1	0	29	42

Source: Author's survey.

Table F Proportions (%) of housing units constructed to Part M of the building regulations, January 2000 to December 2000, as estimated by BCOs.

Units	None	<25%	25–50%	51–75%	76–99%	100%	DK/NA	Total
<100	–	1	–	–	1	–	2	4
101–200	–	2	–	–	1	–	2	5
201–300	1	1	1	–	1	–	2	6
301–500	1	1	–	1	–	–	1	4
501–1,000	1	–	–	1	–	–	1	3
1,001+	–	1	–	1	–	–	–	2
DK/NA	15	–	–	1	1	–	15	18
Total	23	6	1	4	4	0	23	42

Source: Author's survey.

Table G Proportions (%) of housing units constructed to Part M of the building regulations, January 2001 to December 2001, as estimated by BCOs.

Units	None	<25%	25–50%	51–75%	76–99%	100%	DK/NA	Total
<100	–	–	–	2	–	1	1	4
101–200	–	–	1	–	–	1	2	4
201–300	–	–	–	1	1	2	4	8
301–500	–	–	–	–	–	1	1	2
501–1,000	–	–	3	–	1	–	–	4
1,001+	–	–	1	1	1	–	–	3
DK/NA	–	1	–	–	2	2	12	17
Total	0	1	5	4	5	7	20	42

Source: Author's survey.

Table H Proportions (%) of housing units constructed to Part M of the building regulations, January 2002 to December 2002, as estimated by BCOs.

Units	None	<25%	25–50%	51–75%	76–99%	100%	DK/NA	Total
<100	–	–	–	–	1	3	3	7
101–200	–	–	–	2	2	2	1	7
201–300	–	–	1	–	2	2	1	6
301–500	–	–	–	–	1	1	–	2
501–1,000	–	1	1	–	2	1	–	5
1,001+	–	–	–	–	1	1	–	2
DK/NA	–	–	–	–	–	2	11	13
Total	0	1	2	2	9	12	16	42

Source: Author's survey.

References

Aalto, A., 1940, The humanizing of architecture, *The Technology Review*, November, 14–16.

Access Committee for England, 1995, *Letter to the Department of the Environment commenting on the draft proposals to extend Part M to dwellings*, DoE, London.

Administration on Developmental Disabilities, 1990, *Independence, Productivity, Integration for People with Developmental Disabilities: A Summary of Reports Prepared by State Developmental Disabilities Planning Councils*, Washington, DC.

Adorno, T., 1974, *Minima Moralia: Reflections from Damaged Life*, Verso, London.

Age Concern, 1995, *Letter to the Department of the Environment commenting on the draft proposals to extend Part M to dwellings*, 27 April, DoE, London.

Allan, G., 1985, *Family Life: Domestic Roles and Social Organization*, Blackwell, Oxford.

Allan, G. and Crow, G. (eds), 1989, *Home and Family: Creating the Domestic Sphere*, Allen and Unwin, London.

Allen, C., 1999, Disablism in housing and comparative community care discourse – towards an interventionist model of disability and interventionist welfare regime theory, *Housing, Theory and Society*, 16 (1), 3–16.

Allen, C., 2000, On the 'physiological dope' problematic in housing and illness research: towards a critical realism of home and health, *Housing, Theory and Society*, 17, 49–67.

Allen, C., 2004a, Bourdieu's habitus, social class and the spatial worlds of visual impaired children, *Urban Studies*, 41, 3, 487–506.

Allen, C., 2004b, Personal Communication, 22 November.

Allen, C., Milner, J. and Price, D., 2002, *Home is Where the Start is: The Housing and Urban Experiences of Visual Impaired Children*, Joseph Rowntree Foundation, York.

Alwyn Lloyd, 1936, The architect, and housing by the speculative builder, in Betham, E. (ed.), *House Building 1934–1936*, The Federated Employers' Press Ltd., London, pp. 119–136.

Americans with Disabilities Act (ADA), 1991, Rules and Regulations, *Federal Register*, 56, 144, 26 July.

Anon, 1844, Letter to the editor, *The Builder*, 14 September, p. 473.

Anon, 1866, Modern house building, *Building News*, 16 November, 755–756.

Anon, 1873, 'Jerry Builders', letter to the editor, *Building News*, 29 August, 242.

Anon, 1885, Letter to the editor, *The Builder*, xi, 896.

Anon, 1952, Editorial, *House and Home*, 2, 3, 108.

Appiah, K., In My Father's House: Africa in the Philosophy of Cultures, Oxford University Press, Oxford.

Arias, E. (ed.), 1993, *The Meaning and Use of Housing: International Perspectives, Approaches and their Application*, Ashgate Publishing Ltd, Aldershot.

Armitage, J., 1983, *A Survey of Housing, Physical Disability and the Role of Local Authorities*, Shelter, London.

Association of Building Engineers, 1995, *Letter to the Department of the Environment in response to the consultation exercise on Part M*, 10 May, DoE, London.

Bachelard, G., 1948, *La Terre et Les Reveries du Repos*, Librairie Jose Corti, Paris.

Baer, W., 1997, Towards design of regulations for the built environment, *Environment and Planning B: Planning and Design*, 24, 1, 37–58.

Bagguley, P., Mark-Lawson, J., Shapiro, D., Urry, J., Walby, S. and Warde, A., 1990, *Restructuring: Place, Class, and Gender*, Sage, London.

Ball, M., 1983, *Housing Policy and Economic Power*, Methuen, London.

Ball, M., 1996, *Housing and Construction: a Troubled Relationship*, The Policy Press, Bristol.

Ball, M., 1998, Institutions in British property research: a review, *Urban Studies*, 35, 9, 1501–1517.

Bannister, E., 2003, *Interview conducted by Rob Imrie*, 1 March, Bolingbrook, IL.

Barlow, J., 1999, From craft production to mass customisation. Innovation requirements for the UK house building industry, *Housing Studies*, 14, 1, 23–42.

Barlow, J. and Ozaki, R., 2001, Are You Being Served? Japanese Lessons on Customer-focused House building, *Report on a Department of Trade and Industry Expert Mission*, Brighton Science Policy Research Unit, University of Sussex.

Barlow, J. and Ozaki, R., 2003, Achieving 'customer focus' in private housebuilding: current practice and lessons from other industries, *Housing Studies*, 18, 1, 87–101.

Barlow, J. and Venables, T., 2004, Will technological innovation create the true lifetime home? *Housing Studies*, 19, 5, 795–810.

Barnes, C., 1991, *Disabled People in Britain and Discrimination*, Hurst and Company, London.

Barnes, C., Mercer, G. and Shakespeare, T., 1999, *Exploring Disability: a Sociological Introduction*, Polity, Oxford.

Bausch, M., 2000, Testimony to the Housing and Urban Development and Independent Agencies Appropriations Subcommittee, Washington, DC. Reprinted in *Open Doors*, Issue 10; also at http://www.c-c-d.org/od-jun00.hcm (accessed 20 November 2004).

BCIS, 2003, *The Cost of Life Time Homes: a Review of Published Estimates*, BCIS, 3 Cadogan Gate, London, SW1X 0AS.

Beazer Homes, 1995, *Reply to the Department of the Environment's Consultation on the proposal to extend Part M to housing*, Beazer Homes, London.

Beecher, C. and Beecher, H., 1869 (reprinted 2002), *The American Women's Home*, Rutgers University Press, New York.

Belser, S. and Weber, J., 1995, Home builders' attitudes and knowledge of ageing: the relationship to design for independent living, *Journal of Housing for the Elderly*, 11, 2, 123–137.

Bentley, I., 1999, *Urban Transformations: Power, People and Urban Design*, Routledge, London.

Bickenbach, J., 1993, *Physical Disability and Social Policy*, University of Toronto Press, Toronto.

Bickenbach, J., Chatterji, S., Badley, E., and Ustun, T., 1999, Models of disablement, universalism and the international classification of impairments, disabilities and handicaps, *Social Science and Medicine*, 48, 1173–1187.

Bierstedt, R., 1970, *The Social Order*, McGraw Hill, New York, NY.

Binns, D. and Mars, G., 1984, Family, community and unemployment: a study in change, *Sociological Review*, 32, 662–695.

Bishop, J. and Davidson, I., 1989, *Good Product: Could the Service be Better?* The Housing Research Foundation, London.

Blair, J., 1995, *Reply to the Department of the Environment's Consultation on the proposal to extend Part M to housing*, 14 June, DoE, London.

Blair, T., 1997, '*The will to win*', speech at the Aylesbury Estate, Southwark, London, 2 June.

Blomley, N., 1994, Mobility, empowerment, and the rights revolution, *Political Geography*, 13, 5, 407–422.

Bloomer, K. and Moore, C., 1977, *Body, Memory, and Architecture*, Yale University Press, Yale.

Bonnett, D., 1996, Incorporating lifetime homes into modernisation programmes, *Findings: Housing Research* 174, JRF, York.

Booth, C., Batty, E., Dargan, L., Gilroy, R., Harris, N. *et al.* 2003, *Planning and Diversity: Research into Policies and Procedures*, report to the Office of the Deputy Prime Minister, London.

Booth, P., 1982, Housing as a product: design guidance and residential satisfaction in the private sector, *Built Environment*, 8, 1, 20–24.

Borsay, A., 1986, *Disabled People in the Community: a Study of Housing, Health And Welfare Services,* Bedford Square Press, London.

Bournemouth Borough Council, 1998, *Housing Needs Survey*, BBC, Bournemouth.

Bramley, G., Bartlett, W. and Lambert, C., 1995, *Planning, the Market, and Private House Building*, UCL Press, London.

Bratt, R., 2002, Housing and family well being, *Housing Studies*, 17, 1, 13–26.

Brattgard, S., 2002, 1972, Sweden: Fokus, a way of life for living, in Lancaster-Gaye, D. (ed.), *Personal Relationships, the Handicapped and the Community*, Routledge and Kegan Paul, London.

Bright, S., 1995, *Letter to the Department of the Environment on behalf of The Deregulation Unit, Department of Trade and Industry*, 24 April, DoE, London.

Bristol Churches Housing Association Ltd, 1995, *Reply to the Department of the Environment's Consultation on the proposal to extend Part M to housing*, 27 April, DoE, London.

Buckle, J., 1971, *Work and Housing of Impaired People in Great Britain*, OPCS, HMSO, London.

Building Regulations Advisory Committee, 2004, *Briefing paper*, BRAC, London.

Bull, R. (ed.), 1998, *Housing Options for Disabled People*, Jessica Kingsley Publishers, London.

Bull, R. and Watts, V., 1998, The legislative and policy context, in Bull, R. (ed.), *Housing Options for Disabled People*, Jessica Kingsley Publishers, London, pp. 13–39.

Burby, R., DeBlois, J., May, P., Malizia, E. and Levine, J., 2000, Code Enforcement Burdens and Central City Decline, *Journal of the American Planning Association*, 66, 143–161.

Burdett, H., 1883, The dwellings of the middle classes, *Transactions of the Sanitary Institute of Great Britain*, 237–241.

Burnett, J., 1986, *A Social History of Housing, 1815–1985*, Routledge, London.

Burns, N., 2002, Access points and barriers to owner occupation for disabled people. PhD thesis, Department of Urban Studies, University of Glasgow, Glasgow.

Burns, N., 2004, Negotiating difference: disabled people's experiences of house builders, *Housing Studies*, 19, 5, 765–780.

Burns, S. and Mittelbach, F., 1968, Efficiency in the housing process, *report of the President's Committee on Urban Housing*, Washington, DC, Government Printing Office.

Burrows, R. and Wilcox, S., 2000, *Half the Poor: Home Owners with Low Incomes*, Council of Mortgage Lenders, London.

Callado, J., 1995, The architect's perspective, *Urban Studies*, 32, 10, 1665–1677.

Canguilhem, G., 1991, *The Normal and the Pathological*, Zone Books, New York, NY.

Carmona, M., 2001, *Housing Design Quality through Policy, Guidance and Review*, Spon Press, London.

Carmona, M., Carmona, S. and Gallent, N., 2003, *Delivering New Homes: Processes, Planners, and Providers*, Spon Press, London.

Carroll, C., Cowans, J. and Darton, D., 1999, *Meeting Part M and Designing Lifetime Homes*, Joeseph Rowntree Foundation, York.

Cavanagh, S. and Zaveri, A., 2000, *Housing for Independence: Disabled Women Informing Inclusive Design Principles and Policies*, Women's Design Services, London.

Center for Universal Design, 2000, website: www.design.ncsu.edu/.

Chamba, R., Ahmad, W., Hirst, D., Lawton, D. and Beresford, B., 1999, *On the Edge: Minority Ethnic Families Caring for a Disabled Child*, Policy Press, Bristol.

Chapman, T. and Hockey, J. (eds), 1999, *Ideal Homes? Social Change and Domestic Life*, Routledge, London.

Chow, R., 2002, *Suburban Space: The Fabric of Dwelling*, University of California Press, Berkeley, CA.

Christophersen, J., 1995, *The Growth of Good Housing: Promotion and Regulation of Dwelling Quality in Norway*, The Norwegian State Housing Bank, Oslo.

City of Naperville, 2001, *Municipal Code, Supplement Number 41*, City of Naperville, Naperville, IL.

City of Toronto, 2001, Bill 125 *Ontarians with Disabilities Act*, City of Toronto Community Advisory Committee, Toronto.

Clancy, P., 1995, *Reply to the Department of the Environment's Consultation on the proposal to extend Part M to housing*, 27 April, DoE, London.

Cobbold, C., 1997, *A Cost Benefit Analysis of Lifetime Homes*, Joseph Rowntree Foundation, York.

Collins, P., 1965, *Changing Ideals of Modern Architecture, 1750–1950*, Faber & Faber, London.

Commission for Architecture and the Built Environment, 2003, House builders must now go for gold to attract demanding consumers, *Press Release*, 8 July, CABE, London.

Conrad, V., 1964, *Programs and Manifestos on 20th Century Architecture*, MIT Press, Cambridge, MA.

Cooper Marcus, C., 1995, *Houses as a Mirror of Self*, Conan Press, Berkeley, CA.

Council for the Preservation of Rural England, 1995, *Local Attraction: The Design of New Housing in the Countryside*, CPRE, London.

Crossley, N., 2001, *The Social Body: Habit, Identity, and Desire*, Sage Publications, London.

Cruikshank, B., 1999, *The Will to Empower: Democratic Citizens and Other Subjects*, Cornell University Press, London.

Culwell, P. and Kau, J., 1982, The economics of building codes and standards, in Johnson, M. (ed.), *Resolving the Housing Crisis*, Ballinger Press, Cambridge, MA, pp. 321–343.

Curtis, W., 1982, *Modern Architecture since 1900*, Phaidon Press Ltd., London.

Davis, P., 1995, *Reply to the Department of the Environment's Consultation on the proposal to extend Part M to housing*, 22 April, DoE, London.

Dean, H., 2000, Introduction: towards an embodied account of welfare, in Ellis, K. and Dean, H. (eds), *Social Policy and the Body*, Macmillan, London, xi–xxv.

Dean, M., 1999, *Governmentality*, Sage Publications, London.

DeGory, E., 1998, A potential for flexibility. Unpublished MSc thesis in the History of Modern Architecture, Bartlett School of Architecture and Planning, University College London, London.

Denby, E., 1934, Design in the kitchen, in Gloag, J. (ed.), *Design in Modern Life*, Allen & Unwin, London, 61–72.

Department of Employment, 1990, *The Employment of People with Disabilities: A Review of the Legislation*, IFF Research Ltd., London.

Department of the Environment, 1974, Housing for people who are physically handicapped, *Circular 74/74*, DoE, London.

Department of the Environment, 1975, Wheelchair housing, *Housing Development Directorate Occasional paper, 2/75*, DoE, London.

Department of the Environment, 1980, *Development Control – Policy and Practice, Circular 22/80*, HMSO, London.

Department of the Environment, 1991, *English House Conditions Survey*, DoE, London.

Department of the Environment, 1992, *Planning Policy Guidance: Housing, PPG3 (revised)*, DoE, London.

Department of the Environment, 1995, *Draft Proposals to Extend Part M of the Building Regulations to Dwellings*, DoE, London.

Department of the Environment, Transport and the Regions, 1998, *Regulatory Impact Assessment (final) of the Proposed Extension of Part M (Building Regulations) to Dwellings*, DETR, London.

Department of the Environment, Transport and the Regions, 1999a, *Approved Document M: Access and Facilities for Disabled People*, DETR, London.

Department of the Environment, Transport, and the Regions, 1999b, *Planning Policy Guidance 3: Housing*, HMSO, London.

Department of the Environment, Transport and the Regions, 2000, *Our Towns and Cities: the Future*, HMSO, London.

Department of the Environment, Transport and the Regions and the Commission for Architecture and the Built Environment, 2000, *By Design, Urban Design in the Planning System: Towards Better Practice*, DETR, London.

Department of Health, 1970, *Chronically Sick and Disabled Persons Act*, DOH, London.

Department of Health, 1989, *Caring for People: Community Care in the Next Decade and Beyond*, HMSO, London.

Department of Housing and Urban Development, 1991, *Fair Housing Accessibility Guidelines*, HUD, Washington, DC.

Department of Trade and Industry, 2000, *Building a Better Quality of Life: A Strategy for more Sustainable Construction*, DTI, London.

Derby City Council, 1988, *Local Plan*, DCC, Derby.

Derbyshire Coalition of Disabled People, 1995, *Draft Part M: Dwellings*, written in response to the Department of the Environment commenting on the draft proposals to extend Part M to dwellings, 19 May, DoE, London.

Dewsbury, G., Rouncefield, M., Clarke, K. and Sommerville, I., 2004, Depending on digital design: extending inclusivity, *Housing Studies*, 19, 5, 811–826.

Dikec, M., 2001, Justice and the spatial imagination, *Environment and Planning A*, 33, 1785–1805.

Disability Wales, 1995, *Draft Part M: Dwellings*, written response to the Department of the Environment commenting on the draft proposals to extend Part M to dwellings, 10 May, DoE, London.

Disraeli, B., 1847, *Tancred, or the New Crusade*, 1, 233–234.

Dobson, E., 1968, Building regulations – a review of the position in some western countries, *National Building Research Institute, Bulletin 54*, NBRI, London.

Downie, R. and Telfer, E., 1969, *Respect for Persons*, George Allen and Unwin Ltd., London.

Dunn, P., 1988. *The Impact of Housing upon the Independent Living Outcomes of Individuals with Disabilities*. Dissertation. Brandeis University, The Heller Graduate School for Advanced Studies in Social Welfare.

Dunn, P., 1997, *A Comparative Analysis of Barrier-Free Housing: Policies for Elderly People in the United States and Canada*, unpublished paper.

Dupuis, A. and Thorns, D., 1996, Meanings of home for the older home owner, *Housing Studies*, 11, 4, 485–501.

Dyos, H., 1961, *Victorian Suburb: A Study of the Growth of Camberwell*, Leicester University Press, Leicester.

Dyos, H., 1968, The speculative developers of Victorian London, *Victorian Studies, XI*.

Edgar, B., Doherty, J. and Meert, H., 2002, *Access to Housing*, Policy Press, London.

Edgar, E., O'Hara, A., Smith, B. and Zovistoski, A., 1999, *Priced Out in 1999: the Housing Crisis for People with Disabilities*, The Consortium for Citizens with Disabilities Housing Task Force, Washington, DC, www.c-c-d.org.

Egan Report, 1998, *Rethinking Construction: The Report of the Construction Task Force*, DETR, London.

Ellis, K., 2000, Welfare and bodily order: theorising transitions in corporeal discourse, in Ellis, K. and Dean, H. (eds), *Social Policy and the Body: Transitions in Corporeal Discourse*, Macmillan, London, 1–44.

Evans, R., 1978, Rockeries and model dwellings: English housing reform and the moralities of private space, *AAQ*, 10, 24–35.

Evans, R., 1997, *Translations from Drawing to Building and Other Essays*, Architectural Association, London.

Eward, F., 1990, Norms, discipline and the law, *Representations*, 30, 138–161.

Ewing Inquiry, 1994, *Housing in Scotland for People with a Physical Disability*, Disability Scotland, Edinburgh.

Fainstein, S., 1995, Justice, politics, and the creation of urban space, in Merrifield, A. and Swyngedouw, E. (eds), *The Urbanisation of Injustice*, Lawrence and Wishart, London, 18–44.

Falconer, C., 2001, Design for Living, *News Release 386*, 11 September, DTLR, London.

Fanning, R., Judge, J., Weike, F. and Emener, G., 1991, Housing needs of individuals with severe mobility impairments: a case study, *Journal of Rehabilitation*, 57, 2, 7–13.

Farrell, T., 2002, *Building for Life: Conference Introduction*, Building for Life, National Conference, London, 3 July.

Finn, M., 1995, *Letter to the Department of the Environment on behalf of Barratts Developments plc*, 27 April, DoE, London.

Forrest, J., 1995, *Reply to the Department of the Environment's Consultation on the proposal to extend Part M to housing*, 9 June, DoE, London.

Forty, A., 2000, *Words and Buildings: A Vocabulary of Modern Architecture*, Thames and Hudson, London.

Foucault, M., 1977, *Discipline and Punish: The Birth of the Prison*, London, Allen Lane.

Fox, J., 2000, *Letter to the Millennial Housing Commission*, Paralyzed Veterans of America, Washington, DC.

Frampton, K., 1989, *Modern Architecture: A Critical History*, Thames and Hudson, London.

Franklin, B., 2001, Discourses of design: perspectives on the meaning of housing quality and 'good' housing design, *Housing, Theory, and Society*, 18, 79–92.

Fraser, R., 1995, *Letter to the Department of the Environment on behalf of Westbury Homes*, 18 May, DoE, London.

Frederick, C., 1913, *The New Housekeeping. Efficiency Studies in House Management*, Doubleday, Page and Co., New York.

Galster, G., 1991, Housing discrimination and poverty of African-Americans, *Journal of Housing Research*, 2, 87–122.

Galster, G., 1999, Open housing, integration and the reduction of ghettoization: the evolving challenge of fair housing since 1968, *Cityscape*, 4, 123–138.

Gann, D., 1992, *Intelligent Buildings: Users and Producers*, ECA/SPRU, Brighton.

Gann, D., Biffin, M., Connaughton, J., Dacey, T., Hill, A. *et al.*, 1999, *Flexibility and Choice in Housing*, Policy Press, Bristol.

Gavin, H., 1850, *The Habitations of the Industrial Classes*, Garland, New York.

Giedion, S., 1929, *Mechanization takes Command: A Contribution to an Anonymous History*, Oxford University Press, New York.

Gilman, C., 2002, *The Home: Its Work and Influence*, Alta Mira Press, London.

Gleeson, B., 1998, *Geographies of Disability*, Routledge, London.

Gloag, J. (ed.), 1934, *Design in Modern Life*, Allen & Unwin, London.

Gold, S., 2000, Philadelphia Housing Victory, www.libertyresources.org/housing/ph.12 (site visited 12 November 2002).

Goldsack, L., 1999, A haven in a heartless world? Women and domestic violence, in Chapman, T. and Hockey, J. (eds), 1999, *Ideal Homes? Social Change and Domestic Life*, Routledge, London, 121–132.

Goldsmith, S., 1997, *Designing for the Disabled: The New Paradigm*, Architectural Press, Oxford.

Goodchild, B., 1997, *Housing and the Urban Environment: A Guide to Housing Design, Renewal and Urban Planning*, Blackwell, Oxford.

Goodchild, B. and Furbey, R., 1986, Standards in housing design: a review of the main changes since the Parker Morris report (1961), *Land Development Studies*, 3, 79–99.

Goodchild, B. and Karn, V., 1996, Standards, quality control and house building in the UK, in Williams, P. (ed.), *Directions in Housing Policy*, Paul Chapman Publishing, London, 156–174.

Gooding, C., 1994, *Disabling Laws, Enabling Acts: Disability Rights in Britain and America*, Pluto Press, London.

Goodman, 1995, *Reply to the Department of the Environment's Consultation on the proposal to extend Part M to housing*, 27 April, DoE, London.

Greater London Authority, 2004, *Accessible London: Achieving an Accessible Environment*, The London Plan Supplementary Planning Guidance, GLA, London.

Gropius, W., 1954, Eight steps towards a solid architecture, in Ockman, J. (ed.), *Architecture Culture*, Columbia University Press, New York, 177–180.

Grosz, E., 2001, *Architecture from the Outside*, MIT Press, Cambridge, MA.

Groves, A., 2002, PPG3 and accessible housing, *Access Journal*, 7, 8.

Gummer, J., 1995, The Way to Achieve Quality in Urban Design, *Department of the Environment Press Release 162*, 30 March, DoE, London.

Gurney, C., 1990, The meaning of the home in the decade of owner occupation, School for Advanced Urban Studies, *Working Paper 88*, University of Bristol, SAUS Publications, Bristol.

Gurney, C., 2000, Transgressing private–public boundaries in the home: a sociological analysis of the coital noise taboo, *Venereology*, 13, 39–46.

Gurney, C. (undated), 'The neighbours didn't dare complain': some taboo thoughts on the regulation of noisy bodies and the disembodied housing imagination, www.cf.ac.uk/uwcc/cplan/enhr/files/Gurney-C2.html.

Guy, S., 1998, Developing alternatives: energy, offices, and the environment, *International Journal of Urban and Regional Research*, 22, 2, 264–282.

Habraken, N., 1972, *Supports: An Alternative to Mass Housing*, Prager, New York, NY.

Haddon, L., 1998, *Consumer research and tenant consultation: a report for Phase 2 of the INTEGER programme*, unpublished report.

Hamdi, N., 1990, *Housing without Houses: Participation, Flexibility, Enablement*, Van Nostrand Reinhold, London.

Hammersmith and Fulham Council, 2002, *Housing Needs Survey*, Joint Client Services Group, HFC, Hammersmith, London.

Hammond, J. and Hammond, B., 1917, *The Town Labourer, 1760–1832*, Longmans, Green and Co., London.

Hannaford, S., 1985, *Living Outside Inside*, Canterbury Press, Berkeley, CA.

Harrison, M., 2004, Defining housing quality and environment: disability, standards, and social factors, *Housing Studies*, 19, 5, 691–708.

Harrison, M. and Davis, C., 2001, *Housing, Social Policy and Difference: Disability, Ethnicity, Gender and Housing*, Policy Press, Bristol.

Harvey, D., 1989, *The Condition of Post Modernity*, Blackwell, Oxford.

Hatch, R. (ed.), 1984, *The Scope of Social Architecture*, Van Nostrand Reinhold, New York, NY.

Haviland, D., 1996, Some shifts in building design and their implications for design practices and management, *Journal of Architecture and Planning Research*, 13, 1, 50–62.

Hawkesworth, M., 2001, Disabling spatialities and the regulation of a visible secret, *Urban Studies*, 38, 2, 299–318.

HBF, 2001, *City of Derby Local Plan Review – First Deposit: Letter of Objection*, Derby City Council, Derby.

Hedges, B. and Clemens, S., 1994, *Housing Attitudes Survey*, Department of the Environment, HMSO, London.

Helen Hamlyn Trust, 1989, Speech by Andy Rowe MP on Lifetime Homes, HHT, London.

Hemm, D., 1995, *Reply to the Department of the Environment's Consultation on the proposal to extend Part M to housing*, 26 April, DoE, London.

Hertzberger, H., 1991, *'Place and Articulation' Lessons for Students in Architecture*, Utigeverij Publishers, Rotterdam.

Heywood, F., 2004, Understanding needs: a starting point for quality, *Housing Studies*, 19, 5, 709–726.

Heywood, F., Oldman, C. and Means, R., 2002, *Housing and Home in Later Life*, Open University Press, Milton Keynes.

Hill, J., 2003, *Actions of Architecture: Architects and Creative Users*, Routledge, London.

Hill, R., 1999, *Designs and their Consequences: Architecture and Aesthetics*, Yale University Press, New Haven, CT.

Hobbes, T., 1996, *Leviathan*, Oxford University Press, Oxford.

Hockey, J., 1999, The Ideal of Home, in Chapman, T. and Hockey, J. (eds), *Ideal Homes? Social Change and Domestic Life*, Routledge, London, 108–118.

Holland, C. and Pearce, S., 2002, Inclusive housing, in Peace, S. and Holland, C. (eds), *Inclusive Housing in an Ageing Society*, Policy Press, Bristol, 235–260.

Hooper, A., 1999, *Design for Living: Constructing the Residential Built Environment for the 21st Century*, Town and Country Planning Association, London.

Hopton, J. and Hunt, S., 1996, The health effects of improvement to housing: a longitudinal study, *Housing Studies*, 11, 2, 271–286.

House Builders Federation, 1982, *Charter for the Disabled*, HBF, London.

House Builders Federation, 1995, *The Application of Building Regulations to Help Disabled People in New Dwellings in England and Wales*, HBF, London.

House of Representatives, 2003, 'Schakowsky introduces the Inclusive Home Design Act to greatly increase number of homes accessible to people with disabilities', *Press Release*, 5 June, H.R., Washington, DC.

Housing Forum, 2000, New homes national customer satisfaction survey 2000, The Housing Forum, London.

Humman, D., 1989, House, home and identity in contemporary culture, in Low, S. and Chambers, E., *Housing, Culture, and Design*, University of Pennsylvania Press, Pennsylvania, PA, 207–228.

Hunt, A. and Wickham, G., 1994, *Foucault and the Law: Towards a Sociology of Law as Governance*, Pluto Press, London.

Illich, I, 1992, *In the Mirror of the Past: Lectures and Addresses, 1978–1990*, Marion Boyars, London.

Imrie, R., 1996, Equity, Social Justice, and Planning for Access and Disabled People: An International Perspective, *International Planning Studies*, 1, 1, 17–34.

Imrie, R., 1997, Challenging disabled access in the built environment: an evaluation of evidence from the United Kingdom, *Town Planning Review*, 68, 4, 423–448.

Imrie, R., 1999, The role of access groups in facilitating accessible environments for disabled people, *Disability and Society*, 14, 4, 463–482.

Imrie, R., 2000a, Disabling environments and the geography of access policies and practices in the United Kingdom, *Disability and Society*, 15, 1, 5–24.

Imrie, R., 2000b, Disability and discourses of mobility and movement, *Environment and Planning A*, 32, 9, 1641–1656.

Imrie, R., 2003a, The impact of Part M on the design of new housing, *Final report to the JRF*, York, 86 pp., available at www.gg.rhul.ac.uk/jrf.pdf.

Imrie, R., 2003b, *Responding to disabled people's needs in the residential environment*, Final project report to the Economic and Research Council, Royal Holloway University of London, Egham.

Imrie, R., 2003c, Architects' conceptions of the human body, *Environment and Planning D: Society and Space*, 21, 1, 47–65.

Imrie, R. (ed.), 2004a, Housing quality, disability, and design, *Special Issue of Housing Studies*, 19, 5, 685–838.

Imrie, R., 2004b, 'Demystifying disability': A review of the International Classification of Functioning, Disability and Health? *Sociology of Heath and Illness*, 26, 3, 287–305.

Imrie, R. and Hall, P., 2001a, *Inclusive Design: Developing and Designing Accessible Environments*, Spon Press, London.

Imrie, R. and Hall, P., 2001b, An exploration of disability and the development process, *Urban Studies*, 38, 2, 231–237.

Imrie, R. and Raco, M. (eds), 2003, *Urban Renaissance: New Labour, Community and Urban Policy*, Policy Press, Bristol.

Isin, E. (ed.), 2000, *Democracy, Citizenship, and the Global City*, Routledge, London.

Israel, M., 1997, Word Origins, in *The Alternative Usage English*, www.yaelf.com.

Jackson, A., 1996, *Reconstructing Architecture for the 21st Century*, University of Toronto Press, Toronto.

Jackson, N., 1981, Built to sell: the speculative house in 19th century London, Unpublished PhD thesis, Department of Architecture, South Bank University, London.

Jeserich, M., 2003, Mandating Accessible Homes: Bills would create more housing stock for people with disabilities, *AT Journal, 73*, 15 May, available at www.atnet.org/news/may03/051501.

Joseph Rowntree Foundation, 2003, *LTH Standards*, JRF, York.

Karn, V. and Sheridan, L., 1994, *New Housing in the 1990's: A Study of Design, Space and Amenity in Housing Association and Private Sector Production*, Joseph Rowntree Foundation, York.

Kashmiri, A., 2003, *Interview with Ali Kashmiri*, access officer, conducted by R. Imrie, London Borough of Harrow, 8 April 2003.

Kelly, B., 1959, *Design and the Production of Houses*, McGraw-Hill, New York, NY.

Kendall, S., and Teicher, J., 2000, *Residential Open Building*, Spon Press, London.

King, D., 1998a, Bovis evades disabled rules, *Building*, 12 June, 262, 7–8.

King, D., 1998b, Raynsford orders Part M inquiry, *Building*, 19 June, 263, 8.

King, N., 1999, Housing circumstances and preferences of wheelchair users: looking at new options, *Housing, Care & Support*, 2, 1, 17–19.

King, P., 1996, *The Limits of Housing Policy: A Philosophical Investigation*, Middlesex University Press, London.

King, P., 2003, *A Social Philosophy of Housing*, Ashgate, Aldershot.

King, P., 2004, *Private Dwelling: Contemplating the Use of Housing*, Routledge, London.

Knesl, J., 1984, The Power of Architecture, *Environment and Planning D: Society and Space*, 1, 3–22.

Kochera, A., 2002, *Accessibility and visitability in single family homes: a review of state and local activity*, working paper, AARP Public Policy Institute, Washington, DC.

Kose, S., 2000, The impact of rapid ageing in Japan on accessibility issues, unpublished paper, Shizuoka University of Art and Culture, Hamamatsu, Japan.

Lafaivre, L. and Tzoni, A., 1984, The question of autonomy in architecture, *The Harvard Architecture Review*, 3, 27–43.

Landis, J., 1983, Why homebuilders don't innovate, *Built Environment*, 8, 1, 46–53.

Laune, L., 1990, *Building Our Lives: Housing, Independent Living and Disabled People*, Shelter, London.

Law, R., 1999, Beyond 'women and transport': towards new geographies of gender and daily mobility, *Progress in Human Geography*, 23, 4, 567–588.

Lawrence, R., 1987, *Housing, Dwellings and Home: Design Theory, Research and Practice*, John Wiley, London.

Lawrence, R., 1989, Translating anthropological concepts into architectural practices, in Low, S. and Chambers, E., *Housing, Culture, and Design*, University of Pennsylvania Press, Pennsylvania, PA, 89–114.

Lawrence, R., 1995, Housing quality: an agenda for research, *Urban Studies*, 32, 10, 1655–1664.

Lawrence, R., 2002, Healthy residential environments, in Bechtel, R. and Churchman, A. (eds), *Handbook of Environmental Psychology*, John Wiley, London, 394–412.

Le Corbusier, 1923, *Towards a New Architecture*, Butterworth, Oxford.

Le Corbusier, 1925, *La Peinture Moderne*, Paris.

Le Corbusier, 1967, *The Radiant City*, Faber, London.

Le Corbusier and de Pierrefeu, F., 1948, *The Home of Man*, The Architectural Press, London.

Leder, D., 1990, *The Absent Body*, Chicago University Press, Chicago, IL.

Lefebvre, H., 1976, *The Survival of Capitalism: Reproduction of the Relations of Production*, Allison and Busby, London.

Lefebvre, H., 1991, *The Production of Space*, Blackwell, Oxford.

Lefebvre, H., 1996, *Writings on Cities*, Blackwell, Oxford.

Leonnig, C., 2001, Disabled sue District for barrier-free housing: shortage of housing units said to violate law, *Washington Post*, Washington, DC, 28 March, p. B01.

Leopold, E. and Bishop, D., 1983, Design philosophy and practice in speculative house building: Part 1, *Construction Management and Economics*, 1, 2, 119–144.

Lerup. L., 1987, *Planned Assaults*, MIT Press, Cambridge, MA.

Letherby, G., 2002, Claims and disclaimers: knowledge, reflexivity and representation in feminist research, *Sociological Research Online*, 6, 4, www.socresonline.org.uk.

Lewin, F., 2001, The meaning of home amongst elderly immigrants: directions for future research and theoretical development, *Housing Studies*, 16, 3, 353–370.

Lewis, C., 1995, *Reply to the Department of the Environment's Consultation on the proposal to extend Part M to housing*, DoE, London.

Lifetime Homes Group, 1993, *Lifetime Homes*, Joseph Rowntree Foundation, York.

Llewellyn, M., 2004, Designed by women and designing women: gender, planning and the geographies of the kitchen in Britain 1917–1946, *Cultural Geographies*, 11, 1, 42–60.

London Borough of Harrow, 2002, *Unitary Development Plan*, Draft, LBH, London.

Luccarelli, M., 1995, *Lewis Mumford and the Ecological Region: The Politics of Planning*, Guilford, London.

Luck, R., Haenlein, H, and Bright, K., 2001, Project briefing for accessible design, *Design Studies*, 22, 297–315.

Lynch, K., 1960, *The Image of the City*, MIT Press, Cambridge, MA.

MacDonald, N., 1991, *Democratic Architecture*, Whitley Library of Design, New York, NY

MacPherson, C., 1997, A Samoan solution to the limitations of urban housing in New Zealand, in Renoel, J. and Rodma, M. (eds), *Home in the Islands: Housing and Social Change in the Pacific*, University of Hawaii Press, Hawaii, 151–174.

Madigan, R. and Munro, M., 1999, 'The more we are together': domestic space, gender and privacy, in Chapman, T. and Hockey, J. (eds), 1999, *Ideal Homes? Social Change and Domestic Life*, Routledge, London, 61–72.

Maisel, S., 1953, *House building in transition*, University of California Press, Berkeley, CA.

Malleris, W., 2000, The accessible housing debate before Congress, *Apt.ITUDES, Summer*, 20–21.

Marks, D., 1999, *Disability: Controversial Debates and Psychosocial Perspectives*, Routledge, London.

Maslow, A., 1970, *Motivation and Personality*, 2nd edn, Harper & Row, New York, NY.

McDowell, L., 1983, Towards an understanding of the gender divisions of urban space, *Environment and Planning D: Society and Space*, 1, 1, 59–72.

McEwan, S., 1995, *Reply to the Department of the Environment's Consultation on the proposal to extend Part M to housing*, 27 April, DoE, London.

McNulty, T., 2003, Forward, in Office of the Deputy Prime Minister, *Planning and Access for Disabled People: a Good Practice Guide*, ODPM, London.

Meijer, F. and Visscher, H., 1998, The deregulation of building controls: a comparison of Dutch and other European systems, *Environment and Planning B: Planning and Design*, 25, 617–629.

Memphis Centre for Independent Living, 2001, Survey of dwellings, *The Declaration*, 7, 1, 3–5.

Mencap, 2002, *The Housing Timebomb*, Mencap, London.

Merleau-Ponty, M., 1962, *The Phenomenology of Perception*, Routledge and Kegan Paul, London.

Merleau-Ponty, M., 1963, *The Primacy of Perception*, Northwestern University Press, Evanston.

Michailakis, D., 1997, *Government Action on Disability Policy: A Global Survey*, Office of the United Nations Special Rapporteur on Disability, Geneva.

Michigan Statewide Council for Independent Living (2001), *Disability Voice Issues, 1999–2001*, MISILC, www.misilc.org/housing9901.htm.

Mikiten, E., 2002, AIA, HUD announces housing and community design award winners, www.aia.org/aiarchitect/thisweek02/tw0712/0712 twaiahud.htm (accessed 12 December 2003).

Mikiten, E., 2004, Personal Communication, 27 November.

Millen, D., 1997, Some methodological and epistemological issues raised by doing feminist research on non-feminist women, *Sociological Research Online*, 2, 3, www.socresonline.org.uk.

Mills, G., 1995, *Reply to the Department of the Environment's Consultation on the proposal to extend Part M to housing, on behalf of the NHBC*, 26 May, DoE, London.

Milner, J. and Madigan, R., 2001, The politics of accessible housing in the UK, in Peace, S. and Holland, C. (eds), *Inclusive Housing in an Ageing Society: Innovative Approaches*, 77–101.

Milner, J. and Madigan, R., 2004, Regulation and innovation: rethinking 'inclusive' housing design, *Housing Studies*, 19, 5, 727–744.

Ministry of Health, 1944, *Design of Dwellings*, HMSO, London.

Ministry of Housing and Local Government, 1961, *Homes for Today and Tomorrow*, HMSO, London.

Morris, J., 1988, *Freedom to Lose: Housing Policy and People with Disabilities*, Shelter, London.

Morris, J., 1990, *Our Homes, Our Rights: Housing, Independent Living, and Physically Disabled People*, Shelter, London.

Morris, J., 1991, *Pride against Prejudice: Transforming Attitudes to Disability*, The Women's Press, London.

Mumford, L., 1928, Towards a rational modernism, *New Republic*, April, 297–298.

Mumford, L., 1966, *The City in History*, Penguin, Harlow.

Naim, M. and Barlow, J., 2003, An innovative supply chain strategy for customised housing, *Construction Management and Economics*, 21 (6), 593–602.

National Association of Home Builders, 2003, *National Housing Quality Award, 2004: Are You Ready*, NAHB Research Center, Upper Marlboro, MD.

National Council on Disability, 1994, *ADA Watch – Year One: A Report to the President and Congress on Progress in Implementing the Americans with Disabilities Act*, NCD, Washington, DC.

National House Building Council, 1981, How to make houses more suitable for elderly and handicapped persons, *Advisory note number 2*, NHBC, Milton Keynes.

National House Building Council, 2001, *New House-Building Statistics*, NHBC, Amersham.

National House Building Council, 2002, *New House-Building Statistics*, NHBC, Amersham.

National Housing Federation, 1998, *Standards and Quality in Development: A Good Practice Guide*, NHF, London.

National Organisation on Disability, 2002, *Annual Report*, NCD, Washington, DC, see www.ncd.org/housing.

Nicol, C. and Hooper, A., 1999, Contemporary change and the house building industry: concentration and standardization in production, *Housing Studies*, 14, 1, 57–76.

Norberg-Schulz, C., 1985, *The concept of dwelling: on the way to figurative architecture*, Rizzoli International Publications, New York, NY.

North Tyneside Social Services, 1982, *A study of people living in North Tyneside in 1980*, North Tyneside Social Services, Newcastle-upon-Tyne.

Nussbaum, M., 1999, *Sex and Social Justice*, Oxford University Press, Oxford.

O'Brien, P., Blythe, A. and McDaid, S., 2002, *Lifetime homes in Northern Ireland: evolution or revolution*, report commissioned by the Joseph Rowntree Foundation and Chartered Institute of Housing in Northern Ireland, JRF, York.

O'Connor, M., 2002, Builder to spend $1 million to settle US disability suit, *Chicago Tribune*, 20 September, p. 6.

O'Hara, A. and Miller, E., 1998, *Going it Alone – The Struggle to Expand Housing Opportunities*.

Office of Population Censuses and Surveys, 1971, *The 1971 Census of Great Britain: General Report*, HMSO, London.

Office of Population Censuses and Surveys, 1987, *The Prevalence of Disability in Great Britain, Report 1*, HMSO, London.

Office of Population Censuses and Surveys, 1991, *The 1991 Census of Great Britain: General Report*, HMSO, London.

Office of Population Censuses and Surveys, 2001, *The 2001 Census of Great Britain: General Report*, HMSO, London.

Office of the Deputy Prime Minister, 2000a, Housing quality indicators: feasibility study, *Housing Research Summary, no. 70*, ODPM, London.

Office of the Deputy Prime Minister, 2000b, Housing quality indicators, *Housing Research Summary, no. 94*, ODPM, London.

Office of the Deputy Prime Minister, 2001a, *Supporting People: Policy into Practice*, ODPM, London.

Office of the Deputy Prime Minister, 2001b, *English House Conditions Survey, Surveyor's Manual*, ODPM, London.

Office of the Deputy Prime Minister, 2002, *English House Condition Survey: Key Facts*, ODPM, London.

Office of the Deputy Prime Minister, 2003, *Sustainable Communities: Building for the Future*, ODPM, London.

Office of the Deputy Prime Minister, 2004, New design rules create homes with built-in flexibility, *News Release*, 10 March, ODPM, London.

Oldman, C., 2002, The importance of housing and home, in Bytheway, B., Bacigalupo, V., Bornat, J., Johnson, J. and Spurr, S. (eds), *Understanding Care, Welfare and Community: A Reader*, Routledge, London, 330–340.

Oldman, C. and Beresford, B., 2000, Home, sick home: using the housing experiences of disabled children to suggest a new theoretical framework, *Housing Studies*, 15, 3, 429–442.

Oliver, M., 1990, *The Politics of Disablement*, Macmillan, London.

Oliver, P., Davis, I. and Bentley, I., 1981, *Dunroamin: The Suburban Semi and its Enemies*, Pimlico, London.

Ownership Options in Scotland, 2002, Evaluation of Ownership Options in Scotland, *Final Report*, OOS, Edinburgh.

Papanek, V., 2000, *Design for the Real World: Human Ecology and Social Change*, Thames and Hudson, London.

Park, W., 1991, Creating and maintaining access to housing: implementing access at the local level, *Report of the CIB Expert Seminar on Building Non-Handicapping Environments*, Budapest, www.independentliving.org/cib/cibbudapest24.html.

Parker, A. and Mirrlees, C., 1988, *Residential Homes*, Age Concern, London.

Paterson, K. and Hughes, B., 1999, Disability studies and phenomenology: the carnal politics of everyday life, *Disability and Society*, 14, 5, 597–611.

Peace, S. and Holland, C., 2001, Housing an ageing society, in Peace, S. and Holland, C. (eds), *Inclusive Housing in an Ageing Society*, Policy Press, Bristol, pp. 1–26.

Percival, J., 2002, Domestic spaces: uses and meanings in the daily lives of older people, *Ageing and Society*, 22, 729–749.

PIEDA, 1996, *A Cost Benefit Analysis of Lifetime Homes*, PIEDA plc, 52 Queens Road, Reading, RG1 4AU.

Pikusa, S., 1983, Adaptability: designing for functional adaptability; a lesson from history, *Architecture Australia*, 72, 1, 62–67.

Prak, N. and Priemus, H. (eds), 1995, *Post War Housing in Trouble*, Delft University Press, Delft.

Price, D., 2003, Interview conducted by Rob Imrie on 1 March 2003, Independent Living Center, Chicago, IL.

Pugh Associates, D., 1969, Facilities for handicapped people, *Architects Journal*, 5 March, 649–654.

Purcell, M., 2002, Excavating Lefebvre: The right to the city and its urban politics of the inhabitant, *GeoJournal*, 58, 99–108.

Rabinowitz, H., 1996, The developer's vernacular: the owner's influence on building design, *Journal of Architectural and Planning Research*, 13, 1, 34–42.

Rakoff, R., 1977, Ideology in everyday life: the meaning of the home, *Politics and Society*, 7, 1, 85–104.

Rapoport, A., 1977, *Human Aspects of Urban Form*, Pergamon Press, Oxford.

Rapoport, A., 1982, *The Meaning of the Built Environment: a non verbal communication approach*, University of Arizona Press, Tucson, AZ.

Ravatz, A., 1995, *The Place of Home: English Domestic Environments 1914–2000*, Spon Press, London.

Rawlings, P., 2002, Barrier free housing, *Ontario Home Builder Magazine*, online journal (accessed 21 October 2004), www.homesontario.com/ohbmag/2002summer/.

Reinders, H., 2000, *The Future of the Disabled in Liberal Society: An Ethical Analysis*, University of Notre Dame Press, Notre Dame, Indiana, IN.

Richards, J., 1973, *Castles on the Ground*, London, J. Murray.

Ridgway, P., Simpson, A., Wittman, F.D. and Wheeler, G., 1994, Home making and community building: notes on empowerment and place, *Journal of Mental Health Administration*, 21 (4), 407–418.

Robertson, N., 2001, Interview conducted by Rob Imrie on 4 November, Harrow, London.

Rogers, L., 1994, Gazumping the housebuilders, *RIBA Journal*, 101, 11, 6–11.

Rookard, Mrs., 1995, *Reply to the Department of the Environment's Consultation on the proposal to extend Part M to housing*, 26 April, DoE, London.

Rose, D., 1995, *Reply to the Department of the Environment's Consultation on the proposal to extend Part M to housing*, 27 April, DoE, London.

Rostron, J., 1995, *Housing the Physically Disabled*, Ashgate, Aldershot.

Rowe, A. (ed.), 1990, *Lifetime Homes: Flexible Housing for Successive Generations*, Helen Hamlyn Foundation, London.

Rowe, P., 1993, *Modernity and Housing*, MIT Press, Cambridge, MA.

Royal Association for Disability and Rehabilitation, 1995, *A response to the application of the building regulations to help disabled people in new dwellings in England and Wales*, 15 June, RADAR, London.

Rubinstein, R., 1989, The home environments of older people: a description of the psychosocial processes linking person to place, *Journal of Gerontology*, 44, 45–53.

Salmen, J. and Ostroff, E., 1997, Universal design and accessible design, in Watson, D. (ed.), *Time-saver Standards for Architectural Design Data: the Reference of Architectural Fundamentals*, McGraw-Hill, New York, NY, 1–8.

Sangster, K., 1997, *Costing Lifetime Homes*, Joseph Rowntree Foundation, The Homestead, 40 Water End, York, YO3 6LP.

Saunders, P., 1989, The meaning of 'home' in contemporary English culture, *Housing Studies*, 4, 3, 177–192.

Saunders, P., 1990, *A Nation of Home Owners*, Unwin Hyman, London.

Saunders, P. and Williams, P., 1988, The constitution of the home: towards a research agenda, *Housing Studies*, 3, 2, 81–93.

Schneider, A. and Ingram, H., 1997, *Policy Design for Democracy*, University Press of Kansas, KS.

Schroeder, S. and Steinfeld, E., 1979, *The Estimated Cost of Accessibility*, US Department of Housing and Urban Development, Washington, DC.

Scott, V., 1994, *Lessons from America: a study of the Americans with Disabilties Act*, Royal Association for Disability and Rehabilitation, London.

Scottish Office, 1996, *Scottish House Condition Survey*, SO, Edinburgh.

Sen, A., 1999, *Development as Freedom*, Random House, New York.

Shantakumar, G., 1994, The aged population of Singapore: Census of Population 1990, *Monograph No. 1*, Department of Statistics, Singapore.

Sharma, N., 2002, *Still Missing Out? The Case Studies*, Barnardo, Essex.

Shepard Homes, 1995, *Reply to the Department of the Environment's Consultation on the proposal to extend Part M to housing*, 2 May, DoE, London.

Shilling, C., 1993, *The Body and Social Theory*, Sage Publications, London.

Sixsmith, A. and Sixsmith, J., 1991, Transitions in home experience in later life, *The Journal of Architectural and Planning Research*, 8, 3, 181–191.

Smith, E., 2003, Interview conducted by Rob Imrie on 28 February, Concrete Change, Atlanta, GA.

Smith, R., 1995, *Reply to the Department of the Environment's Consultation on the proposal to extend Part M to housing*, Midland & General Homes, 19 May.

Somerville, P. and Chan, C., 2001, Human dignity and the 'third way': the case of housing policy, *paper presented at the Housing Studies Association conference on 'Housing Imaginations: new concepts, new theories, new researchers*, University of Cardiff, Cardiff, 4–5 September 2001.

Sommer, R., 1972, *Design Awareness*, Rinehart Press, San Francisco, CA.

Sopp, L. and Wood, L., 2001, *Living in a Lifetime Home: A Survey of Residents' and Developers' Views*, York Publishing Services, York.

Spinelli, E., 1989, *The Interpreted World: An Introduction to Phenomenological Psychology*, Sage Publications, London.

Steering Committee for Experiments in Public Housing (SEV), 2001, *IT Neighbourhood: An Idea for your Neighbourhood or Village?* SEV, Rotterdam, www.id-wijk.nl.

Stephen-Kaye, H., 1997, *Disability Watch: The State of People with Disabilities in the United States*, Volcano Press, Volcano, CA.

Sterling, B, 2002, When environments become really smart, in Denning, P. (ed.), *The Invisible Future: The Seamless Integration of Technology in Everyday Life*, McGraw-Hill, New York, NY.

Steven Winter Associates, 1993, *The Cost of Accessible Housing*, US Department of Housing and Urban Development, Washington, DC.

Steven Winter Associates, 1997, *Accessible Housing by Design: Universal Design Principles in Practice*, McGraw-Hill, New York, NY.

Swain, H., 1961, Building for people, *Journal of the Royal Institute of British Architects*, 68, 508–510.

Thamesdown Borough Council, 1994, *Access: Design for Life*, TBC, Swindon.

Thomas, C., 1995, *Reply to the Department of the Environment's Consultation on the proposal to extend Part M to housing*, Beazer Homes, London.

Thomas, C., 2004, Disability and impairment, in Swain, J., French, S., Thomas, C. and Barnes, C. (eds), *Disabling Barriers – Enabling Environments*, Sage Publications, London, 21–27.

Thomas, P., 2004, The experience of disabled people as customers in the owner occupied market, *Housing Studies*, 19, 5, 781–794.

Tisdale, W., 1999, Fair housing strategies for the future: a balanced approach, *Cityscape*, 4, 147–160.

Toran, K., 1999, *Accessible housing database and manual*, World Institute on Disability, Oakland, CA.

Truesdale, S. and Steinfeld, E., 2001, *Visitability: an approach to universal design in housing*, Rehabilitation Engineering Research Center on Universal Design, Buffalo, New York, NY.

Tudor Walters Committee, 1918, Report of the Committee to consider questions of building construction in connection with the provision of dwellings for the working classes in England and Wales, and Scotland (Cd 9191), HMSO, London.

Turner, J., 1976, *Housing by People: Towards Autonomy in Building Environments*, Marion Boyars, London.

Twigg, J., 2002, The body in social policy: mapping a territory, *Journal of Social Policy*, 31, 3, 421–439.

United Nations, 1974, *Resolution on adaptable housing*, UN, Geneva.

United Nations, 1994, Draft International Convention of Housing Rights, paper prepared by the UN Special Rapporteur on Housing Rights, Geneva.

United Nations Centre for Human Settlement, 2001, *Position Paper on Housing Rights*, UNCHS, Geneva.

Unwin, R., 1936, The value of good design in dwellings, in Betham, E. (ed.), *House Building 1934–1936*, The Federated Employers' Press Ltd., London, 17–22.

UPIAS, 1976, *Fundamental Principles of Disability*, Union of Physically Impaired Against Segregation, London.

Urban Task Force, 1999, *Towards an Urban Renaissance, Final report of the Urban Task Force*, Spon Press, London.

van der Krabben, E. and Lambooy, J., 1993, A theoretical framework for the functioning of the Dutch property market, *Urban Studies*, 30, 8, 1381–1397.

Venturi, R., 1966, *Complexity and Contradiction in Architecture*, The Museum of Modern Art, New York, NY.

Vidler, A., 1999, *The Architecture Uncanny: Essays in the Modern Unhomely*, MIT Press, Cambridge, MA.

Vigar, G., 2002, *The Politics of Mobility: Transport, the Environment and Public Policy*, Spon Press, London.

Vitruvius, 1960, *The Ten Books of Architecture*, Dover Publications Inc., New York, NY.

Volume House Builders Study Group, 1995, *Reply to the Department of the Environment's Consultation on the proposal to extend Part M to housing*, 20 April, DoE, London.

Waldren, J., 1993, *Liberal Rights: Collected papers, 1981–1991*, Cambridge University Press, Cambridge.

Ward, S., 2004, *Planning and Urban Change*, 2nd edn, Sage Publications, London.

Watts, M., 2002, *City of Derby Local Plan Review – First Deposit: Comment on Objections*, Derby City Council, Derby.

Webb, B., 1995, *Reply to the Department of the Environment's Consultation on the proposal to extend Part M to housing, on behalf of Beazer Homes*, 6 July, DoE, London.

Weber, M., 1947, *The Theory of Social and Economic Organization*, The Free Press, New York.

Weeks, G., 2000, Housing and the disability of extreme poverty, *Journal of Common Sense*, 6, 3, 1–3, www.common-sense.org/publications/journal/housing/html.

Wells, H.G., 1993, *Kipps: The Story of a Single Soul*, Orion Publishing, London.

Welsh, J., 1994, 'Tick for Tat', *Royal Institute of British Architects Journal*, 101, 11, 5.

Westbury Homes, 2001, City of Derby Local Plan Review – First Deposit: Letter of Objection, Derby City Council, Derby.

Wheeler, R., 1982, Staying put: a new development in policy?, *Ageing and Society*, 2, 3, 299–329.

William Davis Ltd, 2001, City of Derby Local Plan Review – First Deposit: Letter of Objection, Derby City Council, Derby.

Wimpey Homes Group, 1995, *Reply to the Department of the Environment's Consultation on the proposal to extend Part M to housing*, 27 April, DoE, London.

Woodhams, C. and Corby, S., 2003, Defining disability in theory and practice: a critique of the British Disability Discrimination Act 1995, *Journal of Social Policy*, 32, 2, 159–178.

Wright, G., 1980, *Moralist and the Model Home*, University of Chicago Press, Chicago, IL.

Wright, G., 1981, *Building the Dream: A Social History of Housing in America*, Pantheon Books, New York, NY.

Wright, J., 1983, *Building Control by Legislation: the UK Experience*, Wiley, London.

Wylde, M., Baron-Robbins, A. and Clark, S., 1994, *Building for a Lifetime: The Design and Construction of Fully Accessible Homes*, The Taunton Press, Newtown, CT.

Young, I., 1990, *Justice and the Politics of Difference*, Princeton University Press, Princeton, NJ.

Zola, I., 1989, Towards the necessary universalising of a disability policy, *The Milbank Quarterly*, 67, 2, 401–428.

Index